The

The ethical teacher

Elizabeth Campbell

Open University Press
Maidenhead · Philadelphia

Open University Press
McGraw-Hill Education
McGraw-Hill House
Shoppenhangers Road
Maidenhead
Berkshire
England
SL6 2QL

email: enquiries@openup.co.uk
world wide web: www.openup.co.uk

and
325 Chestnut Street
Philadelphia, PA 19106, USA

First published 2003

A catalogue record of this book is available from the British Library

ISBN 0 335 21218 2 (pb)   0 335 21219 0 (hb)

Library of Congress Cataloging-in-Publication Data
CIP data applied for

Typeset by RefineCatch Limited, Bungay, Suffolk
Printed in Great Britain by Bell and Bain Ltd, Glasgow

Dedicated to my mother and father, whose ethical example and guidance are very much a part of this book.

Contents

Foreword

Teaching today is increasingly complex work, requiring the highest standards of professional practice to perform it well (Hargreaves and Goodson
1996). It is the core profession, the key agent of change in today's knowledge society. Teachers are the midwives of that knowledge society. Without
them, or their competence, the future will be malformed and stillborn. In the
United States, George W. Bush's educational slogan has been to leave no
child behind. What is clear today in general, and in this book in particular, is
that leaving no child behind means leaving no teacher or leader behind
either. Yet, teaching too is also in crisis, staring tragedy in the face. There is a
demographic exodus occurring in the profession as many teachers in the
ageing cohort of the Boomer generation are retiring early because of stress,
burnout or disillusionment with the impact of years of mandated reform on
their lives and work. After a decade of relentless reform in a climate of
shaming and blaming teachers for perpetuating poor standards, the
attractiveness of teaching as a profession has faded fast among potential
new recruits.

Teaching has to compete much harder against other professions for high
calibre candidates than it did in the last period of mass recruitment, when
able women were led to feel that only nursing and secretarial work were
viable options. Teaching may not yet have reverted to being an occupation
for 'unmarriageable women and unsaleable men' as Willard Waller
described it in 1932, but many American inner cities now run their school
systems on high numbers of uncertified teachers. The teacher recruitment
crisis in England has led some schools to move to a four-day week; more and
more schools are run on the increasingly casualized labour of temporary
teachers from overseas, or endless supply teachers whose quality busy

administrators do not always have time to monitor (Townsend 2001). Meanwhile in the Canadian province of Ontario, in 2001, hard-nosed and hard-headed reform strategies led in a single year to a decrease in applications to teacher education programmes in faculties of education by 20–5%, and a drop in a whole grade level of accepted applicants.

Amid all this despair and danger, though, there remains great hope and some reasons for optimism about a future of learning that is tied in its vision to an empowering, imaginative and inclusive vision for teaching as well. The educational standards movement is showing visible signs of over-reaching itself as people are starting to complain about teacher shortages in schools, and the loss of creativity and inspiration in classrooms (Hargreaves et al. 2001). There is growing international support for the resumption of more humane middle years philosophies in the early years of secondary school that put priority on community and engagement, alongside curriculum content and academic achievement. School districts in the United States are increasingly seeing that high quality professional development for teachers is absolutely indispensable in bringing about deep changes in student achievement (Fullan 2001). In England and Wales, policy documents and White Papers are similarly advocating more 'earned autonomy', and schools and teachers are performing well (e.g. DfES 2001). Governments almost everywhere are beginning to speak more positively about teachers and teaching – bestowing honour and respect where blame and contempt had prevailed in the recent past.

The time has rarely been more opportune or more pressing to think more deeply about what professional learning, professional knowledge and professional status should look like for the new generation of teachers who will shape the next three decades of public education. Should professional learning accompany increased autonomy for teachers, or should its provision be linked to the evidence of demonstrated improvements in pupil achievement results? Do successful schools do better when the professional learning is self-guided, discretionary and intellectually challenging, while failing schools or schools in trouble benefit from required training in the skills that evidence shows can raise classroom achievement quickly? And does accommodating professional learning to the needs of different schools and their staffs constitute administrative sensitivity and flexibility (Hopkins et al. 1997), or a kind of professional development apartheid (Hargreaves, forthcoming)? These are the kinds of questions and issues that this series on professional learning sets out to address.

One of the most important but neglected aspects of professional knowledge in teaching is ethical knowledge. There is a massive emphasis in teacher education and educational policy on teachers developing the knowledge that will make them more competent professionals. Yet, while the kinds of knowledge typically demanded of teachers are important, they are also limited. Teachers are urged to develop more knowledge of the subject matter they teach, better pedagogical content knowledge of how to get their material across, and deeper knowledge of how children learn. Curiously, though, almost no attention is paid to the ethical or moral knowledge that teachers need to inform their professional judgments and guide their relations with children, colleagues and others.

In this important new book on *The Ethical Teacher*, Elizabeth Campbell courageously enters this difficult and delicate terrain of ethical knowledge in teaching. Dr Campbell is an experienced teacher and a seasoned researcher of classrooms and schools. As such, she avoids the usual tendency of educational philosophers to indulge themselves in debating ethical choices and dilemmas in teaching through hypothetical and often extreme examples that have no real bearing on what most teachers do. Instead, she dives straight into the moral quagmire of classroom life and teachers' collegial relationships, examining real, compelling and practical cases drawn from her own research. Through them, Campbell shows how teachers make good ethical decisions, how they struggle with the ethical dilemmas of their work when the right course of action is not always obvious, and how and why teachers sometimes fall ethically short, individually or as a group.

The Ethical Teacher is both provocative and challenging. Writing with elegant clarity and unwavering directness, Campbell scolds moral relativists for failing to come clean and take a stand on issues of right and wrong in teaching. She asks educators to be more serious and committed about achieving and applying moral virtues such as fairness, honesty, justice and giving prime consideration to those who are taught above all else. She shows how ethically outstanding teachers apply these virtues in their practice. In the complex work of teaching, she also acknowledges and illustrates how adhering to these virtues is rarely easy, in balancing the needs of the individual child against the interests of the class, for example. At the same time Campbell does not shy away from insisting that some very common teaching practices (that also appear in her data) such as sarcasm or punishing a class because of the actions of one of its members, are ethically insupportable.

Elizabeth Campbell's book is philosophically insistent but never sociologically or politically naive. Ethics, Campbell recognizes, are not always a matter of unconstrained individual choice in a neutral system. Teachers never have the luxury of completely free choice. Instead, their struggle to be ethical occurs in what are often profoundly unethical schools and systems. Campbell shows, for instance, how teachers are required to administer literacy tests that contain disgraceful cultural biases; how administrators can bully their teachers into adopting ill-considered innovations that sacrifice students' learning to the advancement of administrators' own visibility and careers; how teacher union procedures about dealing with colleagues' misconduct towards children promote shameful loyalty to the teacher code of non-interference with colleagues' judgements rather than urging teachers to confront their colleagues in the best interests of the child; and how most systems of professional standards in teaching are ethically vague and evasive and offer teachers little practical guidance in dealing with the concrete realities of their work.

In the end, though, *The Ethical Teacher* is a book of hope, not despair. It demonstrates how ethical standards can be developed in ways that offer teachers better practical guidance on the rights and wrongs of their work. It shows how communities of learning among teachers can focus not only on analysing achievement data in the pursuit of better test results, but also on reaching common agreement on the ethical standards of their work. And ultimately, Campbell urges, when the system or the school remains stubbornly unethical, individual teachers must dredge up the courage to stand up for what is ethically right, even though they may suffer personally or professionally because of it.

Every learner needs a teacher who not only supports them, but also demands the best of them – morally as well as intellectually. Every teacher needs at least one other adult who will do this for them too. Serving this role, Campbell understands and empathizes with the difficult task of teaching, but she does not endorse anything and everything that teachers do. If you are a teacher, or a teacher or leader of teachers, you will certainly recognize your own moral struggles in this book, but you will also have your conscience pricked from time to time as Campbell calls and challenges you to be more morally courageous in your ethical quest to become the best teacher you can be.

Andy Hargreaves
Ivor Goodson

References

DfES (Department for Education and Skills) (2001) *Achieving Success*. London: HMSO.

Fullan, M. (2001) *Leading in a Culture of Change*. San Francisco, CA: Jossey-Bass/ Wiley.

Hargreaves, A. (forthcoming) *Teaching in the Knowledge Society*. New York: Teachers College Press.

Hargreaves, A. and Goodson, I. (1996) Teachers' professional lives: aspirations and actualities, in I. Goodson and A. Hargreaves (eds) *Teachers' Professional Lives*. New York: Falmer Press.

Hargreaves, A., Earl, L., Moore, S. and Manning, S. (2001) *Learning to Change: Beyond Teaching Subjects and Standards*. San Francisco, CA: Jossey-Bass/Wiley.

Hopkins, D., Harris, A. and Jackson, D. (1997) Understanding the school's capacity for development: growth states and strategies, *School Leadership and Management*, 17(3): 401–11.

Townsend, J. (2001) It's bad – trust me, I teach there, *Sunday Times*, 2 December.

Waller, W. (1932) *The Sociology of Teaching*. New York: Russell & Russell.

Preface

Seventeen years ago, when I was still a secondary school English teacher, an incident occurred that later proved to be a partial catalyst for my subsequent academic future as a teacher educator and educational researcher in the area of ethics in teaching and schooling. Briefly, this incident involved me in the distribution and administration of a survey from the local school board to some of the students in my home form class.[1] Assuming that this task was just another of the numerous administrative demands on teachers, I neither questioned its purpose nor reviewed the survey before inflicting it on my students. As soon as I read it over with them, I saw it as being highly intrusive, non-confidential, serious in its intent (as supported by the school-wide public address message that urged us to complete the survey very carefully), and restricted to only those students who came from Vietnam. I could offer them no explanation for what was clearly a suspicious and distressing activity for many of them. If someone told me that I would deliberately and methodically segregate my students on the basis of ethnicity, subject them to an exercise that created in them some level of fear, violate their trust in me, and have absolutely no idea why I was doing any of this, I would never have believed them. And yet that is what happened, and it was wrong. It did not happen because I was a bad person with sadistic inclinations. It happened because, as a relatively novice teacher in a new school, I lacked what is to be discussed in this book as the ethical knowledge needed to enable me to apply my own moral intuition to the context of my professional obligations in this situation. Some may consider this incident a somewhat trivial matter; I see it as extremely significant ethically, in its own right, and as symbolic of the moral complexities that face teachers daily in their professional work and interpersonal relations with children and youth entrusted to their care.

This survey incident haunted me into my doctoral studies and provided the spark for my dissertation on ethical conflicts and dilemmas experienced by teachers and school principals.[2] During the following ten years, as a professor of education, I expanded on this field of study and extended my interest in the ethics of teaching to an investigation of the moral dimensions of schooling, related influences on moral education, teachers' beliefs about their moral agency, the moral foundations of professionalism, and implications for teacher education. My own teaching is informed by my interest in applied professional ethics, broadly conceived of as encompassing all of the above areas.

This book marks the culmination of my work to date, both conceptual and empirical. Its aim is not to make ethically bad teachers into ethically good ones. Rather, it seeks to show good teachers the essence of their goodness and how it is continually both revealed and challenged by the moral complexities of their professional lives. It is not a book designed for the dishonest, the greedy, the selfish, the indolent, the cruel, the careless, or the unjust. Instead, it is intended to celebrate those of good will, the kind, the dedicated, the responsible, the sensitive, the thoughtful, the truthful, and the fair. I believe the majority of teachers fall into this latter group. However, their goodness occasionally may invite their own weakness; from time to time, they may feel pangs of moral cowardice and muddling uncertainty, not necessarily about the core of what is good, but rather about how it connects to their role as teacher and how it potentially infiltrates even the seemingly mundane elements of their professional practice. This book is for them and those who educate them and those who conduct research about their worlds.

Acknowledgements

I wish to acknowledge and thank the many people who have contributed in various ways to the creation of this book.

First of all, I was privileged to work with an extraordinary research team on a study that helped to crystallize the conceptualization of ethical knowledge as it is introduced here. Many thanks to my co-investigator, Dr Dennis Thiessen, and research assistants, Anthony H. Normore and Gillian Rosenberg for their insight, methodological and analytical excellence, commitment, and enthusiasm, and for always being such great fun to work with.

As a team, we are particularly grateful to the Social Sciences and Humanities Research Council of Canada for the financial support that enabled this study. I further thank the Council for its previous generous support of other research that also informs this book.

I am indebted to all of the teachers whose voices and experiences are represented in *The Ethical Teacher*. I will remain forever moved by their professional commitment to teaching and to students; and, I cannot express adequately my respect for them as courageous individuals who were willing to expose and share their philosophies of teaching and ethics, their moral anxieties and fears, and their self-doubts and uncertainties – it is never easy to express oneself on such complex and sensitive issues, and these teachers did so with openness and collegial generosity. Many thanks also to the school administrators who allowed us into their schools to meet such gifted teachers.

This book may not have happened had it not been for the encouragement of my colleague and friend, Dr Andy Hargreaves. I thank him for his years of good will and consistent professional support, and I further thank him and co-editor, Dr Ivor Goodson, for inviting my work to be part of this series on 'Professional Learning'.

At Open University Press McGraw-Hill Education, Publisher Shona Mullen, Commissioning Editor Fiona Richman and Senior Editorial Assistant Anita West have been exceptionally helpful and gracious to me throughout the process of bringing this book to press. I am fortunate to have been able to work with them, and their attentiveness and warmth made the geographic distance between us barely noticeable.

A special thank you to Dianne Gignac for her meticulous preparation of the manuscript. I truly could not have managed without her skills and computer expertise.

On a personal level, I want to acknowledge the teachers with whom I taught in the 1980s, particularly at Jarvis Collegiate Institute in Toronto, Canada. I learned about teaching from them, and I thank them for their professional wisdom and for the fond memories I have of my former days as a secondary school teacher.

Within the Academy, I wish to thank Dr Mark Holmes. Much of this book hearkens back to my earlier work that he was so instrumental in informing.

As well as dedicating this book to my parents, I would like to acknowledge them for the emotional, intellectual, and material support they have given to me over many years – I thank them for sharing my ideas, discussing my work, and offering profound insight, continuing encouragement, and, most important of all, unconditional praise!

And, at last, I have already acknowledged Dennis Thiessen for his indispensable role on the research team; as my colleague and constant mentor, he is also my academic model – intellectually inspiring, analytically provoking, and conceptually rigorous in all ways significant. However, I want to thank him also for being my husband. It was his support, patience, consideration, and love that enabled me to write this book.

Part 1

Moral agency and ethical knowledge

Over the past two decades, the public and academic discussion of the ethical dimensions of schooling has accelerated. Philosophers, researchers, practitioners, and policy makers are all contributing in their own ways to the revival of this area, with its social and intellectual roots in centuries-old debates, which has been seen as a neglected field of study for too long. The urgency of highlighting ethics in education is contemporarily propelled by increasing calls for moral accountability, codes, and professional standards as well as the exploding field of moral education in schools. This book addresses connections among these significant issues from its own perspective of ethical knowledge as a kind of teacher knowledge that is rarely addressed.

Much of the current literature in the field reinforces the importance of regarding teaching as an inherently moral endeavour. By extension, it supports a belief that teachers primarily carry out their professional work without being fully aware of the moral and ethical implications of their actions. While this book accepts the embedded and implicit nature of much of teachers' moral practice, it seeks to make more visible the level of ethical awareness many teachers bring to their formal and informal exchanges and activities in schools.

In their significant investigation of the moral life of schools, Jackson et al. conclude that teachers and school administrators, while for the most part fundamentally good people, remain noticeably unaware and even unconscious of the ethical ramifications of their own actions and overall practice.[1] They ask the following valuable questions:

> And what about teachers? Do *they* need to be aware of the possible moral consequences of what they are doing in order for those

consequences to take place? Again, it seems reasonable to suppose that they do not . . . But having said that, we are left to wonder about the desirability of that state of ignorance, especially as it pertains to teachers. Might it not be advantageous for all educators, no matter what their job or where they work, to become increasingly aware of the moral potency of their actions?[2]

My short answer to them is an emphatic 'yes'. However, I do not believe that all teachers conduct their professional work in a state of unreflective, unaware, unintentional morality. In fact, some are already able to articulate a level of awareness of the moral aspects of their behaviour and intent far beyond that for which they are often credited. It is this insight that provides the basis of ethical knowledge as introduced and explored throughout this book by connecting, conceptually and empirically, a broadly conceived professional ethics with the vision of the teacher as moral agent.

The moral agency of teachers should be regarded as more than an inevitable state of being, created by circumstances that bring adult teachers and children together in a learning environment. Sockett, who equates the professional teacher with the moral teacher, defines moral agency as a state in which 'a person considers the interests of others, does not make discriminations on irrelevant grounds, and has a clear set of principles or virtues in which he or she believes and on which he or she acts'.[3] In keeping with this notion of moral agency grounded in principle and virtue, my discussion of teachers' awareness of their own moral agent role as the foundation for ethical knowledge is presented within a particular philosophical framework. It is one that supports core ethical principles and remains critical of moral relativism, while nonetheless acknowledging the complexities of moral interpretations of virtue, the significance of contextual realities, and the potential legitimacy of differing ethical beliefs.

As a principle-based role, moral agency is discussed here in terms of both how teachers treat students generally and what they teach them of a moral and ethical nature. Its essence is expressed through both their knowledge of what is ethically important for them do in the course of their professional practice and their knowledge about what they want students to achieve, internalize, or learn related to principles of right and wrong and how they can facilitate and inspire such learning. In this respect, moral agency is a double-pronged state that entails a dual commitment on the part of the teacher. The first relates to the exacting ethical standards the teacher as a moral person and a moral professional holds himself or herself to, and the second concerns the teacher as a moral educator, model, and exemplar whose aim is to guide students towards a moral life. These dual characteristics of moral agency are obviously and inevitably interrelated as teachers, through their actions, words, and attitudes, may be seen to be living by the same principles that they hope students will embrace.

Ethical knowledge relies on teachers' understanding and acceptance of the demands of moral agency as professional expectations implicit in all aspects of their day-to-day practice. As it is addressed in this book, ethical knowledge does not grow out of the expansive literature base on teacher knowledge more generally.[4] Much of that scholarship is silent on the ethical dimensions of such things as pedagogical content knowledge, classroom knowledge, and curriculum. Nonetheless, ethical knowledge does share with some of the teacher knowledge work an interest in aligning the notion of a specialized knowledge base with an enhanced sense of professionalism.

More than ten years ago, Gary Fenstermacher astutely noted that all the 'rhetoric' about the need for an identifiable knowledge base to transform an occupation into a profession 'is nearly devoid of talk about the moral nature of teaching, the moral duties and obligations of teachers, and the profound importance of teachers to the moral development of students'.[5] He asks, incredulously, how one can think of teaching as being disconnected from its moral underpinnings. Clearly, one should not try, and my discussion of ethical knowledge is based upon this premise. More recently, David Hansen has cautioned us against applying the language of professional expertise to the description of the moral dimensions of the teaching practice itself.[6] In the spirit of Aristotle, he considers the notion of practical wisdom a more apt depiction of what he refers to as moral knowledge, distinct from technical competence.

Notwithstanding my general agreement that the moral practices of the ethical teacher are not comparable in a generic sense to a proscribed body of facts and theories as may be found in other professions, the concept of ethical knowledge I present here encompasses those practices. And, whether one accepts it as a kind of specialized knowledge, expertise, or practical wisdom, I believe that an expanded recognition of its significance in defining the essence of teaching will, by consequence, heighten our sensibilities towards teaching as a genuine profession. In this respect, my position supports Strike and Ternasky's conclusion on the ethics of educational professionals. They write:

> If there is no arcane knowledge base for teaching, we might ground a teaching profession in the characteristic activities and commitments of its practitioners. Thus, rather than an esoteric body of knowledge we would find the practices and attitudes without which a person could not be said to be a member of the profession . . . [Teaching] may seek the respect it deserves not by comparing itself to other vocations, but by focusing on the role and importance of teachers' moral and intellectual commitments in the lives of students and in society.[7]

It is the aim of this book to clarify the nature of ethical knowledge as expressed in the awareness of many teachers of their own moral agency and to bring this knowledge to the forefront of our thinking about teaching. In making ethical knowledge more visible, even in its layers of complexity and embeddedness, it is my hope that it may enable three avenues of renewal. First, a more transparent sense of ethical knowledge could provide the basis for a *renewed sense of professionalism*, not simply for reasons of status or even accountability, but for the purpose of redefining the collective profession in ethical terms. Additionally, this would support individual teachers by guiding their overall orientation to their work and, when necessary, helping them to grapple with the dilemmas, tensions, and complexities that may challenge a clear conception of this ethical professionalism. Second, as the foundation of a principle-based ethic of individual and collective practice, ethical knowledge may provide also the basis for *renewed school cultures* in which the moral dimensions of all aspects of a teacher's work are discussed, debated even, exemplified, and ultimately used both as the measure of actions, decisions, initiatives, and policies and as the arbiter of disputes and problems. Third, the concept of ethical knowledge should provide the theoretical and practical framework for *renewed teacher education and professional learning* in all their various forms.

Ultimately, this book has an instrumental as well as a conceptual intent. It proposes how teachers themselves may be able to develop and foster a professional culture based dominantly on a foundation of ethical knowledge by accepting and promoting the interconnectedness of moral agency and professional ethics. The organizational structure of the book into three parts and eight chapters is designed to present the concept of ethical knowledge as it is revealed, as it is challenged, and as it may be used.

The first part, which comprises three chapters, introduces a general discussion of applied ethics as well as the concept of teachers' ethical knowledge as related to their awareness and articulation of the moral and ethical dimensions of their practice and behaviour. It examines moral agency as both a formal and informal role, an inevitable state, a collection of aspirations and intentions, a deliberate and a subconscious orientation to teachers' work, and a dual commitment on the part of teachers to be moral professionals, as well as moral models, exemplars, and educators. Within this part, Chapter 1 addresses philosophical complexities of defining ethics and morals, as well as reviewing briefly the overall field of professional ethics, as subtly distinct from regular ethics, in anticipation of the concluding part of the book. It further clarifies the book's overall theoretical perspective, that is critical of moral relativism, while acknowledging that widely differing opinions exist in schools, as elsewhere, regarding the appropriate definition of terms. As is the case with many other current authors in the field of professional ethics, I argue my support for a common core of principles, such as fairness, honesty, kindness, justice, and courage, while accepting that interpretations of these principles vary, and that the translation of abstract virtues into practice is fraught with tensions and uncertainties.

Chapters 2 and 3 are closely related in both their focus on teachers' moral agency and their use of empirical evidence as illustrative of conceptual issues raised in the discussion. At this point, I should clarify my application of qualitative research data from several of my relevant studies. The context of these studies and the specific nature of the participants themselves are not described. This book is not intended in any way to be a research report, per se. Rather, I present data from interviews and classroom observations as individualized snapshots, composite profiles, and creative vignette compilations of 'real life' attitudes, stories, and behaviours in order to illustrate my descriptions of everyday teachers and the moral and ethical realities they face. First-name pseudonyms are used only for the purpose of 'putting a human face' on the descriptive aspect of the book and should not be relied on to portray a consistent or well-rounded account of any individual. This use of data is found dominantly in the second, third, fourth, and fifth chapters.

Chapter 2 illustrates teachers in the course of their daily work with students and others as they try to uphold through their own behaviour those principles they believe to be morally and ethically important. Such principles include the will to be fair, to treat others with respect and care, to be responsible and accountable, honest, and brave. Teachers demonstrate these and other qualities in a variety of formal and informal ways: through their structured lessons and their casual exchanges, their evaluation and discipline methods, their choices of curriculum and pedagogy, and the general character they project in classrooms and schools. This chapter describes this aspect of moral agency and explores the level of self-awareness teachers have about themselves in this capacity, as central to the concept of their ethical knowledge.

Chapter 3 focuses on the teacher's inevitable role as a moral educator in developing in students specific virtues of character. Teachers transmit moral lessons to students about appropriate and inappropriate beliefs and behaviour by direct instruction, spontaneous admonition and intervention, and personal modelling. This chapter explores both the ways teachers do this, as part of their moral agency, as well as their level of conscious awareness and intention.

While Part 1 of the book describes the ethical orientations of teachers in their professional practice as moral agents, the second two-chapter part shows how dilemmas, tensions, and challenges strain and interfere with teachers' sense of moral and ethical efficacy and agency and, ultimately, compromise their professionalism. Within this context, Chapter 4 describes some of the dilemmas and tensions that threaten teachers' self-perceptions as ethical professionals as well as their public identities. Such dilemmas involve school administration and broad issues of policy, students and their parents, and pressures from various segments of the wider community. Other topics of tension addressed here include the ethics of teaching controversial curricula and engaging in the questionable expression of political opinions or positions in the classroom.

Chapter 5 argues that some of the most dominant ethical dilemmas and tensions for teachers are those involving colleagues. Often they feel the anguish of choosing between their moral and ethical obligations to safeguard students' well-being and the perceived or real pressure to maintain loyalty to and solidarity with their colleagues, even those who have violated the trust and moral authority they have by virtue of their position. The tendency for teachers to engage in what I call 'suspended morality' is common.[8] It emanates from the sense of cowardice teachers express and their difficulties in overcoming the pressure of the teacher group, whether it is exercised by formal associations or informal expectations. The powerful impact of teacher unions or federations and the politics of membership in them also inform this discussion. Ultimately, the dilemmas and challenges addressed in this chapter are juxtaposed with the previous description of moral agency to argue that ethical knowledge and the professionalism based on it are endangered by unresolved tensions caused by norms of collegial relations.

The first part of this book discusses ethical knowledge and moral agency, and the second part presents challenges that undermine them and diminish professionalism. Consequently, the third and final, three-chapter, part of the book follows from the two previous descriptive ones and offers recommendations to enhance ethical professionalism and assuage the dilemmas and tensions that thwart it. This part encourages teachers to use their ethical knowledge to minimize their dilemmas and build a more strongly articulated ethical culture for the teaching profession, thus providing a principle-based foundation for professionalism. This part also relates this prescriptive element to issues of teacher education, both preservice and in-service development.

As the introduction to Part 3, Chapter 6 explores contemporary efforts to formalize visions of moral accountability and professionalism in teaching. The trend to develop and enforce ethical codes and standards and to create various bodies, agencies, and professional organizations to regulate them is examined. While fully supportive of the arguments that teaching must be a morally accountable profession and that ethics should underpin all that is recommended, this chapter is largely critical of the belief that formalized statements imposed on teachers will help to build a stronger sense of professional ethics.

Chapter 7 urges teachers to embrace an element of self-determination to govern themselves as ethical professionals. It argues that at least some of them have the knowledge to share, if not the courage, to do this. It recommends how to apply the ethical knowledge of individuals to the collective articulation of new ethical norms in which the primacy of their moral responsibilities to students is acknowledged. These new norms would replace the fear and tyranny of some aspects of collegial solidarity and the sense of powerlessness on the part of those teachers who feel de-professionalized by regulations, legislated standards, and other constraints beyond their control. This chapter argues that principles of ethics should provide the foundation for teachers, as individual professionals and communities of educators, to acquire the moral strength to meet the challenges they face in the course of their daily practice.

Chapter 8 summarizes the book by reinforcing the conceptual and empirical connections between teachers' ethical knowledge and their role as moral agents, professional ethics, and moral education in the broadest sense. It addresses the field of applied ethics as one that should enable the development of new ethical school communities, and encourages teachers to use ethical knowledge to build and foster a deeper sense of professionalism in teaching. Implications for teacher education and professional learning are examined within this scope. Ultimately, the book concludes with a portrait of 'the ethical teacher', a composite profile created to illustrate the practices and dispositions that characterize ethical knowledge in a way that makes it visible, recognizable, and attainable as a professional goal.

In his 1997 book on ethical judgement in teaching, Karl Hostetler writes that, 'Ethics need not, and probably should not, always be at the forefront of teachers' minds. But it persists as the background project, as teachers are continually searching for, and being responsible to, what is ethically right and good. It is in this sense that teaching is fundamentally an ethical activity, not a technical one.'[9] While I concur with his last sentence, I have changed my mind about the rest of the quotation in the years since it was written; I have gone from accepting the implicit nature of ethics as a signal that it may remain embedded in the background of teachers' practice to insisting that it be brought forward, made visible, discussed, debated, and exemplified for all teachers. It is my hope that *The Ethical Teacher* achieves at least part of this mission.

one

Introduction to ethics in teaching

Applied professional ethics

Professional ethics in teaching, as it is presented in this book, is not a concept to be narrowly defined solely by ethical codes of practice and formalized precepts of behaviour and disposition uniquely relevant to the teacher practitioner. Nonetheless, these should indeed embody fundamental core principles of an ethical orientation so essential to overall moral practice. Rather, professional ethics is conceived of broadly as elements of human virtue, in all its complexity, as expressed through the nuances of attitudes, intentions, words, and actions of the professional teacher. Simply, it is the realization of good and the struggle against bad as they apply to the everyday practice of teachers as individuals and as a collective professional group. In this respect, the focus is on more general principles of ethics, such as honesty and fairness, as they apply to teachers' work, than on the identification of particular interpretations of ethics that emanate from the profession itself (such as the oft-quoted imperative to avoid interfering in a colleague's domain of authority).

In his *Practical Companion to Ethics*, Anthony Weston notes that, 'ethics asks us to live *mindfully*: to take some care about how we act and even about how we feel'.[1] He further explains:

> Despite the stereotypes, the point of ethics is not to moralize or to dictate what is to be done. Ethics is not another form of dogmatism. The real point of ethics is to offer some tools for thinking about difficult matters, recognizing from the start – as the very rationale for ethics, in fact – that the world is seldom so simple or clear-cut. Struggle and uncertainty are part of ethics, as they are a part of life.[2]

In our struggle as teachers to contextualize within classrooms and schools our own moral dispositions, problems and uncertainties inevitably emerge. It is at this point that applied professional ethics becomes both a descriptor of the inherent dimensions of moral teaching and a potentially useful guide in the resolution of problems.[3] Referred to also as 'practical ethics',[4] applied professional ethics provides teachers with the means to reflect wisely on the moral implications of what they say or do not say and do or do not do, not only in dilemma-type situations, but also in the course of their routine work.

The emphasis in this book is on the practical expression of ethics and morality in teaching, as opposed to the study of meta-ethics and questions about the character of morality itself. Hence, this is not a study in philosophy in any classical sense, although the issues, realities, and concerns addressed are essentially philosophical in nature. We must address such an area of significance in an accessible way without 'fear of becoming mired in arguments about moral philosophy and moral theory', as some have suggested.[5] The need for this is both fuelled and partially fulfilled by a rapidly increasing body of scholarship that attests to the pervasiveness of the moral domain in teaching.[6] Accounts of the ethical dimensions of schooling provide details about moral agency, moral purpose, the moral authority of practice, and the argument that 'the components of teaching as a knowledge endeavour and as a moral enterprise are essentially inseparable'.[7] As Hansen concludes, 'The notion that teaching is a moral practice constitutes one of the world's most enduring understandings of the work . . . the activity of teaching is itself saturated with moral significance, and it is so in ways that illuminate both the beneficial and the harmful influence teachers can have on students'.[8] While it is the intention of *The Ethical Teacher* to illustrate primarily the former influence, this is often best achieved by juxtaposing some contrasting depictions of the latter.

Given the reality that teaching is inherently a moral and ethical activity, an interesting distinction has been introduced between applied ethics and 'implied ethics'.[9] Todd argues that since ethical principles are not applied, as in laid on to, the conditions of classroom life to make it ethical, the daily details of this life should instead be seen, in and of themselves, as implying ethics. In other words, ethics emanates from the realities of teaching, rather than being applied to these realities. While this observation sensibly captures the embedded and unconscious nature of many of the moral transactions that transpire spontaneously in classrooms, it obscures an important point. That is, professional ethics, as defined by the moral practice and conduct of teachers, should not be left to chance as an inevitable state of being. There are times when professional teachers need to 'apply' principles of ethics to the conceptualization of their work consciously, visibly, and with commitment and determination. And, at the very least, they need to recognize how such principles do actually 'apply' to their work. This double use of the term 'apply' situates the notion of applied professional ethics within the context of ethical knowledge addressed throughout this book.

The concept of ethical professionalism has been addressed more broadly within occupations and professions other than teaching, although educational ethics as an area of interest to policy makers, researchers, and practitioners has received heightened attention in recent years.[10] Within the scope of the professional literature more generally, there is fairly consistent agreement that ethical professionalism is both based on a shared appreciation for a wide range of commonly accepted moral virtues, and grounded in ethics reflective of the professional practice itself.[11] Thus, we may raise the distinction between the specific ethical demands on the professional and the moral responsibilities of any citizen to themselves and other members of society; we may conclude, as MacMillan has, that professionals are 'bound by a sense of the ethical dimensions of the relations among professionals and clients, the public, the employing institution, and fellow professionals . . . [based on] a conception of what constitutes the profession's purposes and characteristic activities'.[12] However, a critical point for my discussion of applied professional ethics is that such ethical obligations are in addition to, not substituted for, the expectations of moral behaviour for any private individual. Bayles refers to this distinction as the difference between professional ethical norms and ordinary ethical norms, and rightly concludes that professional norms can, in no way, be justified if they are independent of ordinary ethical norms.[13] Therefore, the ethical professional is also an ethical person.

But, what of the ethical person who, upon assuming the role of the professional, somehow transforms their behaviour and attitudes in ways that neglect the very dispositions that guide moral action in other non-professional circumstances? As Coombs wisely observes:

> Just as some business persons may not exercise the same sensitivities in their business dealings as they do in other contexts, educators too may leave important moral sensitivities at the school door. Actions they may see as insulting, belittling, arrogant, patronizing, or unfair in other contexts may not be perceived as such in the educational context. Consequently an important aspect of the task of enhancing the moral sensitivity and perception of educators is that of engaging them in a consideration of how the educational context, with its particular constellation of power, authority, and responsibility relations, affects the applicability of their moral concepts.[14]

Perhaps such individuals would be best served by focusing attention more on the 'ethics' aspect of professional ethics than on the 'professional' aspect, if indeed they perceive the two to be separable. They may be strengthened by becoming familiar with Edwin Delattre's excellent explanation of integrity as central to all ethics and the highest achievement of individual character. In maintaining that the principles of right and wrong conduct are the same regardless of whether one is concerned with ethics in private or public life, he states that there is not a 'distinct set of principles that make up something called business ethics in contrast to science ethics in contrast to education ethics, and so forth. Ethics is ethics. We need to know relevant facts about each specific walk of life to understand how to apply the principles of ethics in it, but that does not change the fundamental principles that apply'.[15] Therefore, professional ethics is the extension of everyday ethics into the nuances of the professional's practices. The ethical knowledge of teachers, as addressed in this book, is what illuminates such relevant facts about school life and the teaching role, thus facilitating the application of ethical principles to one's professional work.

This application of ethical principles to practice is one reason why we might conclude that professional ethics, while fundamentally the same as general ethics, also entails certain unique moral considerations peculiar to the profession. As many who have written in this area note, membership in a profession obligates individuals to adhere to the ethical principles and standards inherent in the technicalities of the profession.[16] Their duty to behave in an ethical manner not only includes but also extends beyond the regular moral conduct expected of any person to encompass elements of competence and service ideals. Sometimes dubbed 'professional virtues', such ideals, nonetheless, still have at their core such general principles as fairness, integrity, moral courage, compassion, honesty, patience, and various adaptations of the ancient principles definitive of the medical ethical tradition: autonomy, justice, non-maleficence, and beneficence.[17]

In anticipation of the expanded discussion of formalized ethics and professional associations in Chapter 6, I note briefly that, in all the numerous statements of professional ethics found on various websites for a diverse range of professions, lists of core ethical principles, such as those stated above, are often presented as the foundation of moral practice for the specified profession. They share many of the same virtue-based ethics that one might apply to everyday life. For example, one statement from the medical field highlights compassion, dedication, honesty, integrity, courage, wisdom, and self-sacrifice, and argues that, 'it is difficult to imagine physicians who practise the above listed attributes and values in professional life, but not in personal interactions with friends, family, and other people. Congruence between professional and personal values is essential'.[18] Another offers a framework for universal principles of ethics that divides applied ethics into three co-existent, overlapping, and occasionally conflicting categories: principles of personal ethics, such as honesty, respect for the autonomy of others, and being fair; principles of professional ethics, such as impartiality, diligence, and duty of care; principles of global ethics, such as social responsibility.[19] In each of these cases, there is scope for appreciating how the principle base of applied professional ethics is relevant to the practice of education and the profession of teaching.

In their examination of professional ethics in teaching as principles that should govern the conduct of educators, Strike and Ternasky describe how principles, such as fairness, justice, and care apply directly to routine classroom-based decisions.[20] They ask what constitutes fairness in evaluation and discipline, how a teacher might equitably allocate time and attention to students of differing needs, whether it is ever appropriate for teachers to punish whole classes for the misbehaviour of an individual student, and other similar questions. These kinds of issues, which are empirically illustrated in subsequent chapters, challenge teachers to apply their sense of professional ethics in ways that hopefully make the best use of ethical knowledge. Such knowledge is based on a sound grasp of moral principles and an experiential foundation that provides the link to such principles or virtues.

It is probably apparent that this discussion of principles or virtues assumes a level of universality and a general rejection of ethical relativism. In this respect, it echoes Soltis' assertion that ethical relativism and subjectivism defeat the very notion of professional ethics, and that 'the specter of ethical subjectivism needs to be dispelled if we as a profession are to have an ethic and be genuinely ethical practitioners . . . it would make no sense to teach principles of professional conduct as if they were arbitrary or subjective'.[21] While this is not an uncommon position in the field of ethics, it is by no means uncontentious or without its detractors.

Knowing the difference between right and wrong

Often in discussions about issues of right and wrong, either within academic circles or as part of the wider public discourse, one of the most pervasive questions to surface is 'Whose values, anyway, should define what is right and what is wrong?'. In its most belligerent form, this question is intended to stifle all expression of moral and ethical values by implying that they represent the subjective proclivities of individuals bent on controlling others rather than the accumulative wisdom gleaned from centuries of philosophical reflection, debate, and historical experience. By implication, any reference to virtue is equated with the oppressive imposition of strident, unflinching, and inflexible opinions whose veracity is very much in doubt. When asked relentlessly, the question may render reasonable and rational people, who believe generally that it is wrong to deceive and abuse other people and that it is right to be kind, fair and trustworthy, confused and defensive as they try to explain such principles as something other than self-evident.

Most people of good will do not want to seem like doctrinaire absolutists out to push their moral agenda on others. So, with the best of moderate intentions, they embrace the ubiquitous 'whose values?' question as an apparently legitimate cautionary warning against extremism. If that is all it were, then there would be good reason to consider it. Unfortunately, as an instrument of moral relativism, subjectivism, and nihilism, it also undermines the confidence and conviction of those who exercise a fairly mainstream appreciation of right and wrong, consistent with the laws of the land, informed by reasoned and humane judgement, and supported by a legacy of philosophy and historical precedent, both heroic and horrific in nature. In the moral muddle that ensues, attempts to articulate even core ethical principles that essentially form the foundation of how human beings should treat one another become paralyzed as, bit by bit, we come to stand for nothing, right or wrong, either as individuals or collectively as a society.

For some of those writing in the areas of professional ethics, the moral nature of schools, and moral education, the 'whose values?' question becomes tedious as it advances an implied moral equivalency between zealous fanatics out to indoctrinate others in their own narrow view of the world and benign and thoughtful teachers striving to be fair and kind while showing students that in civil society, we exercise patience in listening to each other, we don't hit someone because they make us angry, we take turns, and we don't cheat and steal from one another. There seems little point in seriously addressing the moral agency of teachers, the ethical obligations inherent in teachers' professional practice, and the overall moral and ethical nature of schooling if one's conceptual starting point maintains the relativity of all moral and ethical principles as self-justified expressions of opinion, feeling, and preference bounded only by the shifting beliefs of individuals and societies and, therefore, not in any universal or objective sense binding on us all.

At this point, it is important to acknowledge a distinction between moral and ethical principles as the focus here and those social norms, customs, traditions, trends, fashions, and biases that may or may not reflect such principles. A tendency to clump all of these together as more or less equivalent 'values' helps propel the 'whose values?' question and the confusion it spawns. In his study of children and adolescents from a range of cultural and religious backgrounds, Nucci identifies the distinct domains of the moral and the social. The moral domain has at its centre knowledge of right and wrong and involves a transcendent universal set of values around issues of human welfare, compassion, fairness, and justice.[22] While the social domain may encompass moral areas of social regulation (hence the term 'sociomoral'), it is defined also by non principle-based conventions or personal preferences, unlike the moral domain which includes only a 'basic core of morality around which educators can construct their educational practices without imposing arbitrary standards or retreating into value relativism'.[23] Nucci found that children across the diverse research sample uniformly made the same distinctions between issues of essential morality, whether or not these are viewed through a religious or secular lens, and conventions, rules, and practices specific to a particular religion or society. Only the former were seen to be universally applicable, and they all related to foundational principles or virtues such as honesty, justice, integrity, respect, kindness, and trustworthiness. It is with these and other virtues as they are woven into the fabric of teaching in all its complexity that *The Ethical Teacher* is concerned.

Increasingly critical of the rampant relativism embraced since the late 1960s that has undermined the articulation of such principles as virtues, many philosophers and researchers interested in the moral dimensions of education assume, as part of varying ideological and conceptual frameworks, that at least a basic distinction between ethical right and wrong does not need a detailed defence. In other words, in insisting that a good teacher is neither cruel nor unfair, we need not haggle over why this is essentially a moral imperative, rather than merely a culturally and socially constructed norm reflecting the interests of some over others.[24] As Fenstermacher states in his identification of honesty, compassion, truthfulness, fairness, courage, moderation, and generosity as among the exemplary virtues expressed in a teacher's manner, 'I leave open here the very important issue of why these particular traits are to be regarded as virtues, doing so with the philosophically lame but empirically compelling claim that the literature, customs and norms of the vast majority of world cultures hold these traits in high regard'.[25]

The theoretical premise underpinning *The Ethical Teacher* similarly adopts such a position. It is based on the assumption that ethical principles embedded in the empirical illustrations presented or addressed in the overall discussion need not be justified as such; rather, there is an expected recognition of their goodness or, as in the case of their violation, badness. In other words, by way of a polarized example, the teacher who addresses students with kindness and respect is assumed to be doing a good thing, and the teacher who ridicules and disparages students is assumed to be doing a bad thing, even if the latter teacher believes it is an appropriate way to exercise one's professional authority. As Clark reminds us, 'In the moral domain, however, one opinion is *not* as good as any other . . . Overarching principles have been agreed on in our society and within the teaching profession – principles dealing with honesty, fairness, protection of the weak, and respect for all people'.[26]

Similarly, others have also generated lists of core ethical principles that should guide human interaction. For example, in their respective accounts of what constitutes the ethical school, Starratt identifies responsibility, honesty, tolerance, loyalty, courtesy, compassion, integrity, fairness, care and respect; while Haynes refers to both the overarching values of non-maleficence (do no harm) and beneficence (promote human welfare, prevent harm) and specific universal values including justice, honesty, respect, and so on.[27] The core ethical principles cited are usually in agreement, although tolerance, for example, is frequently flagged as potentially problematic as a virtue. Understandably, for those of us who believe in more objective and universal orientations to ethics, tolerance is a questionable principle in its own right as it would compel us to tolerate the intolerable, that is, those practices and views that are harmful, dishonest, or unjust.

General consensus on core ethical principles in an abstract sense should not be seen to imply that there is no disagreement over their interpretation and application. It is not in any way inconsistent with the non-relativist framework of this book to acknowledge and accept that reasonable people can and do disagree over issues of right and wrong. In the context of daily life, moral issues may conflict, and we do not always know with certainty how a particular ethic applies to a specific problem or situation. We may have differing interpretations of what it means to be fair or what the essence of caring is. Uncertainty and complexity are inevitable aspects of adjudicating between right and wrong in one's personal and professional life. However, this complexity does not invalidate the concept of ethical right and wrong. As medical ethicist Margaret Somerville states in her rejection of moral relativism and her support for what she calls the secular sacred: 'Recognition of unavoidable uncertainty is not incompatible with regarding some things as inherently wrong'.[28] And in teaching, as in medicine and other fields, that which is inherently wrong is that which harms, deceives, manipulates, deprives, neglects, cheats, intimidates, and uses others for one's own ends.

Clearly, ethics is not simply a matter of private choice or personal satisfaction. As Reitz argues in his discussion of moral crisis in schools: 'When morality becomes a totally private affair, a personal sense of right and wrong diminishes to a point of no return. If I am responsible only to myself, nothing can be wrong'.[29] Contrarily, moral and ethical standards are inherently public; they define what we do to, for, and with one another. Additionally, they influence our treatment of non-human life. Because of this, as Fasching notes, ethical reflection requires us to deliberate with others and engage ourselves in the responsible and reasoned intention to discover what is right. He further claims, however, that we can do this only if we are prepared to be mistaken and 'to recognize both our own fallibility and our common humanity'.[30] On one hand, ethics seems easy and straightforward, especially in the most extreme of situations; on the other hand, it is fraught with tensions and uncertainties that have challenged us for centuries to think deeply about the contextual realities of our lives as they influence our ethical knowledge.

Before addressing ethical complexity as an integral characteristic of teachers' knowledge, I should clarify briefly my use of the terms ethics/ ethical and moral as both expressive of principles of right and wrong. Some scholars and researchers use only the term 'moral' to refer to the nature of teaching, the dimensions of education, and the agency of teachers. Some regard 'moral' to be concerned with the rightness and wrongness of specific conduct or character, while 'ethics' refers to a broader, more universal and all-encompassing understanding of such moral standards and principles. Of these, some use ethics only in what I consider to be an excessively narrow and restrictive sense to mean formalized codes of practice. I too make a small distinction in my use of some terms. For example, I refer to profes- sional ethics, not professional morals, thus acknowledging those who may regard morals as more individually and personally conceived and ethics as more collective and public. Similarly, I refer to an individual teacher's moral agency, not ethical agency. By entitling this book, *The Ethical Teacher* rather than *The Moral Teacher*, I am exercising my preference for the ter- minology of ethics as more strongly indicative of the collective sense of professionalism I hope to inspire by illustrating the moral practice of some individuals.

Nonetheless, having said this, I essentially do not distinguish conceptually between the terms; both address virtue and basic principles of right and wrong as they influence belief, intention, and behaviour. Hence, I frequently refer to the moral and/or ethical nature of teaching, moral and/or ethical dilemmas and issues, and moral and/or ethical exchanges in classrooms, for example. In this respect, the terms are used here, for the most part, interchangeably. There is ample support in both the moral philosophy and professional literature to justify this usage.

One term that I generally choose to avoid, unless it is modified by the adjective form of moral or ethical, is 'values'. Like many others writing in the field of professional ethics and the moral domain of education, I regard values as those non-moral preferences individuals hold in relative ways. As the great conceptual equalizer of all preference, opinion, belief, and attitude, 'values' as a term does not fit well with a virtue-based discussion of profes- sional ethics and moral agency in teaching. As Hunter argues, 'The very word "value" signifies the reduction of truth to utility, taboo to fashion, conviction to mere preference; all provisional, all exchangeable'.[31] *The Ethical Teacher* is not based on a compelling need to justify philosophically why treating students unfairly, for example, is wrong and not merely an individual value choice on the part of a teacher. It is for this reason that the 'whose values?' question introduced at the beginning of this section is seen as potentially so destructive of any collective professional attempt to distinguish between right and wrong in the often complex and uncertain context of teaching.

Ethical complexity as knowledge

If we are to make teachers' ethical knowledge more visible as exemplary of virtue-based professional practice, we must recognize and accept the moral layeredness of teaching, the complexities of classroom and school life, the occasional uncertainty of teachers striving to respond to conflicting demands in ways that are fair and caring to all, and the fact that people in teaching, as elsewhere, have varying and competing perspectives on what constitutes right and wrong, good and bad. Ethical knowledge encompasses divergent orientations, but is not so diffuse that it ignores its fundamental rootedness in core principles or virtues such as honesty, justice, compassion, dedication, diligence, integrity, courage, and other components of moral pluralism. However, disagreement over the interpretations of such principles and confusion as to their applicability to specific contextual situations are inevitable in teaching as they are in wider society. As Hostetler argues, 'A teacher's ethical world simply isn't precise. However . . . such imprecision does not mean that ethical judgment is irrational, arbitrary, or merely subjective and that even if situations exist to which there is no one right response, that does not mean we cannot identify wrong responses'.[32] The point of illuminating ethical knowledge is not to attempt to eliminate such imprecision, but rather to illustrate how teachers may work within it, despite conflict and disagreement, to enhance moral agency built on an appreciation of how moral principles are embedded in practice in a variety of ways.

As has been claimed by many philosophers in education and in other fields, it is not in any way inconsistent to hold to a belief in objective ethical principles while accepting that reasonable, rational individuals of good will and thoughtful intention may hold differing views about morality. In some instances, they may not know what to believe. I would assume that most of us have experienced such uncertainty and lack of clarity even though we have not lost faith in the abstract value of core virtues. As Sirotnik reminds us, in his defence of moral imperatives, 'An antirelativist position, however, does not automatically resolve fundamental questions, dilemmas, and issues'.[33] It is perhaps because of this that public discourse, consensus, and debate over ethical concerns have prevailed since the era of Aristotle. The exploration of teachers' ethical knowledge replicates such moral deliberation as it applies to the contextual realities of teaching and the interpersonal dynamics in schools.

While teachers as professionals may agree on the objective principles of fairness and honesty, for example, they may, within the context of their own individual schools and classrooms, interpret them differently in the course of their daily practice. What one teacher may regard as a caring alternative to treating all students equally because some are more needy than others, another teacher may see as a violation of justice that demands impartial and equal treatment of all. Furthermore, an individual teacher may believe both of the above and function in a fluctuating state of dissonance and self-doubt about inconsistencies in their own practice. While two teachers may fundamentally agree on the need to be honest, one may be more sensitive than the other to a potential conflict between telling the truth about a child to another teacher and the principle of confidentiality and respect for the privacy rights of students and their families. Two teachers, both believers in the virtue of loyalty, may become opponents in a situation that tests one's collegial loyalty against the moral expectation to safeguard the well-being of students. Teachers' own philosophical orientations, conscious or not, to moral and ethical issues will ultimately determine how they interpret their professional obligations and their role as moral agents.

Inevitably, discrepancies among perspectives are based, either deeply or superficially, on the philosophical and ideological complexities of competing conceptual paradigms. One's view of ethics may be rooted in neo-classical objective principles of universal worth, as is the case in this book. Or, it may reflect a more constructivist orientation that defines ethics relationally and situationally as perspectives. Within these two broad approaches, one may be a neo-Aristotelian virtue ethicist, a utilitarian consequentialist, a Kantian advocate of deontology, a care theorist who, while sharing much of the respect for virtues that virtue ethicists have, nonetheless sees care not as a virtue per se, but as a relation-centred concept, or a social justice ethicist rooted in political critique and critical theory, just to identify several competing frameworks.

The Ethical Teacher deliberately situates its discussion of ethical knowledge, moral agency, and applied professional ethics within the contextualized practice of teaching. Moral and ethical principles are both embedded and engaged in the complexities, and often uncertainties, of this practice. While I appreciate that principles and virtues have broader significance in the realm of moral philosophy, I have chosen not to engage in an expansive theoretical description or analysis of specific paradigms, such as those mentioned above.[34] Rather, the focus is on the ethical dimensions of teaching and teachers' understanding of how these relate to their own professional work in both formal and informal ways.

While the behaviours and beliefs of teachers may encompass a variety of theoretical perspectives, ethical knowledge as it is described here relates to attitudes and interpersonal dynamics that essentially speak to a concern for right and wrong as embedded in what I have been referring to as core principles or virtues. In this respect, I do not use the term 'principle' to mean a law, precept, or maxim. Principles are not positioned here as motivators of action, but rather as descriptors of the knowledge and conduct of the ethical teacher.

If we are to embrace ethical knowledge as the knowledge base for a renewed professionalism in teaching, we must continue to accept and describe the embedded nature of much of what teachers do to reflect virtues and core principles. Many of the most prolific scholars who have addressed over an extended period of time the moral dimensions of teaching, such as Gary Fenstermacher, David Hansen, Robert Nash, Nel Noddings, Kevin Ryan, Hugh Sockett, Kenneth Strike, and Alan Tom, view ethics as central to the very essence of teaching, not as a by-product of the teaching process. Nonetheless, rather than leaving such dimensions embedded as part of an overall description of the inevitable moral nature of teaching, we must also draw heightened attention to them through the practice of some teachers more than others. In making moral practice visible, teachers themselves may explore the ethical implications of their work. They could build on the knowledge that some teachers (who can articulate clearly and precisely in ethical terms their behaviour and beliefs) exemplify, in order to harness such ethical knowledge to inform and enrich the profession as a whole.

Sockett describes professional teachers as 'experts' precisely because of their 'professional virtue', which he defines as 'a sustainable moral quality of individual human character that is learned'.[35] In sharing their ethical knowledge as it is grounded in the realities of practice, teachers may further learn from one another more about the connectedness between their own moral dispositions or intuitions and the work that they do in schools. Similarly, Carr claims that:

> The knowledge and understanding which should properly inform the professional consciousness of the competent teacher is . . . a kind of moral wisdom or judgement which is rooted in rational reflection about educational policies and practices and what is *ethically*, as well as instrumentally, appropriate to achieve them.[36]

Presumably, this knowledge is, in one respect, what all moral people should possess, yet it is necessarily seen as professional knowledge in a specialized way because of its application to the context of teaching in all its complexity and uncertainty.

If ethical knowledge is to become recognized and promoted as the cornerstone of professionalism in teaching, then the inevitable embeddedness of the moral dimensions in schools should not be equated with a lack of awareness or consciousness on the teacher's part. As Sizer and Sizer emphatically declare, teachers have a profound moral contract with students and therefore ought to be aware of what they are doing.[37] Heightened alertness to the nuances of practice and policy seen through the lens of more widely shared ethical knowledge may advance this professional obligation.

As is probably apparent, in both its title and its conceptual orientation, the focus of *The Ethical Teacher* is on the singular individual's moral practices, ethical perspectives, and professional obligations both as an individual and as a member of a collective body of other professional teachers. This is quite distinct from a focus on institutional and systemic realities within which individuals exist, and where a critique of organizational structures supplants a concern for individual moral responsibility. While I do not discount the significant influence that contextual elements of an organization's culture have on the attitudes and behaviours of individuals, my discussion of ethical knowledge is situated not as a statement of institutional culpability, but as an exhortation to teachers to examine the ethical realm of their work and foster with other teachers a collective sense of professionalism based on the principles and virtues embedded in their own practice. This is entirely consistent with Sommers' sharp criticism of the ideology that views the 'seat of moral responsibility' as being found in society and its institutions rather than as a matter of individuals' virtue. She writes strongly against 'the shift away from personal morals to an almost exclusive preoccupation with the morality of institutional policies'.[38] This position raises some provocative questions about whether one could be an ethical teacher in an unethical school and, conversely, whether one could engage in immoral behaviour in an environment based on a seemingly moral foundation. My immediate answer that both scenarios are entirely possible will be explored in greater detail in the latter part of the book.

Interestingly, at the time of writing this book, some members of the business community in North America were coming under close scrutiny, moral condemnation, and, in some cases, legal prosecution for gross breaches of ethics that threatened the companies under their control and robbed shareholders and members of the public of millions of dollars. Ironically, some of these companies had been singled out for praise in the past for championing currently trendy causes and public relations schemes identified as being ethically (equated with socially) responsible. Yet, it is the behaviour of individuals, the clear violation of such ethical principles as honesty and integrity, that put the well-being of others most at risk.

The Ethical Teacher is concerned with the moral and ethical complexities of the practice of teachers as individuals and as members of a larger professional group, as well as their unique interpretations of these complexities. In the chapters that follow, illustrative snapshots of teachers' practices, reflections and beliefs are offered as empirically grounded descriptions of moral agency in teaching. However, as stressed throughout Chapter 1, ethics, while straightforward on one level, is rarely simple in application. For example, what one teacher regards as a morally charged critical incident, another may interpret solely in terms of classroom management strategy. As Halstead and Taylor confirm, 'The indirect moral influence on children is deeply embedded in the daily life of the school, either within normal teaching activities or within the contingent interactions at classroom level . . . The process is further complicated by the fact that the same incident may have moral meaning to one observer and not to another'.[39] So how does one discern between the moral and the non-moral?

When describing the moral nature of classrooms and the ethical dimensions of teaching, one should resist the temptation to over-interpret all nuances of teaching as morally significant in and of themselves and, thus, be conscious instead of narrowing the interpretation. However, I also agree with Hansen's sensible observation that 'not everything that teachers do *necessarily* has moral significance, but any action a teacher takes *can* have moral import'.[40] From my point of view, the moral and ethical character of a teacher's demeanour, attitude, expression, or behaviour becomes evident once we clearly associate it with either the advancement or the violation of core ethical principles or virtues.

Once we see a teacher's prompt return of assignments as a sign of respect and care for students, rather than a mark of efficiency, we are getting a glimpse of moral agency. Once we recognize a teacher's efforts to allow all students time to answer questions in class as a quest for fairness, rather than a sound pedagogical strategy, we are made conscious of the moral complexity of teaching. Once we see a teacher temper the disciplining of a badly behaved child with compassion and understanding of the child's unhappiness, we cease to see only a classroom management technique. Once teachers themselves see such things, they start to define the foundation of a virtue-based applied professional ethics, they start to claim as their own what is explored throughout this book as ethical knowledge in teaching.

two

The teacher as a moral person

Teacher character as moral agency

The ethical teacher is, by necessity, an ethical person. One who lies and cheats for personal gain or who is callous towards the feelings of others is unlikely to transform into a principled person of integrity upon becoming a teacher. And, the teacher who strives to empathize with students and colleagues, who aims to be fair, careful, trustworthy, responsible, honest, and courageous in the professional role probably understands and appreciates the importance of such virtues in everyday life as well. The moral and ethical principles that teachers themselves uphold in the ways that they interact with students and others and in their approach to their professional responsibilities provide the basis of one aspect of their moral agency.

As a double-pronged state entailing a dual commitment on the part of teachers, moral agency concerns both what teachers hold themselves to ethically and what they seek to impart to students as contributing to their moral education. This chapter focuses on the former, those ethical principles reflected through the teacher's overall demeanour and specific behaviour, whether deliberate or not. This element of moral agency is primarily important on the grounds of a nonconsequential imperative. It is simply that students (and others in the professional teacher's world) have a moral right to be treated fairly, kindly, honestly, and with competence and commitment. Also important is the associated, but more consequential, consideration that students learn lessons about morality through their experiences with teachers. They can sense when teachers genuinely care about them; they can sniff out hypocrisy in a flash; and they are alert to differences between the supercilious and the authentic. Ultimately, the moral impact on students of what they see and hear around them is significant.

While the role of teacher carries with it its own moral expectations, the character of the individual teacher 'goes to the heart of the teacher's moral responsibilities', as Wynne and Ryan claim in their discussion of morality in teaching as exemplified by the daily actions of teachers.[1] And, character, as manifested in all its complexity, is central to moral agency. In an Aristotelian sense, the ongoing acquisition of virtue builds one's character in such a way as to habituate the person into a virtuous life in which good thoughts and good acts become a second nature extension of the kind of person they have become.

In defining character as a reliable inner disposition to act in a morally good way, Wiley refers to the character required of teachers who face daily moral decisions, and claims, 'Ethical behaviour is more important than any other aspect of teaching. An ethical teacher needs to have an awareness of moral issues, a sense of right and wrong, good judgment, integrity, and courage.'[2] By way of empirical example, one of the teachers in my study of moral agency in teaching recounted an anecdote from her own teenage years when she worked as a sales clerk in a women's clothing store. She explained, 'Some poor guy comes in and needs to buy something small for his wife, and another saleslady kind of took over and sold him the whole big thing. I didn't feel good about that. I thought he got suckered into more than he came in for.' As a result of this incident, the teacher said she quit this job. While this story does not seem to relate to teaching, it actually does define this person as the teacher she has become. She used this example to speak about her moral intuition regarding how to treat other people with honesty, care, and respect. She showed early on in her life a clear disposition towards being sensitive to morally charged situations, and she applies this same sensitivity to her treatment of students, as was observed in the dynamics of her classroom interactions. In her formal and informal conduct, she displays what Hansen identifies as 'moral sensibility'.[3] Reflective of her inner character, this sensibility is not a tool she uses to achieve success with her students. Rather, it is simply the way she is, and her judgement about her position as a teacher merely flows from the person she is.

More than a decade ago, Gary Fenstermacher identified the concept of a teacher's moral character as a kind of manner. More recently, he and Virginia Richardson, along with their research team at the University of Michigan conducted a significant project entitled 'The Manner in Teaching Project'.[4] Grounded in the philosophical assumption that one acquires virtue by associating with virtuous people, this project sought to 'understand how teachers display (or fail to display) the moral and intellectual virtues in their classrooms'.[5] They further define manner as 'the relatively stable dispositions of a teacher, expressive of his or her character as person and professional'.[6]

Their findings focus on such moral virtues as justice, fairness, compassion, humility, and tolerance expressed through teachers' 'manner' within the contextual complexity of the classroom. This study is consistent with my own investigation of teachers' moral agency, as it empirically informs *The Ethical Teacher*.[7] Both studies concentrate on the individual teacher as a moral person/moral professional and how ethical principles exemplifying this are revealed in the nuances of teaching, rather than on the aspects of the teaching role itself that are inherently moral.

The character or manner of the teacher, when shown in both small and large ways in the classroom, can affect students profoundly. In their review of recent literature on moral education and the teacher's role and responsibility, Halstead and Taylor, citing numerous sources, conclude:

> It is through relationships that children learn the importance of qualities such as honesty, respect and sensitivity to others. Children are most likely to be influenced by teachers whose qualities they admire. Such qualities include tolerance, firmness and fairness, acting in a reasonable manner and a willingness to explain things and, for older pupils, respect and freedom from prejudice, gentleness and courtesy, and sensitivity and responsiveness to the needs of pupils.[8]

One may note that such qualities are, at their core, moral and ethical principles that underpin the conduct of the professional teacher as moral agent. From this perspective, professional ethics is nothing more and nothing less than virtue in action.

In her discussion of moral intelligence as the 'capacity to understand right from wrong; [the] means to have strong ethical convictions and to act on them so that one behaves in the right and honorable way', Michele Borba describes the seven essential virtues as being empathy, conscience, self-control, respect, kindness, tolerance and fairness.[9] She further claims that moral philosophers have identified more than four hundred virtues. Clearly, of these, concepts share nuances of meaning. For example, compassion and empathy may be similar, justice and fairness are often, but not always, equated, courage and integrity are not so discrete as to be necessarily itemized separately, and respect for others could be seen to embody all other virtues. Note the overlapping commonalities among virtues and principles most frequently identified with professional ethics and specifically the moral qualities of teachers: fairness, justice, consistency, impartiality, trustworthiness, honesty, integrity, courage, commitment, diligence, respect, responsibility, empathy, kindness, care, compassion, gentleness, patience, understanding, friendliness, humility, civility, open-mindedness, and tolerance.

However, character is not merely a checklist of these and other associated virtues, but rather a dynamic reflection of the layered complexity of human experience in which ethical principles both overlap to complement each other and conflict to challenge one another. Even the most virtuous people may not know exactly how the principles so deeply embedded in their character relate to the situational realities of the workplace or the context of professional expectations. How to draw on such principles to give one the moral strength to deal with the daily unknowns is not straightforward. A conceptualization of the ethical teacher of good character fulfilling obligations as a moral agent accepts this uncertainty not as a problematic barrier but as an enabling descriptor to help us reframe teachers' practice in ethical terms.

Such a conceptualization has as its starting point practical examples of teachers' conduct and expressed beliefs. From these, moral and ethical principles are exemplified as elements of the teacher's character that infiltrate the classroom and school contexts in often seemingly mundane but nonetheless critical ways. The examples addressed in the following section are organized mainly around four multifaceted and intersecting ethical principles that the teachers themselves most often identified as being important to uphold: fairness, kindness, honesty, and respect.

In the classroom: moral messages

Moral messages abound in classrooms and schools where teachers' actions and attitudes towards others, most notably students, demonstrate varying levels of sensitivity to a range of moral and ethical principles. When viewed through a virtue oriented lens, formal and informal routines, interactions, and practices become more than academic objectives, efficiency strategies, control techniques, and effective planning and policy measures (although it clearly may be argued that such concerns, especially those relating to the intellectual responsibility of the teacher to be a responsible and effective teacher, are also themselves ethical in nature).[10] In this respect, the curriculum choices teachers make in structuring lessons, the pedagogical decisions they take, their casual social exchanges with students as well as their more formalized approaches to discipline and classroom management, their methods of evaluation, and many other discretionary aspects of their work all have the potential to influence others in profound moral and ethical ways.

For example, when grade six teacher Gina selects reading material for her class, her choices are not only curriculum based; they also reflect her attentiveness to the emotional well-being of her students, as she lets compassion and empathy guide her. She explains:

> There are stories that, even though they are offered in the text book, I'll say, 'no, I'm not going there. The students don't need that.' If you know

that someone doesn't have a mother or father, then there are just certain stories you won't read. I don't care if they're in the book. Because it could bring back bad memories for a child, and it could hurt them. I am not going to bring that into the classroom.

For the same reason, she, like grade three teacher Alan, modifies a combined writing and art lesson that culminates in the crafting of a Mother's Day or Father's Day card. Appreciating the complicated and troubled home lives that many of their students have, they emphasize that the cards can be made for anyone special to them. What for some teachers may start as a fairly ordinary writing unit becomes for others an exercise fraught with moral tensions.

The pedagogical tradition of requiring students to raise their hands in class has the obvious instrumental purposes of establishing classroom order, testing student comprehension of content by maintaining a disciplined climate conducive to answering questions, and facilitating group discussion. Morally, however, it regulates turn-taking which inevitably involves issues of fairness, respect for others, patience, and self-control. How a teacher navigates in such routine situations is ethically significant.[11] Thoughtlessly done, it may project the image of a teacher who discriminates, favours, or just does not care about students. Thoughtfully carried out, turn-taking may enable the teacher to ensure fair participation as well as protect both the less vocal students who may need some gentle and kindly encouragement and the more vocal ones who may become targeted for abuse by other students who grow to resent them.

Another common pedagogical strategy, small group work, is morally laden, given that the process of determining group membership necessitates some kind of selection among individual students. The ethical teacher must make academically and morally sound decisions about how groups are formed and how individuals within a group context should be evaluated. Issues of fairness and care need to be considered.

Theresa has a problem with one of her grade ten students who is very upset at being split up from her best friend for a group exercise that Theresa has assigned. Normally, Theresa will encourage students to be responsible by allowing them to form their own groups. On some occasions, like this one, however, she will make the choice for them. In this case, she knows the student, who seems insecure with others, will benefit in the end by this action even though she is initially distressed. Theresa takes her aside, explains her reasons gently and kindly, and then watches as the student, now liberated from the shadow of her more outgoing friend, gradually emerges as a group leader in her own way with an enhanced sense of confidence and self-worth. Theresa explains:

I also want to give students a chance to work with people who may not have the same values and opinions as their friends and themselves. This way, there is more sharing; they grow in knowledge and they meet each other on a different level. It allows them to show off their best side so that by the end of class, they feel valuable and can say, 'I have lots to offer this class, after all, and so does everybody else.'

Theresa's spontaneous private exchange with the student in the above scenario, as she calms and reassures the girl, reflects one of an infinite number of ways teachers can exude genuine care and respect for their students. Often instantaneous, seemingly involuntary, the actions and reactions of teachers send subtle messages to students about how they are thought of as people, not simply learners. Upon realizing that he has inadvertently missed a student when passing out math tests, Robert apologizes to the grade seven student and hands him a test (note the word 'hands'. He does not throw it on the student's desk or make the student come to him for it). On a hot spring day, Lori asks her students if they are comfortable or whether they need more windows open before commencing class. Surprised by the sudden strength of the smell from the candles she just lit as part of a science demonstration, Jean immediately abandons the exercise, apologizes to her grade four class and ensures that no one feels ill before moving on to the next activity. Such fleeting situations consistently reinforced by the civility of the teacher go a long way to setting the tone in the classroom as one of consideration, understanding, care, and respect.

Classroom management and discipline are layered in moral complexity and raise questions that leave teachers uncertain, angry, guilty, saddened, disappointed, confused, and feeling a range of other emotions. The rightness and wrongness of policies, such as zero tolerance policies, and practices, such as entire class punishment as a management strategy, should be considered by teachers as part of this complexity. By way of example, Gina describes her elementary school's policy of issuing infractions to students for a variety of misdemeanours with a cumulative effect on consequences ranging from phoning parents to suspension (for example, three infractions and the child gets a detention, five and the child is sent to the office). Notwithstanding what I consider the morally questionable nature of such a policy itself and its fair implementation, the immediate problem for Gina is, as she explains:

> I use infractions to help curb the wrongdoing by my students. But I have to be careful too because sometimes if you are working with a student and he's never received an infraction and is really hardworking, but something dumb happens and he does something but is really embarrassed by it. You don't do something to make him even more embarrassed, and it can be really devastating for him to get an infraction. And then there are other children where it's 'look it's been three times this week that you've done this; now I have to call your parents'. But

then, the kids say 'why did I get a major infraction, but you didn't give him one for the same thing?' Then the parents phone and say that I deal with students differently. But for some kids, a minor infraction is like the end of the world for them, and for others, they need them.

What Gina grapples with as part of her ethical judgement is a common concern of teachers: how to balance kindness and understanding with fairness and impartiality, all virtuous principles, in situations where they may seem, at least to some, to conflict.

Similar tensions emerge in the complex area of student evaluation. The principled desire of the caring and sympathetic teacher striving to encourage, support, and reward the failing student who tries hard can transform into a dishonest inflation of the student's academic accomplishment that is fundamentally unfair to everyone, especially the student himself or herself. As Ross explains, 'you can't give somebody an A if they obviously didn't understand the concepts. I can't feel sorry for you and say, "you're going to get the A because you really worked hard". But you can write comments such as "outstanding effort", and you can encourage.' Some teachers agonize over such situations, and the grey areas can get more grey. The important thing is that they at least recognize them as moral issues and not just assessment ones.

The moral and ethical principles embedded in these brief examples include the interwoven virtues that teachers of character most reflect: the will to be fair, to be kind, to be honest, and the all-encompassing will to show respect for others by having the courage to commit themselves to these and other virtues of responsibility and integrity. The rest of this chapter expands on some of the concepts raised by these and other examples as they illustrate the complexities of such principles when applied to practice.

The virtue of fairness is rooted in the fundamental ethical principle of justice and implies other associated moral qualities such as consistency, constancy, equality, impartiality, and equity that are not necessarily interpreted in the same ways by all people. For teachers, the need to treat students fairly is an all-pervasive moral imperative that extends into all aspects of their professional practice. It influences such things as enforcing school and class rules, marking and assessing students, displaying their work publicly, assigning tasks, granting favours, calling on them to respond to questions in class, arranging them in groups and seating patterns, engaging in personal exchanges with individuals, assigning and enforcing test dates and homework deadlines, just to name a few. The days of regarding the idea of a 'teacher's pet' as a harmless idiosyncrasy of a crank teacher should be well and truly over. As Jackson et al. argue:

> Of all the moral qualities a teacher might possess, a habit of being fair is surely one of the most highly praised. The rules of fairness call for

treating all students alike, at least insofar as granting favors and privileges is concerned, although they usually also allow special awards to be given to acknowledge outstanding performance of some kind.[12]

Similarly, David Bricker identifies fairness or justice as the first virtue of public life; calling it also the first professional principle, he notes that teachers regard fairness as something 'mandated of them by the ethics of their profession'.[13]

However, the interpretation of what fairness actually means in practice is often the source of confusion and dispute. As Colnerud remarks, in her study of teachers in Sweden, ethical conflicts confront teachers torn between deciding whether fairness requires 'equal or differential allocation and treatment' of students.[14] Teachers in my studies of moral agency and ethical dilemmas also spoke at great length about fairness as necessitating equal treatment or special and different treatment. For most, it involves a sensitive and commonsensical combination of both. Teachers are unique among professionals in that they, for the most part, engage with their primary stakeholders or 'clients' (to use the language of the professions) in groups rather than individually. Given this context, issues of comparative fairness are of immediate and obvious significance as teachers strive to balance the perhaps conflicting needs of individual students with a dedication to fostering a sense of common good and well-being for the class or school as a whole. It is a complex and morally demanding objective, and teachers who carry it out well deserve much admiration.

At a very routine level, Shannon, like many elementary school teachers, ensures that classroom chores or duties are allocated equally to all students. Such things, as listed on the 'monitor board', include taking the attendance record to the office each morning, fetching the gym key, being a row monitor, handing out paper, books, glue and scissors, tidying up the room, and cleaning the blackboards. While students volunteer for these jobs, Shannon ensures that the same student does not always do the same duty and that all students participate. She also tries to balance and share all duties between the boys and the girls equally. She comments that, 'I feel at their age they see that as a fairness issue'. What is noteworthy here is that the teacher recognizes what otherwise may be seen as a functional routine of daily school life as a morally embedded activity, and that she both empathizes with the students' sense of fairness and applies it to her practice as a teacher.

For secondary school teacher Marissa, 'treating each individual with respect and dignity' is a matter of fairness. She explains further: 'I try to be equitable with them all. We do tend to like students or be more fond of or quick with certain students than with others. But I try not to let that influence me, for example in enforcing the uniform rule, and coming in late and getting a late slip, and so forth; and it's a constant battle, but I try to be equitable, treat them equally and with respect.' On another occasion, when asked what she would like students to say about her as a teacher, Marissa replies, 'I guess that I was kind to them and compassionate and fair. I want them to say that I was fair and that I treated them equally. For example, if you give a test to your period one class but not to your period four one even though they're doing the same work, that's not fair.' So, for Marissa, fairness means equal treatment. On many occasions, she is observed attempting to make visible for students her efforts to treat them fairly. In one situation, she asks one of a group of three students who are frequently disruptive in class to move her seat; it is evidently not the first time this has happened. She explains gently and calmly: 'Maria, I know it isn't just you. I know you're not the only one talking today, but I need you to move and work somewhere else. I'm asking you because you're in the middle. If Ellen was in the middle, I would have asked her to move.' Upon hearing this explanation, Maria moves her seat.

Marissa acknowledges that maintaining equality is not always easy. She speaks of occasions where she may insist a student do something while letting another student 'off the hook'. It may be because of differences in their ages or grade levels (she is more lenient with the older students) or because some students are constantly challenging the rules and in need of firmer guidance. She remarks, 'each individual is different, which challenges me then on the equality issue. So you see, as much as I say I try for equality, there are still boundaries. Although I said I try to be equal, it gets challenging, and it is difficult to do.' Her conscious attempts to treat students fairly and explain to them her reasons for her actions and choices are observed as a matter of daily occurrence. While she claims that certain students may feel 'picked on', they are always the ones who are most disruptive of others and challenging of the school rules. Efforts on Marissa's part to apply the rules fairly to all are perceived by such students to be persecution because of the added attention their behaviour attracts.

Unequal or differential treatment of students is seen by teachers as fair treatment when it corresponds to a level of equity or when, as Fallona found in her research, they 'attempt to be fair by attending to those students whom they feel need their attention the most'.[15] This is consistent with Nucci's claim that 'treating others fairly may mean treating people unequally in the sense that equity requires adjustments that bring people into more comparable statuses'.[16] He further notes, in citing Kohlberg, that children start to become aware around the age of 8 years old of differences in needs and capacities of individuals who should therefore be treated differently.[17]

However, while teachers recognize that it is not necessarily unfair to treat students differentially, realistically drawing the line between when it is or isn't appropriate is not ethically unproblematic. Theresa worries that the poorly behaved students get disproportionally more of her energy and attention; they are asked to sit near the front of the class, leaving the other well-behaved students near the back to be potentially ignored. Similarly, with respect to her special needs students who are integrated into her class, she believes that, 'when I deal with the autistic child, it obviously takes away a chunk of classroom time for everyone. Although I feel that these children have a right to be in the class and a right to their education, I don't always have an appropriate activity, and then all students end up getting short-changed on one level or another. So that's really an ethical issue for me.' Sean sends daily notes home with one of his most troubled, behaviourally and academically, grade three students. He knows that some of the other students would also like this little bit of extra attention. With some frustration, he comments, 'Maybe I can't treat everybody equally. Maybe for the sake of the class and for the sake of me and my ability to teach, I have to pay more attention to him. Maybe it will serve a greater good eventually. I would like to sit down everyday and write a note for everybody, but I need to prioritize, and, in the end, the more difficult students do get more attention.' Erica, who teaches grades two and three, explains the issue this way:

> I would like to say that the rules apply equally to everybody, but I know that they don't. And that's because there are certain ways you have to handle some kids and certain ways you have to handle others. And I have certain expectations for some students that I don't have for others, and whether or not that's fair, I guess anyone can judge. But I certainly can't have the same expectations that I have for Joey morally as I would for Dan, which is why when Dan yelled out today in class, he got sent to his desk, whereas Joey yells out constantly. I can't send Joey to his desk because he won't go, and the time that I spend getting him to his desk would disrupt everybody else.

She further justifies her differential treatment morally and notes that 'Joey needs me in a different way than the other students. The other kids in my class know that I spend a little bit of extra time with him but they understand that there's a reason for it.' Nonetheless, she admits the complexity involved by referring to another student who was upset by her special treatment of Joey: 'He explained to his mother, who told me, that this makes him sad. Maybe in a lot of ways it's not fair, but in a lot of other ways, I see it's really hard when you're one person and you have 25 kids.'

Most teachers accept that fairness is best achieved when they are equally attentive to each student's capacity and needs; as needs differ, the level of attention differs as well. Widely differing treatment, however, can become very unfair regardless of the good intention or motive behind it, and the struggle for the ethical teacher is to be ever conscious of balancing the need to be fair to individuals and the need to be fair to the group. An added complexity is signalled in situations where other moral principles, those relating to the will to be kind, caring, and compassionate and those compelling us to be honest and trustworthy complicate the moral pursuit of what is just and fair. While this is often experienced by teachers most poignantly in their professional obligation to evaluate students, such ethical concerns pervade all aspects of school life.

Much has been written about an essential conflict between the ethic of justice and the ethic of care as two distinct ethics having different moral aims.[18] On one hand, a focus on the just application of impartial and consistent standards is criticized for potentially ignoring human differences in ways that negate genuine sensitivity to the needs of others. On the other hand, the goal of caring in its responsiveness to the shifting relational and situational demands of others may be seen as fostering gross unfairness by being neither impartial nor equal. Some, such as Michael Katz, argue that, 'At the core of teacher-student relations . . . is a potential tension between two different moral orientations that are bound up with a teacher's effort to treat students well – the tension between being fair and being caring'.[19] Others, such as Kenneth Strike, criticize such a dualism.[20] Rather, he advocates moral pluralism as a preferable means of conceptualizing complexity and conflict in which a wide range of moral goods, including fairness and care but necessarily involving other interwoven virtues, characterizes the moral life in both conflictual and compatible ways. Such a pluralism is an apt descriptor of the experiences and moral orientations of teachers portrayed in *The Ethical Teacher*.

Care, as a principle, embodies associated virtues and a manner of behaving towards others with kindness, compassion, sensitivity, empathy, gentleness, and understanding. By sharp contrast, Reitz offers the following bleak, but not uncommon, depiction of the teacher as the impersonal professional:

> The unnecessary distance some teachers put between themselves and their students, the cold objectivity of the well-constructed lesson plan, and the impersonal adherence to every jot and title of a curriculum guide destroy trust and deliver an unfortunate message to students. The impersonal teacher is saying in effect: 'I am here because I am paid; you are here because you have to be. We will both be satisfied if you get passing grades. I can't be concerned about how you develop as a person or what you do in life with the information I am communicating. I teach what I am told to teach and that is the limit of my responsibility for you.'[21]

Fortunately, caring teachers need not sacrifice either their formal authority or academic rigour while exuding a sense of kindness and humanity that influences the climate of the classroom in perhaps small, but nonetheless significant, ways.

Theresa is conscious of always trying to make eye contact with her high school students. During one lesson, she notices she had not yet made such contact with a student sitting off to the side of the room. She says to her in front of the class, 'Oh, I feel like I've been ignoring you because I haven't looked at you', and she apologizes. She continues to worry about this and makes plans to move the student to another seat within her sight range. Also, when she moves around the classroom to help individuals or groups, she puts her body at eye level by either sitting on a desk or chair or by kneeling on the floor. She explains, 'You're not in the conversation if you're standing and they're sitting. It takes that power thing away, I think, and is part of caring. It says to the students that I care enough that they're worth bending down for or sitting down with.' At the elementary level, Shannon does similar things to put herself at her students' eye level; for her too it is a matter of wanting students to feel valued and cared for.

For many teachers, like Sean, it is very important for them to protect students' dignity and avoid embarrassing them in front of their peers. In one class, a student is humming, and he simply asks whomever it is to please stop. No effort is made to discover who it is. He later explains, 'This is not a witch hunt . . . I try not to single people out unless I really have to, and sometimes I do and feel bad about it. I try to be respectful of their feelings.' He empathizes with students, as does Tracy. In her home form class, there are several students who are not allowed by the principal to attend a special school assembly, for disciplinary reasons. Rather than reading off their names, she discretely indicates those who could attend, as she dismisses the class: 'I wasn't going to say "the following students must stay with me" and I wasn't going to use public humiliation as the means of punishment.'

Contrary to the image of the teacher as a severe authoritarian, suspicious and disdainful of students, the ethical teacher projects the image of a kindly and caring person. Such a teacher may do so in any number of ways: by anticipating sensitive situations and heading off undue emotional harm to students, by smiling at them, by speaking to them not as 'chums', but as fellow human beings, by being consistent and reliable in temperament, by being attentive to students' anxieties, and by recognizing that kindness does not equal weakness – the teacher's lingering fear of being seen as a 'push-over' is groundless if in fact it is moral strength, not timidity or cowardice, that makes him or her seem caring, kind, compassionate, and empathetic. These qualities should drive, not compromise, the conviction to be also fair and, as needed, firm.

The fair and kind teacher should be someone to trust. And trust is built, at least in part, by an expectation of honesty. 'Students are very, very intuitive. You cannot lie to them and get away with it. If you try, you're mincemeat. I don't have any pity whatsoever for a teacher who tries to pull the wool over these kids' eyes,' says secondary school teacher, Carol. This indictment of those who treat students dishonestly in an interpersonal sense is echoed by many teachers. It is really quite simple, as Erica explains: 'If you do have a sense of moral judgement and you do have a sense of the difference between right and wrong, and you're honest with yourself and honest with your kids, then that will come across.' The virtue of honesty also encompasses the capacity to be sincere and genuine about what one says and does.[22]

The moral imperative that teachers behave honestly involves not only the relational aspect of teaching, but also the intellectual or academic focus. It prohibits them from misrepresenting either the curricular content they are teaching or the students' understanding of it. It is a mark of respect for the student to respect also the integrity of the content.[23] While correcting students' errors may seem at times to conflict with the caring teacher's desire to be kind and supportive of students' feelings, even the well intentioned corruption of intellectual truth, in all its possible forms, is nothing less than fraudulent. And, it deceives the very students intended to be the object of one's care.

In terms of evaluation, Erica states:

> I have to be very ethical when I'm marking them. I can't give them a mark because I like them as human beings; I have to give them a mark based on what they do in my classroom. An example is Joey. He's a great kid, and I totally have sensitivity to his family problems and his needs on one moral level. But on an ethical level, I have a responsibility that when he can't do his reading or he can't do his writing to give him marks that accurately portray that. I have to be honest.

However, as she notes, teachers should correct students either formally through assessment or informally during the course of classroom discussion always with sensitivity, kindness, and encouragement. As Theresa comments, 'When I must fail a student, I never feel good. But I also never let them walk out of my room without talking about it. I'll sit down with them and say "I'm sorry but you failed." And we usually talk about why and what to do.'

For Marissa, another aspect of evaluation that connects to the obligation to be honest concerns the students' right to be informed of their marks for everything they do and their right to question the teacher, without fear, about any errors in the grading or calculating of marks. She is appalled by the number of teachers she sees who often do not give back tests, homework, or assignments; she expresses distress at the fact that many students have 'absolutely no idea how they've been evaluated'. This is an ethical issue not only of honesty, but also of respect.

As an ethical principle, respect may be seen to envelop most other virtues in its broadest sense. If one is respectful of oneself and of others, one is responsible and diligent in fulfilling commitments, one is courteous and civil, kind and caring, reasonably modest yet confident in one's convictions, thoughtful and trustworthy, honest and fair-minded. This is quite distinct from the loose interpretation of 'respect' as one of the most misused terms in popular culture. Respect for others does not translate into unconditional subservience and awe, and real self-respect is never based on shallow conceit and self-aggrandizement. Both teachers and students, who seem to use the term repeatedly, need to appreciate these distinctions in the expectations they have of one another.

Some argue that, 'A moral classroom begins with the teacher's attitude of respect for children, for their interests, feelings, values, and ideas. This respect is expressed in the classroom's organization, in activities, and in the teacher's interactions with children.'[24] Respect, on the part of the teacher, is manifested in multiple and varying ways by avoiding negative actions or what Dunn also identifies as 'unprofessional behaviour' (which includes such things as being late, gossiping about students, and being careless with student grades).[25] It is also reflected through the many positive steps teachers take to respect the dignity of their students as human beings.

Teachers from kindergarten and early elementary to senior secondary classes argue that it is ethically critical that teachers do not publicly 'embarrass', 'humiliate', or 'single out' for the purpose of derision or ridicule individual students. Some speak of their alarm at hearing colleagues do just this as misguided teaching and control strategies or as illustrative of their sardonic efforts at being humorous. By contrast, the respectful teacher may be seen engaging in 'one-on-one' conversations with students in hallways for a variety of reasons, but always, with the purpose of protecting students' privacy.

Other fairly routine illustrations of teachers' realizations of the principle of respect include Terry, who is willing to share with a student another's assignment in order to help the first student understand why he had difficulty; however, he always ensures that he first removes from the assignment all identifying information to protect the confidentiality of the other, and he is always honest with students about this practice. Bob refers to the need to respect students by marking their work with care and returning it promptly. Judith regards the manner in which teachers dress to be significant; she argues that sloppily dressed or casually clothed teachers send negative messages of 'disrespect' to students. She states, 'Maybe it's very traditional, but the way you dress reflects how you feel about where you are. It's something that the students notice, and parents have mentioned it to me.' Many teachers model respectful and polite civil behaviour seemingly effortlessly and automatically; they are heard to say 'please', 'thank you', and 'you're welcome' to students and colleagues. Others are inclined to apologize when appropriate. Gina always checks that her students can see the blackboard or overhead slides she uses; she also makes sure that she wears her glasses some days instead of her contact lenses so that the two or three students in her grade six class who are self-conscious of having to wear glasses themselves would 'feel better'. Respect is an expression of mutual understanding and trust. Theresa explains, 'If I don't want kids to yell at me, then I have to make sure I don't yell at them. It's as simple as that. If I want them to care about each other, then I have to show care towards them; so sometimes I do things for them. As a simple example, if a kid drops her pen, I'll get it for her. I don't say, "Well, you dropped your pen, get it yourself." ' Judith summarizes what these teachers address in relation to the ethical obligations that they require of themselves: 'I have to model proper ethical behaviour in terms of fairness, in terms of respect, in terms of honesty and just generally instilling some sense of kindness really. I mean the obvious point is to treat the students as I would want to be treated.'

Such an allusion to the 'Golden Rule' is a common reference point for teachers of character whose overall manner in the classroom sends moral messages to students that, among other things, they are being treated fairly, kindly, and honestly, and that both they as people and the work they do are respected by their teachers. While two teachers may differ in their approaches to practice, both may be seen to fulfill their professional responsibilities as moral agents if, in fact, they are able to defend their actions and attitudes on ethical grounds alone. Some teachers are more aware of their moral potency than others; while many of the nuances of virtue they display are seemingly spontaneous and even involuntary on their part, such teachers recognize the moral dimensions of their work. They see instructional, interpersonal, disciplinary, evaluative, and curricular moments as potentially morally-laden expressions of their ethical obligations as professionals. Such awareness contributes to the foundation of ethical knowledge in teaching.

Self-awareness as ethical knowledge

If ethical knowledge is to be conceptualized as the basis for a renewed sense of professionalism in teaching, then teachers need to be aware of the moral nature of what they do. They need a well developed 'conscience', defined as something which 'provides us with *knowledge* about what is right and wrong. However, conscience is more than just a passive source of knowledge. Conscience involves *reason* and critical thinking, it also involves *feelings*. Conscience not only *motivates* us; it *demands* that we act in accord with it.'[26] However, the ethical teacher's well developed conscience must transcend everyday knowledge of right and wrong to be able to apply such knowledge to the professional context of teaching practice. An intuitive sense as a moral person must be brought to bear on the teaching role so as to influence actions and interactions. And, for it to be regarded as knowledge, it must be conscious. While teachers need not necessarily weigh every word and action in terms of the moral and ethical principles underpinning them, they should be able to rely on their ethical knowledge to regulate such daily behaviour. And, ethical knowledge requires that they at least have a solid appreciation for their moral agency role and a clear awareness of how that role is manifested in their overall practice.

In their noteworthy study, Jackson, Boostrom, and Hansen argue that teachers are not generally aware of the moral strength of their actions. Indeed, they claim that teachers do not consciously intend to act as moral agents, and that it is only by virtue of being essentially good people that they can have a kind of 'rubbing off' impact on students. They state, 'The unintentional outcomes of schooling, the ones teachers and administrators seldom plan in advance, are of greater moral significance – that is, more likely to have enduring effects – than those that are intended and consciously sought.'[27] Similarly, in a separate discussion, David Hansen refers to the habitual way teachers act; not fully self-conscious of their behaviour as expressions of virtues, they enact the qualities embedded in the kinds of persons they are – moral meanings are 'unwilled' and 'unintended'.[28] He offers by way of example a description of a teacher who navigates her way through a class discussion by calling on students to take turns. She is praised for her sensitivity and fairness, and is characterized as a person who just happens to be sensitive, rather than a teacher who intends to demonstrate her sensitivity in class. Given the spontaneity of the context and the lack of any scripted lesson plan, such a conclusion makes sense. However, there may be an additional angle from which to look at such a situation that in no way dismisses the idea of spontaneous, habitual, second-nature type of behaviour on the teacher's part.

This teacher made a point of mentioning to her students the reasons for what she was doing as she was doing it, thus showing some level of awareness and intent, or alertness, as Hansen acknowledges. If she were anything like the teachers quoted here in the previous section of *The Ethical Teacher*, she would have been able in an interview to articulate moral reasons for conducting her class this way; if asked for an example of fairness or sensitivity, she might well have identified this scenario. While such an after the fact awareness of one's moral practices would not necessarily diminish the often unplanned nature of their execution, it should be seen to situate the practices in a realm other than that of the fully unintended or the unwilled because there *is* an overarching intention on the part of the teacher to be fair and sensitive to students generally. As the teacher acknowledges how this intention informs the specifics of her practice, she reveals her ethical knowledge.

Some teachers, such as those previously quoted, can articulate with depth and intention what they hope to achieve morally and ethically in their class-rooms and how they hope to facilitate it. In this regard, it seems that a level of ethical knowledge has been acquired by at least some teachers who demonstrate a self-conscious awareness of what they try to do in their capacity as moral agents. With thoughtful intent, they express a reflective acknowledgement of the virtues and principles that guide their practice. They are mindful of the good. So, while their daily acts of fairness, kindness, honesty, and respect – as well as the complex subtleties of interacting with students – may still be largely spontaneous and habitual, some teachers nonetheless do seem able to perceive and explain them within a moral and ethical framework to an extent greater than that with which they have been previously credited.

One may recall Thompson's point that 'no teacher acts without some concept of professionalism and the ethical basis of teaching. Every teacher has an "educational platform." '[29] Such a claim is echoed by grade three teacher, Shannon, who states: 'I can't imagine a classroom that doesn't have moral and ethical dimensions. I think that every word you say to a student has moral or ethical value.' Similarly, in his research on teachers' beliefs in practice as they relate to morality, Sanger sought to understand how primary teachers view morality and their own moral agency.[30] He concludes that the teachers he studied have substantial beliefs about morality as well as a rich and complex understanding of how it unfolds in the classroom. I am reluctant to believe that all teachers have either an appreciation of the ethical foundations of teaching or the capacity to acquire such an appreciation; however, those who do have a keen sense of their own moral agency and how it influences their professional practice possess the ethical knowledge that when shared and augmented may prove to be a catalyst for applied ethical professionalism in teaching.

Some teachers who seem to express a heightened awareness of themselves as moral agents and their classrooms and schools as arenas of dynamic ethical complexity recall their own past experiences as students. They refer to teachers who had bullied and humiliated them, and how haunted memories of such experiences contribute in part to their consciousness of how they, themselves, treat students. As secondary school teacher, Carol, recounts:

> My grade seven and eight teacher was the worst teacher. Oh, my goodness, gracious! And, he became a principal. How a man could do that to children! So many bad things that man did. He taught all kinds of things. He taught me not to do any of those things. You know, I'd put up my hand, and he'd say, 'Oh, here comes another stupid question.' He'd say, 'Martin,' that's my maiden name, 'what do you want? It must be something stupid if you are going to say it.' This man was so mean. Not just to me. He was just not a good teacher, not at all. And I had him

for two years. I took his abuse for two years. Oh, he shut me up. I had no self-esteem. And, he produced something in me that I hate. He produced hatred in me. I hated him. Now I make sure I don't have any hatred in my classroom.

Carol spoke of another teacher who used to call on her to read aloud in class often even though she knew how embarrassed Carol was that she could not pronounce certain English words because of her strong French Canadian accent. Given the choice of words in the poem she was asked to read, as well as the teacher's manner, Carol was convinced that she did this deliberately: 'She could have picked someone else to read those ones. I was so hurt that she did it. It's extremely important to me that I don't do that to any student.' Even if Carol's teacher was not being deliberately cruel, she reflected flawed ethical judgement and a lack of sensitivity in this case. Ethical knowledge demands a more heightened awareness on the part of teachers.

Marissa describes a similar experience:

We're all such delicate human beings, and teachers play such an influential role in a student's life. I remember my grade nine English teacher; I think I'm glad I had him because I know from him what not to do as a teacher. He said that my handwriting was horrible and it was too big. Well, you know, I had problems with my eyes, and I needed new glasses, and he was so insensitive to that to say in front of the whole class, 'Redo it because your writing is too big.' This crushed me, and I don't want anybody in my class to ever feel that way.

During my interviews with Marissa, she frequently anticipated questions about the moral and ethical significance of certain circumstances. She identified with great precision the very examples of her practice, illustrative of her moral agency role, that I previously observed, before I had a chance to ask her about them. She was able to explain exactly why she does certain things in class that highlight her ethical intentions. She understands why she promotes the virtues that she does in the classroom. She spoke often about her own sense of fairness and kindness; she expressed regret that she has not developed a level of courage that would enable her to speak out against what she occasionally perceives as collegial injustice towards students. She seemed aware of her own gentle and compassionate manner in the classroom. Marissa believes she is intuitive. While much of what she does as a teacher may indeed be an intuitive and spontaneous extension of her own character, she reflects a level of conscious ethical knowledge that she calls on to explain her practice. In this respect, it is significant to recognize that her role as moral agent is neither a surprise to her nor a fluke of her subconscious. It is an identifiable element of her professional being.[31]

Marissa is not alone in this regard. Many teachers speak of their ethical intentions and judgements about their successes and failures in meeting self-established standards for being fair, kind, honest, and respectful to students. They spend a good deal of time and energy adjudicating in their own minds what these and other ethical principles mean in the complex and varying circumstances of school life. And they are able to articulate moral rationales for their choices. For example, Theresa struggles to keep her students' creative projects left in her classroom at the end of each year despite a clear lack of storage space. She explains, 'I won't throw the project out as long as the student is still at this school. It is a creation of that student and if she comes looking for it a year later and I've thrown it out, that can be very hurtful. I think it says a lot for kids that you care about their stuff that you would keep it safe for them.' What may be for some teachers a somewhat trivial issue of clearing out one's classroom becomes for Theresa a moral issue requiring her to show care and respect for students' property and, by extension, for the students themselves. The fact that she mentions this as a conscious decision she makes on moral grounds despite the inconvenience to herself says much about her ethical knowledge and how it is revealed even in seemingly minor and routine situations.

Even those teachers who may be seen as essentially moral people and who have a heightened awareness of the ethical dimensions of their professional responsibilities as well as their own actions, may experience partial lapses in self-awareness. For the most part, such teachers work from within a conscious moral framework and articulate their intentions and actions in terms of ethical objectives. However, given the complexity of school life, the multiple and often conflicting demands on teachers, the need to respond quickly to spontaneous situations involving students and others, and the obvious and rather trite observation that teachers are, after all, only human, it is hardly surprising that even the most morally-intentioned teacher may misjudge a situation in a way that may transmit unforeseen negative moral messages.

By way of example, Marissa – who is ever-conscious of being fair and kind towards students – allows extensions on assignments, accepts students late to class, and permits students to determine test and assignment due dates. She explains that she does this consciously as part of a moral objective to foster in her secondary school students a sense of self-responsibility and self-worth. It is also for Marissa illustrative of her respect for students. While there are usually consequences to be paid for delinquent behaviour (she insists on students providing late slips for admittance to class; she may deduct marks for late assignments, etc.), these are admittedly fairly gentle and benign. Marissa does not chastise students; part of being self-responsible means for her an understanding that those who cheat or take advantage of her good nature are only cheating themselves. One wonders whether the other students who always arrive to class in a timely manner and get their homework and assignments completed to meet deadlines may feel a sense of unfairness when they see negligent classmates treated so apparently softly and with care. Similarly, those who lose the class vote on when tests are scheduled may feel that they could accept a mandated date from the teacher more easily than a majority rule decision based on classmates' preferences.

When asked about whether her efforts to accommodate students in this way could be seen as unfair to some, Marissa replies that she has never had a complaint about it:

> I've been conscious of that because I was one of those kids who used to get everything done on time even if I had to stay up late to do it, and then the teacher would say, 'Don't worry, I'll collect the assignments tomorrow instead of today.' And I hated that so much. I think if any student addressed that with me I probably would have to look at it and say, 'Okay, maybe we could look at giving you a bonus for handing it in.' But, I've never had any one tell me it's unfair. So they don't see it, I don't think, as an injustice; they see it as helping another student along.

Could Marissa be mistaken about this? Do such scenarios imply a tension between one principle, such as care and sensitivity to individuals' circumstances, and another, such as justice and equal treatment of all? Is the fact that the students have not complained even relevant if the practices themselves are inherently flawed in an ethical sense? As discussed previously, different perspectives on how the ethic of fairness, in this particular case, is manifested in action may raise such questions that could challenge the teacher's awareness and interpretation of her practice. For some teachers, this and other such scenarios create tension and uncertainty that may result in ethical dilemmas. As is explored in Part 2 of *The Ethical Teacher*, dilemmas potentially undermine a teacher's sense of ethical knowledge.

Teachers who have a conscious awareness of their moral agency are not immune from situations where their ethical knowledge fades, and their awareness of the moral dimensions of their actions diminishes. Buzzelli and Johnston, who similarly argue that teachers do have a moral sense, a deep awareness of the moral significance of their choices, refer to such lapses in awareness as 'blind spots in our ability to perceive the moral in situations'.[32] They recommend the continual cultivation of moral perception on the part of all teachers, new and experienced. The latter part of *The Ethical Teacher* addresses how the collective sharing of ethical knowledge as it influences the peculiarities of specific circumstances in teaching may best enable teachers to hone their awareness in even more ethically perceptive ways.

By contrast, there are other teachers who seem oblivious to the moral impact of their own practices and attitudes. The faulty self-awareness of those lacking ethical knowledge is most clearly revealed in situations where the embedded moral messages are negative and possibly even harmful. To be clear, this is not a reference to the (hopefully) small number of teachers who are cruel or unfair by design and intent; rather, this is meant to indicate those teachers who simply fail to appreciate the nature of moral agency and how their own actions, while not malicious, are nonetheless in violation of the spirit of moral agency. They do not reflect on their professional life in ethical terms.

For example, Kenneth Strike describes the response he received from teachers to an article he wrote in which he argued that, in classrooms, group punishment is fundamentally unfair. Most of the reactions failed to address this issue in an ethical sense at all and, instead, focused on it as being a matter of the strategic effectiveness of classroom management techniques. Strike writes, 'They did not assess the desirability of the ends sought. They did not judge their preferred means by any standard of fairness.'[33] He further describes another situation in which the names of recalcitrant students are listed daily on the blackboard of each classroom in an elementary school, as part of a new initiative in school discipline. During a parents' evening at the school, Strike noticed that in most classes, the lists of names were still on the boards as a leftover from the day's business (it was not the deliberate intention to display the names to parents). Apparently it had occurred to no one, including the principal, to erase the names for the sake of privacy and the protection of individual students. This is a good example of the kind of day-to-day occurrences that challenge the objectives of moral agency simply because of those who lack the conscious ethical knowledge to connect core principles of moral and ethical virtue to the context of their practice.

The following is a compilation of some of the incidents and situations observed in one teacher's elementary classroom that demonstrate the teacher's lack of ethical knowledge, her inability to judge her own actions in terms of their moral significance. One may argue that such an itemization obfuscates the context of her classroom; however, from my perspective, no level of contextual understanding could justify ethically these behaviours as being inherently moral. Context can not make a disrespectful action suddenly respectful. Context can not transform rude and inconsistent treatment of students into satisfactory behaviour just because, as the teacher says, students learn to read her moods: 'Something will push a button with me one day and I'm furious, and they'll do the same thing on another day and you know I'm okay.' Once we see inconsistency of treatment not merely as inept pedagogy, but as a sign of disrespect for students, we see some of the ethical dimensions of teaching. The following scenarios relate to concerns about respect, fairness, kindness, honesty, and associated moral principles and should not be viewed only as issues of pedagogy, discipline and general aspects of classroom organization:

- One little girl's pencil sharpener fell to the floor and it opened, making a mess. The teacher ordered her to clean it up. While the girl was on her way to get the broom, the teacher said, 'Can we do it quickly without day-dreaming'. Her tone was rude and abrupt, and her comment was harsh and judgemental.
- The teacher told students working on an assignment that she would give them five minutes to finish the task and pack up before going to the next activity. However, she never stopped talking at them, and after only two minutes went right to the next lesson, expecting students to 'change gears'.
- During small group activities, the teacher switched two girls into a new group for no obvious or explained reason. The result was that these girls were behind the others on the new activity. During this time, the morning snack arrived in the classroom, as scheduled. It was muffins. The teacher told the girls who were behind the others to continue their work and that they would get their snack afterwards so as to avoid getting their hands greasy while working. She did not follow up on this, and the girls never did get their muffins that day.
- The teacher states that she avoids apologizing to students because she believes it would undermine her authority and diminish students' trust in her. On one occasion, a boy apologized to the teacher for speaking out in class; however, she did not accept his apology and instead reprimanded him by saying, 'You have to show me sorry. It's meaningless without acting sorry.' Ironically, the teacher later blew over by accident a few pages of an assignment that one of the girls had been working on; this time, the teacher did apologize in passing but failed, herself, to show what it means as she walked away abruptly without helping the girl who was trying to pick up the papers off the floor.
- During a whole class discussion, the teacher called on one of the boys to respond to her questions. Another student complained that this boy always got to talk. The teacher replied, 'I don't think so. You have equal time too.' However, later in an interview, the teacher admitted that she calls on the first student more than the others because he 'helps the topic move along'.
- To establish classroom culture, the teacher develops terms of reference by picking on personality or behavioural quirks of her individual students and then by referring to them by the student's name. For example, she will tell students 'not to do a Mario' and they will know that they should not start giggling in the middle of their answer to a question. She claims that the students love this humorous practice and do not see it as a put-down 'because they've gone down in history for having a character trait'. One may contrast this practice with those of teachers who consciously try to avoid singling out individual students for fear of embarrassing them in front of peers.

- The teacher's use of humour occasionally includes poking fun at students. In one example, she was laughing at her own mispronunciation of a student's name by saying it over and over in a deep voice. The students found this funny and laughed with her. The student whose name was being ridiculed was not in class that day. I wonder how he would have felt; I also wonder what kind of teasing he may get from the others when he returns to class. Ironically, in a previous interview the teacher stated that she would not tolerate students making fun of names or sounds.

- The teacher gave a test to her class based on the previous night's home-work assignment. After she handed it out and told them to do it on their own, she left the room. Instantly, one of the more behaviourally difficult students started bothering other students and cheating by looking at the answers on a worksheet the teacher had left on her desk. Several students noticed this and called out about it – that he should not be cheating. The teacher returned to class, and the boy yelled out, 'finished!' The teacher joked that he was only finished because he was copying. She obviously knew what he was doing but didn't correct him on his cheating or yelling out which showed disrespect for the other students who were still trying to finish the test, despite the teacher's disruptive ongoing banter with the student.

- When students work either individually or in small groups, the teacher rarely circulates to provide contact and support. On many occasions, she leaves the room entirely in the hands of a teacher's aide or student teacher. When she is in the room working at her desk, she either ignores students' questions or replies to them without stopping her own task or looking up to make eye contact with students.

- The teacher states in an interview that on the last day of school, 'I didn't have time to connect with the kids. There was a lot of paperwork to do.' The class had planned a party and students brought in treats or snacks. They tried to play music and they got a video to watch from the library, 'but it really wound up with them watching the video and me finishing my paperwork'. Contrast this scenario with the last day of school in Erica's grade three classroom: 'We attended a morning assembly for the whole school, then in class we sang songs and finished our reading of *Charlotte's Web*. I planned a barbecue for the class so we all went outside and played soccer, had hot dogs, and I made sundaes for them. The kids in this room this year – I felt so very connected to them.'

My point in describing these classroom incidents is to offer a negative comparison with the other practices described in this chapter as virtue-based; it is not to condemn the teacher as a person lacking moral character for I cannot make such a judgement. However, unlike the other teachers quoted and depicted, she seems completely unaware of the moral and ethical implications of her actions and lack of actions. In this respect, she fails to demonstrate a level of ethical knowledge that would make her more reflective and deliberative about her practice in moral terms. As Strike and Ternasky conclude in their discussion of professional ethics, 'As moral craft, teaching will require not just that teachers treat their students fairly and with respect. It will also require that teachers comprehend the complexity of the ethical landscape.'[34] And, many teachers grapple with this complexity on a daily basis. As grade six teacher, Gina, states:

> We [teachers] have a lot of moral obligations to our students and we are very serious about them. I don't come here to collect a pay cheque and go home. Everybody works because we all need to get paid. But, there is some sense of satisfaction in what you do when I can walk out of here feeling good about what I do. Sometimes, however, I feel terrible because I worry that I wasn't fair to somebody during the day or that I didn't get back to somebody who needed to talk to me. I'm always scared of giving messages to students that might be taken the wrong way. Some kids need help, and others always are interrupting. So, you find that your day is all over the place and you think, what did I do today? What did I get accomplished because it just seemed like such a hectic day? I'm not a superhuman being, but I too have to make sure I make good choices.

A significant aspect of moral agency is framed by the character or manner of the teachers themselves as moral persons whose intuitive sense of fairness, kindness, honesty, respect, and other related ethical principles is embedded in their professional practice. However, the moral messages such teachers express and demonstrate are not merely haphazard extensions of their personal nature. For many, degrees of self-awareness and self-questioning combine to heighten their conscious and deliberate intentions to honour in their approach to teaching those principles that they so value. Those who appreciate that their role is one of moral significance and understand how their agency plays out in the nuances of often routine actions and reactions help to define ethical knowledge in teaching.

three

The teacher as a moral educator

Moral education as moral agency

For centuries, the concept of the teacher as a moral educator of the new generation has endured as both a stated objective of the professional role and an implicit inevitability of its moral agency since, 'teachers are already teaching ethical behaviour and attitudes both by their example and in the multitudinous informal ways they interact with children and youth'.[1] Moral education, as it is broadly conceived, includes both what teachers as ethical exemplars model in the course of their daily practice and what moral lessons they teach directly either through the formal curriculum or the informal dynamics of classroom and school life. As the second element of the dual nature of moral agency, as it is discussed in *The Ethical Teacher*, moral education is based not on programmes but on the teacher as a person who intentionally promotes, as well as exemplifies, ethical virtues such as honesty, fairness, respect, and kindness. In this regard, what teachers teach students in a moral sense connects closely to the previous chapter's discussion of the virtues teachers hold for themselves as important characteristics of their practice.

As I have written elsewhere:

> Moral educators are all teachers who understand the moral and ethical complexities of their role, who possess a level of expertise in interpreting their own behavior and discerning the influence that this behavior has on students, and who, as a consequence, strive to act ethically within the context of their professional responsibilities.[2]

They also have an expectation that students should acquire virtues necessary to live a moral civil life, and they assume a professional responsibility for nurturing this development. Those who do it well weave moral lessons into the fabric of their daily teaching in seemingly effortless and spontaneous ways that nonetheless respond to the social and conceptual complexities of the classroom. Kevin Ryan astutely notes that, 'To engage students in the lessons in human character and ethics without resorting to preaching and didacticism is the great skill of teaching'.[3] Those who achieve this with purpose and intent demonstrate another facet of what is discussed throughout this book as their ethical knowledge.

In their classroom-based study of the moral life of schools, Jackson et al. identify several categories of formal and informal instruction and activities in which moral lessons are taught or transmitted by implication; these include official curricula, rituals and ceremonies, visual displays of moral content, spontaneous interjections or moral commentary, and rules and regulations.[4] Similarly, Berkowitz lists elements of 'generic moral education initiatives' that include the promotion of a moral atmosphere, role modelling of good character, discussions in class of moral issues, and curriculum lessons in character.[5] Multiple empirical examples of such dimensions of moral education as well as a vast array of theoretical literature from varying ideological perspectives exist in the field of education. As the primary focus of *The Ethical Teacher* is not on moral education, per se, but rather on the attitudes, practices, and awareness of teachers in their role as moral agents, my own presentation of empirical illustrations in the subsequent sections of this chapter is necessarily abridged.

In the classroom: moral lessons

I see quite a bit of meanness among students, and I'm not going to tolerate it because we're two months into the school year now, and I think they should know right from wrong in a basic sense. Of course, you're going to get more complicated issues where naturally I'll help them through it, but they should know by now that if somebody drops something, you don't kick it. Also, when you keep disrupting you are disrespecting. You are telling the children around you that it doesn't matter to me that I'm stopping the whole class for attention or I'm stopping the whole class from their learning. What matters is that I want attention and I want it now. And, that's an ethical issue because students have to come to some understanding, maybe not at the moment, but eventually, that you can't function in a society like ours if you're constantly speaking out and you're not listening to others.

(Shannon, grade three teacher)

From junior kindergarten to senior secondary classrooms, teachers engage students in often continuous and repeated moral lessons about what are and are not appropriate attitudes and behaviours, in both their formal interactions and informal exchanges. For students, classroom life is usually their first experience of a structured societal context beyond the family, and there is much to learn about the complexities of civil reality. For many teachers, their recognition of this is not simply a reactionary response to a need to establish classroom order, but rather it is the intentional quest to help students develop a sense of empathy for others, self-discipline, personal responsibility, patience, tolerance, and an internal commitment to these and other related virtues. They spend an enormous amount of time and energy in their efforts to maintain in their classrooms a climate of respect in which they respect students, students respect them, and, significantly, students respect themselves and each other. As an echo from the previous chapter, it should be stressed that unless the first of these conditions is met, it is pointless and ethically problematic for a teacher to insist on the rest.

Richardson and Fallona refer to the moral virtues teachers seek to develop in students as being primarily social – learning to be nice and work with others – and their study attests to the frequency with which teachers will interrupt what they are doing, including conducting formal lessons, to reprimand students who deviate from this expected principle of classroom behaviour.[6] Such an emphasis on mutual respect, empathy, tolerance, and sharing is part of what Fenstermacher describes as the construction of classroom communities as one method for fostering moral conduct.[7]

For grade two teacher, Tatiana, a classroom community of peace and friendship is of the utmost importance. One day, after multiple fights and squabbles during lunch, she gathers the class together. Visibly upset, she declares:

> Everyday we talk about friendship, about being friends, how to get along with one another. We had so many problems at lunchtime. Remember about peace and friendship? What do we learn about this? Do you know what you did was *wrong*, or did you think it was *right*? No, it wasn't right. Tomorrow, be ready to write in your journals something good that you did for somebody, how you helped each other. I want to hear only of positive things. I don't want to hear of fights. I want to see more friends in this class. It's too bad we need to talk about all this again.

The next day, Tatiana follows up on this with the journal writing topic of 'How to be a friend'. Also in a grade two classroom, Farideh is explicit in explaining that 'being quiet while others are working', 'waiting patiently until everyone is finished', and 'sitting with good body language' during tests are signs of how 'we show respect to the other people in the class'. She praises students for their 'good manners' when they thank her or others; she frequently refers to them as being 'good' and equates this with being 'respectful of each other'. When lining up, students are told of the proper procedures not simply as abstract rules but as moral imperatives since, as Farideh reminds them, 'this school is not just for you – it's also for a lot of other students'. Underpinning her expectations of respect are the ethical principles of thoughtfulness for others, self-discipline for the benefit of all, and general consideration.

For Farideh, as well as many teachers, such consideration should be extended also to others beyond just the students and teachers. She explains to her class that the reason they have to push in their chairs at night is because 'it makes it easier for the janitor to clean the room'. Similarly, Sean asks his grade three students to pick up the scraps of paper from the floor and put them in the recycling bin in order 'to help the custodian'. Theresa stops a grade twelve student who is about to discard her drinks can as she leaves the room by saying, 'if there is still anything in that can, you shouldn't throw it in the garbage because that would be disrespectful to the custodian'.

As early as the kindergarten years, some teachers concentrate almost fully on guiding children through the moral complexities of the classroom as a community.[8] For Sarah, it is a matter of cultivating in them a sense of 'conscience'.[9] In his account of moral intelligence, Coles explains:

> The conscience is the voice within us that has really heard the voices of others (starting with our parents, of course) and so whispers and some-times shouts oughts and naughts to us, guides us in our thinking and our doing. The conscience constantly presses its moral weight on our feeling lives, our imaginative life. Without doubt, most elementary school children are not only capable of discerning between right and wrong, they are vastly interested in how to do so – it's a real passion for them.[10]

For Coles, the elementary years are when a child's conscience is or is not developed. Among the strategies Sarah uses in her classroom is the repeated reference to selected phrases and maxims such as 'if you don't have anything nice to say, don't say anything at all', 'you can't say you can't play', 'let him/ her have a turn', 'friends are a gift you give yourself', 'think before you speak', and 'how would you feel if someone said that to you?'. With an age group this young, she does not believe in using the words 'wrong' or 'bad' and she does not allow the children to use them either. Often when referring to someone's unacceptable acts in the class's public forum known as 'circle', she says that the student 'is still learning to share', or that the student 'has forgotten how we behave'. These and other such phrases are expressions of conscience for Sarah that become classroom reference points to trigger the students' awareness of virtues they should internalize.[11]

At the other end of the schooling continuum, Carol frequently discusses with her grade twelve students how important it is to be kind to one another. In her own words, she 'pounces on' opportunities in class to use language such as, 'rudeness is unacceptable', 'make loving decisions', 'building positive relationships', 'respect for self and others', 'respect for privacy', 'integrity', 'honesty', and 'truth'. Like many other teachers of all grades, she especially reacts when she hears a student tell another to 'shut up' or refer to another as 'stupid', even in jest; these are the words that many teachers identify as the most intolerable.

The ethical teacher's will to create a respectful and kind climate in the classroom is, in itself, a moral intention, not only because of what it contributes to the overall ongoing moral education of students, but also because it implicitly has the effect of protecting students in the immediate context of classroom and school life. For example, during one grade nine class, Marissa assigns groups for an exercise, much to the dismay of some who want to choose their own groups and who complain loudly about being matched up with certain classmates they do not know. Marissa tells them, 'We have to respect everyone, not just our friends, and we have to be nice to everyone, not just our friends. I don't want you making comments that can offend other people or hurt them. You don't want to hurt their feelings. I know you don't mean to, but it can hurt'. On two other occasions, Marissa is seen to have students clean out their desks even when they are not the ones who left them messy or cluttered: 'Who is going to come and clean up that piece of paper, if not you? We have to be responsible. You have to have a bit of pride where you're not sitting in garbage. Let's clean it out, and isn't that nice to do for the next person who comes to sit in that desk?' Marissa herself helps them in the clean-up.

Such behaviour on the part of teachers usually occurs spontaneously in response to something students say or do or to various circumstances as they arise. It is by no means uncommon to hear teachers say, as Theresa did to her grade ten class, 'I know there are people talking. It's a sign of disrespect. When you talk while someone else is talking, it says to them that they aren't saying anything worth listening to and you're going to have your own conversation. That's not what we're going to do here.' In seizing so-called teachable moments to promote an ethical perspective on specific classroom incidents, teachers engage in moral education repeatedly throughout the school day. Such moral lessons may take the form of strict reprimands or friendly reminders or admonitions.[12] Fenstermacher, who refers to such efforts to foster moral conduct in the classroom as 'call outs', explains that, 'They serve not only to call the non-obedient student to account, but to refresh everyone else's memory of what is desired in the setting. We found call outs to be one of the most obvious and frequently used ways teachers signal their expectations for student conduct, particularly in moral domains involving cooperation, fairness, and regard for others.'[13]

Many teachers comment about the fine distinction they must make between using such 'call outs' to discipline individual students, while at the same time reminding the entire class of what is inappropriate behaviour, and singling out students in ways that could be possibly embarrassing or hurtful to them. The ethical teacher is sensitive to the subtle line between the two and exercises moral judgement about when to use call out strategies and how far to push certain issues. Prolonging the focus on a negative incident may not only embarrass the perpetrator, but also other innocent parties affected by it. For example, Marissa's reprimand of her grade nine students who complained about being matched up with certain classmates for a group assignment is a fine example of a teacher not allowing a rude and insensitive situation to pass without comment; however had she been less general in her rebuke and dwelled on the incident as it related to specific students, the unwanted classmates matched with the complainers may well have felt hurt and embarrassed for being highlighted as the unpopular victims in this scenario. Teachers need to be aware of the ethical complexities underlying such layered situations in order to anticipate and head off potential harm. They need to attend to multiple moral demands inherent in the will to correct bad behaviour while protecting the student's sensibilities, to send moral messages to the class as a whole as part of their overall moral education, to ensure that students not centrally involved in the critical incident are not inadvertently treated unfairly, and to accomplish all this often as a split-second reaction to the incident while maintaining attention to the flow and objectives of the lesson being taught or the task being executed.

Grade three teacher, Shannon, finds that by shifting attention away from the errant student and onto herself, she can transmit her intended moral message effectively while protecting other students. For example, she explains:

> I have a student who has a speech problem. And the kids do tease him. The other day, a student said he was stupid. And I guess that's where the empathy, the understanding, the caring and inclusiveness come in. I told the class that I have a speech problem, which I do. I said, 'I have a slight lisp on S's, and you probably can't hear it, but I have it. And when I was in grade school, my friends tried very hard not to tease me about it and to understand that it had nothing to do with my ability'. So, I thought that's something that they could understand, and that the student who is teased could relate to with me, so he'd feel better.

Many teachers share personal anecdotes that start to resemble parables developed with the intention of sending moral messages to students. As

Noddings notes, 'To be effective as models, however, teachers have to be real people, people whose life experiences, desires, and disappointments seem real and lead students to believe that they can also become educated persons – without becoming alien creatures.'[14] She also claims that, 'It is hard to exaggerate how much it might mean to a particular student to hear a teacher say, "That happened to me once too".'[15] However, teachers must use moral judgement when revealing aspects of their own experience to students. Sensitive storytelling or casual and spontaneous recollections of incidents or feelings for the purpose of exemplifying a moral point or empathizing with students in order to be caring or fair is part of the intricate and moral interpersonal relationship between teachers and students. This should not be confused with teachers who gossip, boast, or pontificate about personal, sometimes intimate, details of their private lives as part of a self-glorification practice. Some do this to titillate students, others do it with the misguided belief that it will make them seem 'cool', others do it as a control mechanism. In some cases, it is pathetic; in all cases, it is unprofessional. The ethical teacher knows the difference between this kind of behaviour and self-referencing as non-egotistical moral modelling or illustrative of a sound moral lesson.

While much is transmitted of a moral nature through spontaneous admonition, intervention, and other elements of interaction between students and the teacher as ethical exemplar, moral lessons are also taught and reinforced by means of more formalized direct instruction. Otherwise referred to as 'didactic instruction', this method of teaching moral lessons is explicit, often, although not necessarily, grounded in formal curricula such as life skills programmes, and presented in such a way as to leave no doubt about the ideals and principles being promoted.[16]

Some teachers support this method with visual aids in an effort to establish a moral classroom tone in a physical as well as intellectual sense. For example, Sean has several posters on the wall of his grade three classroom and he refers to them often when teaching. One, entitled simply 'Values', lists commands such as 'be caring', 'be fair', 'be honest', 'be responsible', 'be helpful', 'respect the feelings of others', 'cooperate with others', 'respect people's differences', and 'share with others'. Another list of 'Cooperative Group Rules' instructs students to 'take turns talking quietly', 'listen to each other's ideas', 'help each other when asked', 'praise each other's ideas', and 'talk about how you worked well together and how you can improve'. Another poster is called 'People's Characteristics' and includes such qualities to develop as being 'trustworthy', 'reliable', 'responsible', 'sensitive', 'friendly', 'brave', 'persistent (doesn't give up)', 'hopeful', and 'positive'.

Some teachers teach direct lessons about how human virtues should be extended in situations not only involving other people, but also with respect to non-human life. For her reading programme, Shannon explains, 'I always look at the books that come into my classroom to make sure that animals are not being mistreated in the books. It's a matter of respect again, that we treat animals with care and that we look after animals because they are part of our world. It's very important to me, and I teach this directly to my students'. Similarly, Gina precedes her grade six science lesson which involves using insect specimens with a lecture on how to handle the specimens in such a way that shows care and respect. She explains, 'It's a dead living organism. You have to show respect for a life in all forms'. Unlike Sean's posters that use blunt commands to teach virtues directly as the sole purpose of the instruction, Shannon and Gina weave their direct lessons about moral principles across other curricular objectives. In their cases, reading and science provide opportunities to engage in direct moral education in a more integrated manner.

For many teachers at both the elementary and secondary levels, the use of story books and literature provides not only scope to teach language, writing, reading, and elements of literary history and style, but also a rich trove of human experiences and characteristics from which to divine moral lessons. For example, as a follow-up to a science unit on spiders, Erica chose to read *Charlotte's Web* to her grade two/three class. Her choice, however, was not solely based on a desire to integrate the reading programme with the science one; it went far beyond that as she engaged her students in numerous discussions about human moral virtues, the development of empathy, the fostering of kindness, and the essence of true friendship. Described as ethically comparable to Aristotle and Homer, this book 'presents both a lesson in friendship and a compelling vision of the goodness of goodness itself'.[17] Erica knew this as she asked her students to consider how Wilbur, the pig, might feel when he was cold, hungry, and alone, and what they could do to help him; when talking about Templeton, the pack rat, as someone without a moral conscience, Erica asked her students to consider how his character develops and grows and whether 'he really is completely a bad character' or whether 'he made some bad choices'. From this, she uses Templeton as an ongoing point of reference when talking to her students about bad and good life choices relating to issues as diverse as lying and cheating to drug use to helping others to being responsible for one's actions. Much has been written from a range of ideological perspectives on the benefits of using literature in the classroom as a way to sensitize students to issues of moral significance. Both 'character educators' and their critics support this practice, albeit in different ways.[18]

As a direct and formalized means of instruction in principles of moral virtue, the character education movement has acquired much attention in recent years, and use of its related programmes has gained momentum in the field. Often associated with the work of such scholars as Thomas Lickona, Kevin Ryan, Edward Wynne, and Madonna Murphy, character education has inherited much from 'traditional virtue centered approaches' to educa-tion that have existed for centuries that promote the notion of universal common values such as 'being honest, generous, just, kind, and helpful, and having courage and convictions along with tolerance of the views of others'.[19] Grounded in a repudiation of ethical relativism, character education assumes the existence of 'rational, objectively valid moral requirements to which all people are accountable'.[20] This common core of ethical values transcends human differences and is based instead on human similarities. Furthermore, 'character education differs from other forms of moral education in that it describes and prescribes what is meant by right and wrong (good and bad), and it is meant to help children behave in morally good ways'.[21]

Critics of the character education movement often accuse the programmes aligned with it as promoting drill, unreflective and unquestioning acceptance of overly simplistic interpretations of values, preachiness, and gimmicky processes that are destined to be ineffectual as well as intellectually suspect. Some, notably those critics from the radical ideological left vilify character education almost totally in political terms as a neo-conservative plot to indoctrinate children. Some, more reasoned voices such as Nel Noddings and Robert Nash level criticism at the specifics of character education while, at the same time, recognizing the importance of sound ethical principles, although they contextualize them differently.[22]

The conceptual basis of *The Ethical Teacher*, as addressed in Chapter 1, supports the anti-relativist stance of the character educators and accepts the promotion of basic human virtues that enable people to live rational, civil, and responsible lives marked by a commitment to core principles such as honesty, kindness, fairness, and respect for others. Nonetheless, I do find the criticism of some of the character education methodologies to be quite sens-ible; schemes such as showcasing a 'virtue of the week' in schools or having students daily compliment classmates as part of a ritualistic exercise seem vacuous in comparison to the caring and fair teacher engaging students regularly in reflecting deeply on the essence of their humanity in all that they do together in class. One would be wise to heed Kevin Ryan's frequent cautions against character education's faddish and sloganed tendencies.

It is not the purpose of this book to argue the merits of one form of moral education over another or even to delve deeply into the area of moral educa-tion itself. Rather, the concern is with teachers' perceptions of their inevit-able position as moral educators and ethical role models as an implicit aspect of moral agency in teaching. Bearing this in mind, those who embrace their professional responsibilities to students and others with a commitment to exemplify and transmit moral and ethical principles or virtues have an overarching intention to be good, do good, and teach good. This intention and the teacher's awareness of it contribute also to the basis of ethical knowledge.

Awareness of intention as ethical knowledge

Ethical knowledge relies on teachers' awareness of how their intuitive sense as moral persons seeking to be fair, honest, kind, and respectful influences their treatment of students and others as well as the execution of their professional responsibilities. Some teachers seem to articulate with insight how aspects of their virtuous selves guide their daily practice. However, ethical knowledge is also motivated by the moral intentions of teachers striving to impart valuable moral lessons to their students. Similarly, some teachers seem aware enough to express with purpose and intent what they want their students to internalize of a moral nature and how they guide their learning in this area.

Much has been written about teachers' lack of awareness of their potential influence in this regard, especially in relation to their responses to student behaviour; they are seen to be driven more by a rule-oriented need to maintain social order in the classroom than by a deeper moral purpose to foster virtuous conduct in their students.[23] However, such a portrayal underestimates at least some teachers who, even if not attuned to every nuance of each interaction with students, have clearly defined intentions in their capacity as moral educators. Some of them have been introduced previously in this chapter. As Marissa explains after she addresses her reasons for some of the things she says and does: 'I'm planting the seeds, and the seeds will at some point in time in their lives, they'll blossom. Maybe not right now; maybe one student out of the 28 may get it now. Who knows, but I'm optimistic, and if I can reinforce in them the right behaviour, at some point in their lives, they'll get it. They'll understand.'

By contrast, Brian McCadden describes Mrs Hooper, a kindergarten teacher whose 'understanding of what she was doing as a moral enterprise was flickering'.[24] Focused on the instrumental purposes of her effective interactions with children rather than on their moral importance, she is judged to be fairly typical of most teachers. However, this is quite different from Sarah, the kindergarten teacher whose morally embedded orientation to teaching is entirely devoted to cultivating in her students what she herself refers to as moral 'conscience'. Grounded in principles of fairness, honesty, mutual respect, and kindness and framed by an understanding of how students become more conscientious through teaching strategies that encourage the development of empathy, responsibility, and independence, Sarah's orientation to both deliberately planned events and routines and unexpected incidents is responsive to the different ways in which students develop their understanding of moral principles.

Nonetheless, this is a complex objective for any teacher, even those who have a heightened awareness of their own moral agency. Sometimes, even the best of moral intentions cannot stave off ethically problematic unforeseen results of a teacher's specific response or initiative. For example, Sarah believes that certain incidents between students, both positive and negative and frequently both, should be brought to the entire class's attention in the public forum known as 'circle'. In discussing the incidents publicly, she uses them as 'teaching tools' to help students more generally understand how they can improve on their capacity to be kind to others, cooperative, and so on. Those students in the right in such incidents appear to appreciate the positive recognition. For the sake of those in the wrong, Sarah has to guard against prolonging or increasing their feelings of guilt or upset. She always seeks permission from both parties to bring incidents to 'circle', and she is ever mindful of the need to handle the discussions with considerable care and sensitivity. However, consider the following scenario:

Katie, Julia, and Jessica were colouring together at a table. Julia leaned closer to Katie and whispered 'something bad' about Jessica. Katie refused to whisper back so Jessica's feelings wouldn't be hurt. Later Katie told Sarah: 'Julia whispered something bad about Jessica and I wouldn't whisper back. Now Julia is mad at me.' After speaking with both girls, Sarah sought permission from them to bring the incident to circle. During the discussion, Sarah said to the class, 'So this kind of thing won't happen again?' Julia was the first to respond that it wouldn't. Sarah added, 'You know sometimes we forget'. Julia smiled and said, 'I forgot'. Sarah praised Katie for her refusal to whisper and listed it as an 'act of kindness' on the 'friendship moments' chart hanging prominently on the wall. Throughout this little drama, the silent and seemingly forgotten person was Jessica, who may well have been unaware that she had been either the victim of Julia's nastiness or the object of Katie's kindness, and whose permission to discuss this publicly was never sought. Treated as 'Exhibit A' in a situation not of her own making, Jessica may have found such a public revelation humiliating and far more hurtful than the initial incident had been for her. The lapse in Sarah's ethical knowledge that enabled her to overlook this possibility is not an indictment of her otherwise often clear awareness of herself as a moral agent and moral educator. It does, however, underline the moral complexity of classrooms and the need for teachers to be ever attentive to and reflective of their practice.

In another incident, Theresa senses a need to cultivate a deeper feeling of community and care in her all girls grade twelve values and lifestyle class. She introduces an exercise in which each student is given a piece of paper with her name on it to fold into a fan. The fans circulate throughout the class, and the students write comments on them to each other. These include such phrases as 'I've always appreciated your humour in class' or 'it was great getting to know you this year so far'. Comments may be signed or left anonymous, however only nice comments are permitted, given the double entendre of the word 'fan'. Theresa explains that if a student doesn't have anything nice to say about another, then she may pass the fan on to the next person without writing anything. What is intended to be a warm and fuzzy exercise in appreciation and empathy in order to build individual self-esteem and group cohesiveness could, however, become an emotional nightmare for the student whose fan is returned to her with few or no comments at all on it. Similarly, how many elementary school teachers treat Valentine's Day with some trepidation, realizing that what is supposed to be a happy day of friendship, gift giving and card exchanges can potentially be a crushing experience for the less popular students in their classes? Simply making arbitrary rules that either everybody or nobody gets a card is not really a moral lesson in fairness and is unlikely to fool anyone about the reality of their peer relationships. Teachers may not be able to protect students from all cruelty from their classmates; however, at least they should not be implicated in officially sanctioning or enabling it through in-class practices, no matter how well intentioned they start out to be. Such concerns are moral issues, and the ethical teacher who views them first and foremost as such is consequently better equipped to anticipate the effects of individual actions, decisions, and reactions.

Thus lies the professional challenge to build a knowledge base to share, referred to here as ethical knowledge, that expands on the morally intuitive sense that at least some teachers have at least some of the time in relation to their work as moral agents. Reflective awareness of moral agency provides the genesis for ethical knowledge. And moral agency is manifested in the principles or virtues teachers bring to their overall treatment of others, most notably, but not exclusively students, as well as to their practice as ethical models, exemplars, and moral educators.

Part 1 of *The Ethical Teacher* has concentrated on championing real examples of teachers' ethical knowledge in practice, while also hinting at some of the tensions and challenges that may arise from moral complexities in teaching. It has been heavily classroom focused. However, as Berkowitz comments, people's treatment of one another is central to a conceptualization of moral education, and 'this clearly includes how students treat each other and how teachers treat students, but also must include how teachers treat each other, how other staff and administrators treat each other and how they treat teachers and students, etc.'.[25] Teachers' moral agency in the classroom may be strengthened or weakened by interpersonal interactions and critical incidents that both occur within and extend beyond the classroom. The following part of this book focuses on the 'weakening' side of this equation by addressing some of the moral and ethical dilemmas, tensions, and overall challenges that diminish a teacher's sense of moral agency and that, if left unresolved, jeopardize any professional attempt to enhance teachers' collective ethical knowledge.

Part 2

Challenges to ethical professionalism

Schools and the people in them are caught up in a host of contradictions and the inevitable conflicts between individual and group interests and well-being. One would hope that teachers and administrators are well prepared to deal with these contradictions and conflicts in steadfastly fulfilling their educational mission. Unfortunately, they are not.[1]

In the thirteen years since Goodlad and his colleagues expressed this conclusion relating to the moral dimensions of teaching, very little has changed. Teachers continue to experience conflicts and complexities, dilemmas and tensions that strain and interfere with their sense of agency as both moral persons and moral educators. By undermining the moral agency of teachers, such challenges diminish the ethical knowledge of individuals and thus compromise the quest for a collective appreciation of ethical professionalism.

While the ethical teacher is, by necessity, an ethical person, as argued previously, the reverse is not necessarily the case. Even those of good character, will, and intention may fail to grasp how the moral principles they strive to uphold apply to the contextual realities and details of their daily professional practices. And, even those who possess a keen moral sensibility that enables them to make conceptual connections between their moral intuition and the demands of their professional work, may find in actuality that their actions and reactions become paralyzed by the uncertainty caused by tensions and dilemmas.

Some define ethical dilemmas as situations 'in which two or more courses of action (moral choices) are in conflict, and each action can be plausibly defended as the "good" one to take'.[2] Conversely, others see ethical dilemmas as negative by definition and define them as 'situations in which we are compelled to choose between equally undesirable alternatives'.[3] Yet others combine the positive and negative and conclude that, 'In a moral dilemma, no matter what solution we choose, it will involve doing something wrong in order to do what is right'.[4] Regardless of variations in defining the term 'dilemma', the meanings are essentially similar, and, as Knutson argues, 'true ethical dilemmas are very rare'.[5] She further notes that ethical problems, issues, and predicaments are, on the other hand, all too common and often described loosely as 'dilemmas'.

It is such a loose use of the term that underpins the following two chapters as teachers themselves use it to describe ethical scenarios that confront them with varying levels of intensity and tension to cause both internal and external conflicts. From the perspective advanced in this book, such conflicts contribute to the threatening of teachers' self-perceptions as ethical professionals as well as of their public identities.

The empirical illustrations reported here identify issues raised by elementary and secondary school teachers, including some who were introduced in the previous two chapters and others who participated in a study exclusively concerned with ethical dilemmas in schools. This study, which exposed individuals' feelings of anxiety, hypocrisy, conscience, guilt, and integrity concluded that, 'Although more teachers than principals were aware of moral and ethical conflicts in their professional lives, neither group was shown to be able to translate objective and fundamental moral beliefs into meaningful action'.[6] Many of their responses to the dilemmas reflect what is discussed in the latter section of this part of *The Ethical Teacher* as suspended morality, false necessity, and the tyranny of the group; such responses illuminate mostly negative corruptions of consequentialist and nonconsequentialist theories of ethical decision making, as addressed by Strike and Soltis.[7] They also exemplify the following observation offered by William Hare in his review of Hostetler's book on ethical judgement, dilemmas, and decision making in teaching:

> [The book conveys] the complexity of ethical issues where one must somehow assess the relative importance of conflicting moral principles and try to balance ethical ideals against contextual factors and consequentialist concerns, in situations which are immediate and often emotionally charged. Judgment is needed, and must be developed, in order to deal effectively with messy and imprecise problems which defy a formulaic response.[8]

Often, responses to dilemmas are made, and decisions in schools taken, with the moral invocation that the choice must serve first 'the best interests of the student'.[9] However, as Keith Walker wisely cautions us, this maxim has the potential to do both good and harm.[10] He further refers to the ubiquitous and sententious use of the phrase 'best interests of children' to justify 'everything from teacher strike action to time tabling decisions, dress code policies, and assessment decisions'.[11] The ethical teacher is conscious of students' best interests and holds this maxim as a professional first principle, even in all its complexity, while remaining vigilant against its use to serve other ends of a private or ideological nature. While self protection, personal benefit and convenience, and subjective beliefs are important to the individual, they should never obscure the professional obligation to serve others.

Part of the point in exposing ethical dilemmas, challenges, and tensions of moral import must certainly be to enable and encourage teachers to reflect, individually and collectively, formally and informally, on how they can serve their students' interests morally; such service should not be used as a secondary means of garnering support for a primary personal or political agenda, but rather as a principle-based expression of daily conduct teachers bring to bear on all aspects of their practice and interpersonal relations within schools. As a consequence of this argument, the following two chapters not only describe specific moral incidents, circumstances, and dilemmas identified by teachers, but also expand on this discussion to include broader issues that I believe significantly challenge the ethical professionalism of teachers. Such issues include the complexities of dealing with controversy in the classroom and the promotion of political positions, as well as concerns about how unionization affects the teacher's moral authority.

As McCadden observed about the teachers he encountered while conducting his research, they 'sincerely wanted to do the right thing (in contemporary language), and to seek the good (in classical language), as they understand it. However, understanding what the good is at a given time and then acting on it are not things that anyone found easy to do'.[12] This is not an atypical reality. Good teachers do indeed have virtuous aspirations and intentions that can get thwarted by ethical dilemmas and challenges that they, for the most part, must face alone and with minimal guidance beyond their own moral intuition and the pressing norms, both positive and negative, of their workplace associations. Some of their experiences are described in the subsequent two chapters.

four

Dilemmas in teaching

Moral uncertainty: when ethical knowledge fades

> Generally, teachers must operate without specific guidance or collective wisdom as to what constitutes ethical conduct. Consequently, teachers are in the difficult position of having to make ethical decisions without much guidance. If they use or are accused of using poor judgment, they may find themselves called to account before an administrator who also has little guidance regarding an appropriate course of action.[1]

Ideally, when faced with ethical decisions, individual teachers who are astutely aware of their role as moral agents would draw on an extensive body of personal and professional ethical knowledge to provide guidance and direction. However, as those who write about ethical conflicts in teaching can attest, this is not the case as teachers struggle to react and respond to often complicated situations and dilemmas that occur haphazardly and usually without warning.[2]

One may recall the Preface to *The Ethical Teacher* in which I describe a personal experience where I lacked the ethical knowledge to connect both conceptually and in practical terms my natural will to be a good, fair, kind, and empathetic teacher with a routine administrative task. Such an incident is not an isolated occurrence in schools. On another occasion, I recall how a class of fairly calm 14-year-olds erupted into an unruly and unhappy group within minutes of having to fill in a form for the school's records on which they were to list their home address and contact numbers for their parents or guardians. What I had not realized was that at least half of these students came from families with divorced parents, and some of them spent their weeks alternating between two homes. Such a mundane exercise suddenly became a painful reminder of personal grief, as one student explained in frustration as he tried to squeeze two addresses into a box on the form designed for one, before bursting into tears and refusing to complete the form. I wish I had had the foresight that is honed through ethical knowledge to anticipate such an incident and take steps to avert the tensions created when we fail to see what teachers call 'administrivia' as potentially being morally charged.

In another class, this one a grade ten English class, I remember teaching a poem that was about a teenager who committed suicide. I recall one 15-year-old boy who seemed to get more sad, more silent, and more withdrawn as the class progressed. I have no idea how that poem affected him, but I think it did. The dilemma for me was how to make things better for him and other students who deserved more sensitivity. The moral tension that arose from that situation bothers me still. What a shame it was, that in the department meetings where my colleagues and I planned the curriculum and made choices about material, no one thought to discuss this poem in ethical terms rather than literary ones. Perhaps if we had, we would have all been better equipped to anticipate the moral implications of what we teach and how we teach it and to frame our lessons accordingly.

And then there was Pat. Like many of the rest of us, he disliked the computerized report cards that we had to use in which prefabricated comments, such as 'works hard in class' or 'needs to be more attentive to homework', were our only choices for remarking on our students' progress. For him, however, this was an ethical concern, a dilemma, one in which he felt that he betrayed his students and their right to more personalized assessment by following this system-wide process. So, Pat made a professional decision. He told his students they could, if they wished, bring their report cards to him so he could write special additional comments on them. This was his way of being more caring and ethically responsive, even though it required of him much more work. This was indicative of Pat's ethical knowledge. It had not occurred to me, a novice, that teachers had the moral authority to make such a decision; had we worked in a less isolated school culture where Pat would have freely shared with the rest of us this practice as an ethical solution to the perennial problem of preparing report cards, we might have collectively been able to serve the best interests of more students by adopting Pat's individual response as our own collective practice.

These brief examples illustrate a mere fraction of potential moral scenarios in which daily and often routine aspects of teaching can create ethical dilemmas, tensions, and challenges for teachers whose ethical knowledge is limited or fades away to be replaced by moral uncertainty about what constitutes the right response to a given situation. Such uncertainty also curtails one's ability to recognize and anticipate the situation as morally problematic in the first place until one is confronted head-on with an obvious dilemma. In lacking a sound moral and ethical foundation as a guiding principle for their professional practice, teachers may become confused about how sometimes conflicting principles of right and wrong in practical terms apply to such dilemmas.[3] In other instances, they may know clearly what the right choice is but remain unsure of how to implement it. In yet other situations, teachers may know both what is right and what to do about it, but for personal reasons of security, convenience, efficiency, or advantage, they may choose not to act on this knowledge. They may be intimidated by what Reitz describes as school climates that impress on teachers not 'to rock the boat. [Where] peace at any price seems to be the order of the day'.[4] For his teacher respondents, this reality fed their uncertainty about what constitutes ethical criteria and how to apply them to their in-school dilemmas.

This parallels what Bev, an elementary teacher, remarked after recounting a series of dilemmas she experienced as a result of conflicts with administrators, teacher colleagues, official policies, and normative practices in the school:

> In the regular context they all seem as isolated incidents; then when you pull it all together and base it all on moral values and ethics, it's interesting how they all string together in an underlying current. I think a lot of incidents occur, and you think of them at the time, and then they're brushed under the carpet. But when you think of a few of the incidents I've mentioned, it gives you a sort of uncomfortable feeling in your stomach thinking, 'this is happening', and maybe these things are totally off-the-wall, maybe this isn't an average school, maybe there are worse things happening in other schools, but I think there are a lot of unknowns out there and a lot of things that aren't discussed or brought up.[5]

The kinds of ethical dilemmas and challenges that Bev and other teachers address are not, for the most part, the type of more sensational issues reported by the press. Admittedly, there are teachers who have been found criminally and/or professionally guilty of such behaviour as abuse, negligence, theft, the acceptance of bribes, nepotism, misrepresentation of qualifications and other forms of dishonest practice.[6] While *The Ethical Teacher* recognizes such examples as serious and grievous breaches of ethical principles, its concern with professional ethics, moral agency, and the dilemmas that compromise ethical knowledge is more firmly rooted in the complexities of the daily practice of teaching, those seemingly routine, sometimes mundane, and frequently spontaneous occurrences that should challenge teachers to reflect on the ethical implications of their decisions.[7] It assumes that the abusive or deceitful teacher is unlikely to experience any real sense of moral angst or dilemma (or at least not of the kind with which this discussion is interested); this teacher's main concern is to avoid being identified for such behaviour. On the other hand, such individuals may indeed cause a great deal of moral anxiety and confusion for their more honest colleagues who struggle with the dilemma of how to react to know-ledge or suspicions about collegial misbehaviour.[8] This book is concerned mostly with this majority of essentially good-willed teachers who are faced with moral uncertainty as they strive to cope with ethical tensions either caused by others or created by the circumstances in which they work.

Tensions and dilemmas of an ethical nature may threaten teachers' self-perceptions as moral people and ethical professionals. As Lyons notes, the many dilemmas that fill a teacher's work life and that are fundamentally moral and ethical problems may in fact not be solvable; they must be simply only managed.[9] And the way teachers manage their dilemmas may be not a source of decisive comfort to them, but rather a lingering catalyst for self doubt and criticism. For example, grade two teacher Erica recalls the following painful incident:

> I had a really bad student teacher, and I was told by the university preservice supervisor that I had to pass him. I was the last to hand my evaluation to the office, and I gave him low marks and not great com-ments because I kept asking myself over and over again why I should pass him, and it wasn't fair. He missed six days of the session. He also made fun of my students behind their backs to make the others laugh. All the work I put into building a rapport in class, and this was a nightmare. Ella [one of the students] sees a therapist on a regular basis, and she got up and had to do something in front of the class. She didn't know the answer, and he made fun of her. She came to me and cried, and I had to keep her aside from the class. She kept asking me, 'When is he [the student teacher] going away? When are you teaching us again?'

Erica regrets to this day that she compromised her principles to give the student a passing grade because she felt the pressure to conform to a solution that would cause the least conflict for her and her school. In passing him, she essentially contributed to his smooth transition into a career as a certified teacher even though she found this to be ethically and professionally objectionable.

Sharon Todd poses the following relevant and significant question: 'Does becoming a teacher necessarily mean learning to make certain concessions to rules and routines that might be hurtful, at times, to students in the class?'[10] By way of example, she describes a student teacher's account of how she had to comfort a grade one student, who started to cry (apparently, but unnoticeably, because she had wet herself) during the morning classroom ritual of standing to attention for the national anthem, while the host teacher ignored the child. The account makes a contrasting distinction between teacher as an 'institutional figure' (the host teacher) and teacher as a 'compassionate person' (the student teacher). It is not difficult to criticize the apparent callousness of the host teacher; however, what we do not know from this story is whether he personally was experiencing in this sudden and fleeting situation a sense of internal dilemma and anxiety as he weighed in his own mind the rightness of attending to the girl immediately or of maintaining classroom order and attention focused on the anthem rather than on the girl who might have become further embarrassed by his intervention at this point. His choice to refrain from reacting sooner may have in fact rattled both his conscience and his sense of himself as a kind and responsive moral agent to his students. Or, perhaps it may not have; the point of making this conjecture is to illustrate the potential for ethical uncertainty and anxiety on the part of teachers in experiencing the nuances of their life in classrooms.

For grade twelve teacher, Marissa, moral anxiety is the result of a personal feeling of spiritual hypocrisy. As a teacher in a Catholic school, she is expected to uphold and impart the 'gospel values'; she does this, not only in her religion classes, but in all her classes by exemplifying the virtues of compassion, self responsibility, patience, and faith. For her, the essence of goodness is spiritual, not based on rigid or doctrinaire ritual. She does teach formally the religion curriculum, but she also expands her vision to encourage students to 'have a seeking spirit', 'to develop an unselfish relationship with God', to appreciate that prayer comes in a variety of forms, and to be empowered by the sense of living an open and good life. She rejects a notion that religion should be based on fear of God, and is alarmed by some of the ways the students see religion as strict and punishing. She admits, 'I don't share a lot of the Catholic Church's teachings, their views. I don't. But as a professional, I would present those views in an unbiased manner, and open up for their [students'] own responses to certain things'. Her lessons reflect this. In the past several years, Marissa has become a practising Buddhist, a fact she does not mention to either students or colleagues. Combined with her reservations about the Catholic Church, this initially was a source of internal tension for her ethically since she felt she was living a hypocritical life teaching in a school system she did not support. She overcame this dilemma once she realized that her lifestyle and teaching philosophy are perfectly compatible with the best of Catholic principles. Marissa's experience is illustrative of those situations in which teachers feel torn between their own ethical beliefs and the need to fulfil the demands of professional life, be they related to honouring the curriculum or adhering to other policies, rules and routines, when the two imperatives appear to be in conflict.

In her description of the ethical school, Felicity Haynes states that, 'Part of what it means to be a professional is not be someone who follows the rules automatically, but someone who is competent and intelligent and ethical in their practice . . . Yet the professional is also bound by legal and professional requirements articulated out of a need by various people over time, even where it is as apparently petty as a requirement for a teacher to wear either a tie or stockings to class'.[11] While the designation of what is petty and what is not may be in dispute, teachers report that they frequently experience a range of ethical tensions and dilemmas as a result of administrative decisions and actions as well as school policies and overall practices. Often in such cases, the central dilemma for teachers is whether to obey administrative directives and accept without complaint policies and procedures they find morally objectionable. For the most part, they do, although some teachers try to cope by modifying their acceptance or subverting a policy as long as they can do so without incurring personal blame or engaging in open conflict.[12]

From his study of 300 teachers who were asked to identify in anecdotal form behaviours they had observed personally in school that could be characterized as 'questionably ethical' or 'clearly unethical', Reitz generated a list of 64 separate categories of unethical behaviour. He concluded that 'in almost all instances the unethical conduct reported was either encouraged or enforced by the building administrator, or in some instances by organizational policies and procedures'.[13] In ways that parallel many of these categories, the subsequent empirical examples offer a descriptive glimpse at some issues teachers find morally troublesome as a result of routine incidents stemming from decisions made by or interactions with administrators, of policy-related circumstances, and of concerns about evaluation.

Many teachers describe the difficulty they have in accepting the ways administrators discipline their students. For example, Shannon recalls with regret how, after she found one of her grade eight students reading a pornographic magazine, she reported him to the principal: 'And I don't think it was dealt with very well. The boy was made to feel terrible like what he did was really awful and that he was a bad person'. Morally, she had trouble with this outcome and afterwards tried to comfort and reassure the student; however, she did not say that she disagreed with the principal for fear that he would 'tell' and get her 'entangled' further. She also did not tell the principal about her disagreement. Furthermore, she might be reluctant in the future to report on other students due to this incident; unfortunately, this reaction is neither courageous nor honest and does nothing to help show the principal how he might treat students with more regard. In contrast, secondary school teacher Karl challenged his administrator for being too lenient in a morally charged situation that he believed required a firm stand. He explains:

> I got into another problem, but this one is really something – it ties in with racism. A boy transferred into my class, and the vice-principal told me, 'Well, this kid comes from a family that has a history of bigotry. And this boy had a black teacher. In order to avoid any problems, we

switched his timetable'. And I looked at him – and he was also the representative for race relations at our school! – and I said, 'You mean to say that you're accommodating his point of view? What you should tell this kid is either he behaves or he is out of there!' Now to me, that is a very serious moral issue.[14]

A further tension for Karl was that by retaining the student in his class, he felt that he was seen to be implicitly endorsing the vice-principal's decision that he actually saw as objectionable on ethical grounds alone.

As in the above case, school administrators are often perceived by teachers to pursue various courses of action with the seemingly laudable objectives of ensuring a smooth running, peaceful, and efficient organization or advancing a desirable initiative without thinking about the possible ethical ramifications of the action itself. This, in turn, may create ethical tensions for the teachers who are most affected by the actions or who are expected to implement administrative decisions. Daniel offers an example:

> Little things happen – occasionally decisions will be made haphazardly by a vice-principal or principal who's under a lot of stress. So you just modify it because it's a problem. For example, to save time this year, instead of home form teachers phoning up students to tell them they failed courses, they set aside a day where everyone was to come in, and home form teachers would tell those students who failed that they failed and would have to register for summer school. And that was ridiculous [to announce failures in front of the entire class]. That was something that was not thought out. The decision lacked imagination. They didn't realize that you would be stigmatizing kids for having failed subjects in front of their peers. So what I did was I told the students that if they didn't hear from me they didn't have to come in. And I phoned kids over the weekend to let them know they had failed so it wouldn't be so embarrassing for them.[15]

As integral to his sense of moral agency, Daniel is aware of how the administrative decision might compromise his duty to protect students from emotional harm in his classroom. As a consequence of this ethical knowledge, Daniel, on his own initiative, takes an action that may well have served a greater number of students had it been addressed more openly with colleagues as a kind of professional use of ethical knowledge. They too may have found this new procedure troubling for similar reasons, but remained uncertain as to how to deal with it.

Another incident that might have been avoided had either the school administrators or classroom teachers applied ethical knowledge to a routine procedure confronted Tatiana as she handed out information forms to her grade two class to take home to their parents. Given the multicultural composition of the school, the forms were printed in a number of languages, each on a coloured page. The English version was on plain white paper. Tatiana had a list of which students should get which coloured form. As she proceeded to hand them out, some students got very upset and insisted that their parents could read English; many wanted an English version as well as their first language one, but the office had not provided enough copies to accommodate this request. Some students started teasing each other over their linguistic backgrounds, and others started fighting over the forms. In a school that prides itself on fostering the values of multicultural inclusion and tolerance of diversity, no one had considered how what was to them a simple administrative matter could become morally problematic for its singling out of individual students. Tatiana's response to the chaos in her classroom did not leave her feeling that she had either prepared her students for this situation or cared for their general well-being.

Of all the normalized routines in schools, one of the ones I find most annoying is the constant and intrusive use of the public address system to announce on a daily basis even the most trivial of messages at the convenience of the office administration. For me, and for many teachers I have observed and interviewed, this is an ethical issue that violates principles of respect, consideration for others, and care for the academic tasks of the school. These announcements (as well as frequent telephone calls to the classroom from the office and numerous knocks on the classroom door from students sent on missions from other teachers or staff seeking the teacher's response to an often insignificant issue that could well wait until a suitable break in the day) have an unsettling effect on students trying to concentrate on their tasks and on teachers trying to keep student attention focused. In one grade two classroom, we counted in the course of one day 13 such interruptions: seven public address system announcements, four internal telephone calls, and two knocks at the door. This was apparently an average day. Teachers spend much of their time reinforcing the message to students that speaking out and interrupting one another are rude and disrespectful; ironically, the school environment does nothing to support and everything to negate this moral message. As grade twelve teacher Theresa explains:

> I think the PA system does undermine what I do because, look what happens with announcements in the morning or at the end of the day, not to mention all the others. I don't think the office means to be disrespectful because they have no sense of what's happening in classrooms. But the students see it as a sign of disrespect.

Sadly, while many teachers express similar concerns, they all accept the situation as an almost inevitable feature of school life. Instead, their collective ethical knowledge that enables them to view this as a moral, rather than merely a procedural, concern should be used by them to raise this issue substantively with school administrators who have the ability to remedy it. Why are teachers, if they are to be seen as professionals, so uncertain in their moral authority to do this?

Perhaps, it is in part because they share, and are resigned to, secondary school teacher Judy's view of schools:

> Fairness and equity aren't used as guiding principles, and I find as a practising teacher, you have very little power . . . I get very upset by what I see going on in classrooms – treatment of students by staff and administration, and treatment of staff by administration. It comes home very personally when you're in a situation where you feel you've been treated unfairly. On a personal level I get very upset by what happens in schools.[16]

Many teachers describe situations in which they perceive leadership in schools to be 'arbitrary', 'unrealistic', and 'heavy-handed' in that it infringes on their ability to do 'what is best for students'. They speak of these issues in terms of fairness and care, but also express reluctance to complain since principals can punish them, for example, by assigning undesirable courses or classes, difficult timetables and inferior classrooms in awkward locations and by withholding resources, books and money for departmental or programme needs. One teacher, Paul, referred to such treatment as not uncommon, and described it as 'part of the unethics of administration'.

By way of example, Audrey, an elementary school teacher, describes her opposition to a school board initiative that she regarded as a violation of children's privacy and fundamental rights. It was a pilot project on assessment that required the videotaping and audiotaping of students at work in classrooms. Despite her objections, she felt compelled by the principal to attend meetings with parents and pretend to be supportive of the project. She found this deceit ethically difficult to accept on a personal level, but ultimately remained silent about it.

Theresa also spoke about the unfairness of having to accept administrative decisions even though they may not be in either the teachers' or the students' best interests. Her specific example deals with the sometimes routine practice, in secondary schools especially, of juggling around the timetable and course assignments so most teachers have more or less comparable schedules, even if it means assigning them to teach subjects they are not formally qualified to teach. She comments: 'Instead of going with people's strengths and gifts, you make everyone suffer in the name of equity. Equity isn't always fair'.

I am struck by how early in their careers teachers come to relinquish their moral sensibilities in response to administrative imperatives and the pervasive climate in schools, as mentioned previously, to avoid 'rocking the boat'. Almost without exception, when my student teachers return from their practicum placements in schools, at least a couple of them report that an administrator asked them to cover the classes of an absent teacher. This way, the school can avoid the hassle and expense of arranging for a supply teacher or can free up regular staff who do not then need to be 'on call' for their absent colleague, and in some cases can avoid recording the teacher as actually being absent. As student teachers are not yet qualified, certified, or hired with formal permission by the school, this practice is neither legal nor professional, however it is commonplace. The student teachers, who are not in a very good position to resist such requests, report back on this experience with the same sense of moral uncertainty that more experienced teachers express when they find themselves caught in the ethical tension of being pulled between one's conscience and the power of normative school practices.

While the previous empirical examples illustrate a hodgepodge of incidents teachers recounted about routine or sometimes haphazard and unpredictable administrative actions and decisions in schools, teachers also describe circumstances in which they experience moral dilemmas relating to the expectation that they enforce school policies or other formal regulations. As Colnerud found in her study, teachers may experience considerable moral anxiety when part of their sense of professionalism dictates that they must punish students for breaches of what they consider to be unfair rules or policies.[17] Some of the more sensational stories relating to the extreme and often ridiculous, if not unethical, applications of zero tolerance policies against violence and weapons or drug possession, are reported publicly.[18] However, for the most part, teachers identify policies such as those relating to more daily issues of attendance, lateness, discipline, and dress codes as being potential catalysts for tension between their sense of moral responsibility to students and the dutiful enforcement of rules. For example, elementary teacher Barb explains:

> In this school district, there is an automatic 15-day suspension for any child caught making racial slurs. Now, I certainly don't agree with tolerating racism, but I don't think you can make hard, fast rules. So I would deal with it but it puts me in an awkward position: Can you see suspending a 7-year-old child?! So, I would talk to the child, but I wouldn't report him. I would be breaking the rule. But, in this case it would not be a public breaking of the rule. It's a more subtle form of rebellion, I guess.[19]

While teachers can modify policies in practice to reflect more closely their own ethical judgement in specific cases, most are aware that, regardless of their justifications, their respect or lack of it for school rules sends implicit messages to students about appropriate conduct. Ethical teachers must be thoughtful about this, although it is often difficult for them to be fully confident in all situations. For example, a secondary school teacher describes a school's late policy that compels teachers to bar from class any student who is late after three previous 'lates' per term. The success of this policy relies on uniform compliance and consistent implementation by all teachers. In one instance, a chronically late student, who has been struggling academically but finally is showing improvement and enthusiasm for her work, arrives to class ten minutes late for a group presentation that she and her peers have worked hard to prepare. According to the policy, the teacher should not allow her to attend the class. To make an exception would set a negative precedent for others, and to subvert the policy would be risky in professional terms. Yet, enforcement of it would have an adverse effect not only on this student but also on the others in her group who rely on her contribution and would be punished indirectly by her exclusion through no fault of their own. The teacher considers this unfair and is torn between doing what she thinks might be right in this case (by ignoring the rule) and the expectation that she fulfil her responsibility to implement the policy.[20] While she selects the former course of action, both choices in this dilemma are an unresolved source of moral uncertainty for her.

Some of the complexities and uncertainties teachers face in the evaluation and assessment of students are addressed in Chapter 2, in which teachers are seen to weigh internally seeming conflicts between such principles as fairness, honesty, and care. Similar conflicts are heightened considerably when the presence of an external force, such as a school administrator or the imposition of high stakes standardized testing, serves to augment the teacher's sense of moral anxiety over correct courses of action.

Teachers describe what they call 'mark tampering', 'mark inflation', and 'the flipping over of marks' as significant ethical problems for those of them who are conscientious in marking, yet are coerced by principals into changing students' marks or reports for reasons other than the assessment of academic and classroom performance. For example, secondary school teacher Karl complains:

> There's something causing trouble right now. The principal has maintained that a 20% failure rate in grade nine math is excessive, and that he intends to do something about it in our school. He feels the rate should be about 10%. So he asked me (as acting department head) how I was going to make things better. And I took exception to his use of the word 'better'. I said, 'We know that to have any effect on the failure rate, we have to dramatically lessen the expectations of the kids now, and that would really do an injustice to the kids who are very capable who are put out in a competitive situation'. So he's trying to look good as far as I'm concerned. I'm fighting this. I want him to give a rationale in writing for his conclusions. But I don't think he will. He's afraid to

commit himself to paper which would set up a confrontational situation beyond the school level. So this is where we are now. In fact, I'm not going to apply for the permanent headship here because of his position on this thing. When you sell out your top students, then you're not doing much good at the lower end either. That to me is a moral situation.[21]

At the elementary level, Barb and Daphne offer the following respective perspectives:[22]

I've had situations where I was asked to change a student's mark. This came from the principal. And I made sure that I had that in writing, that I was not in support of the change of mark and that it would be doing the student a disservice. But the principal has the final say.

The principal wanted me to soften some remarks on a report card. He stood there and stopped me from doing it [sending the report out unchanged]. He said he would not sign it. I said, 'It's going home the way it is'. But I had to relent because he's the boss. I had to take the comment out. As a consequence of this principal, I'm going to have to transfer out of the school at the end of next year.

The fairly recent introduction of province-wide standardized testing at the grade three level presents some Ontario teachers with the dilemma of having to administer what they regard as an unfair test to their students without trying to help them answer the questions, which would be seen essentially as cheating. Two teachers in a multicultural, inner city school discuss this issue in ethical terms. Erica comments:

The reading test has words on it like antibiotics, penicillin and Velcro – all these words that mean nothing culturally to these students. Maybe in their countries, they don't even have such things. So they come here and they have no idea what they are, and they're upset because they want to do well because they see this as a test and everyone knows that tests are important, and they can't do it. And it's devastating for them. And it's not a fair way to test the child. It's not a fair way and it's not an ethical way, and you know what, it doesn't tell you anything about them as a learner.

Jasmine refers to the math test that asks students to calculate a problem regarding slats in a picket fence. As she says, 'My kids are urban kids. They've never seen a picket fence. When they look out their windows they see chicken wire or rod iron fences'. As a result, they cannot visualize the problem and answer the question despite having the mathematical skills. So, Jasmine made a 'judgement call' and drew a picket fence on the blackboard so the students could understand. When asked whether she admitted doing this, when the principal asked if the test had been administered properly, she said, 'I don't want to burden people with that as long as I'm broadly keeping to the main rules. Those are my decisions, and I don't need to bother anybody else's conscience'.

The previous empirical anecdotes describe dilemmas, tensions, and challenges that teachers face in their interaction with school administrators and as a result of policies, procedures, and practices that are indicative of both peculiar circumstances and fairly normative school based processes. Often such dilemmas leave teachers uncertain about the rightness of their responses or lack of responses or frustrated in their efforts to fulfil professional responsibilities as moral agents. The point of these descriptions is not to assess either the moral value of the incidents per se or whether the teachers behaved ethically. Rather, it is to highlight various sources of ethical tension for teachers. Additional moral challenges are presented to them by situations involving students and their parents.

As mentioned previously, Chapter 2 addresses ethical challenges to teachers as they try to balance principles of fairness, care, and honesty in their evaluation and disciplining of students, among other exchanges. Challenges may develop into significant dilemmas when incidents occur where teachers suspect students of cheating on assignments or tests. In some cases, these events are further complicated by a variety of contingent circumstances. For example:

> An English teacher discovers that one of his senior students has plagiarized a major essay assignment that counts for a significant proportion of the final mark. The student has near perfect marks in his science courses and is aiming to get a scholarship that would enable him to enter the medical research field at university. He needs at least a B in English to have a chance at the scholarship; and a failure on this essay would reduce his mark to a C-. The student, a recent immigrant whose first language is not English, holds down a part-time job to support his mother since his father died last year. The teacher knows that personal circumstances have adversely affected the student's ability to improve his grades in English. However, the school policy on plagiarism leaves no doubt to its intent. The penalty is automatic failure on the assignment with no chance to make up the mark. The moral message from the school is quite clear on this issue. Other students have been punished for this kind of cheating. For all the teacher knows, they too may have been trying for scholarships and may have been affected by personal hardship. What is the right and fair thing to do?[23]

Theresa describes another evaluation issue that she finds morally complex. It involves her assignment of a 20% participation mark to her grade 12 students for attentiveness, homework completion, class contribution, and so on. While she essentially supports the principle of such an assessment measure, she finds the subjectivity of it something to agonize over in her efforts to be fair and honest in her judgements. This is often further complicated by students who challenge her because of their perceptions of favouritism and bias on her part. Additionally, Theresa acknowledges that such marks may be used for the purposes of classroom management, and while this practice may be effective, it is ethically suspect. So, it bothers her even as she does this.

Regarding discipline and classroom management concerns, Marissa recounts a dilemma she faced in trying to uphold the principle of fairness even in the face of potential violence and threats to her safety by a student who was 'a local gang leader who said he hated women, had a terrible attitude, and constantly tried to demean me'. In this case, she applied, rather than compromised, her ethical knowledge to resolve the situation. She explains:

> He would change seats to bug everybody, and I wouldn't allow them to sit out of their seats because I put them in alphabetical order, and he would just think he could sit where he wanted. And then he would sleep in class. So with the fear of what would happen, I could have just let him sleep in class, ignore what he said, let him sit where he wanted, you know. I could have let it all go and I wouldn't have gotten the verbal abuse, I wouldn't have gotten any of that. But I knew it was wrong. I knew that because I'm asking Mandy to get a late slip, and I'm asking Tony to go back to his seat, that he should too. It was very scary, but there was something inside me that just said, go with what is true and right, and I won't get hurt, I won't get my tyres slashed. So, I persisted. I was firm but kind. I never degraded him, and I never humiliated him. In fact, none of his other gang members or anybody ever bothered me. Initially, there were dirty looks, but at the end, they were even saying hello to me.

For Marissa, fairness as equitable treatment reflects the embedded principle of respect for the dignity of individuals; even under a most adverse condition, she resolved to adhere to it. For her, it is an ethical matter of building trust between herself and her students.

Grade two teacher Erica, who also speaks about the ethics of building trust, discusses the moral pangs she experiences when she is compelled to 'break a child's trust', even when it is for the ethically right reasons. For example, every year she, like many other teachers unfortunately, are told personal things by students 'in confidence' that may involve abuse or neglect at home; at this point, the teacher is morally and legally required to report it to the proper authorities.[24] However, as Erica says, 'It's really difficult when you have that child looking up at you and telling you something that's very private to them, and you tell them that you have to tell others about it – when you report, you're breaking this child's trust'.

In her research on teachers' ethical conflicts, Colnerud found that the 'most essential value' in conflict with other moral imperatives such as 'respecting parents' integrity' is the need 'to protect pupils from physical or mental harm'.[25] Grade three teacher Shannon discusses both sides of this issue in moral terms. Regarding parental integrity and the rights of parents to be informed of matters relating to their children, she states: 'Sometimes, the students say to me, "Please don't tell my dad." And I say, "I can't promise you that." So, I've learned through experience that that's what you have to say because if you tell them, "No, I won't tell," and you do, then later they'll say you broke your promise. I feel it's my moral obligation to be quite honest'. On the other hand, however, teachers such as Shannon need to be ever conscious that students' requests that teachers keep some things a secret from their parents may indicate a genuine fear on their part that they will be harshly punished at home for reported behaviour at school. As Shannon recounts, 'I had a boy in my class who was explosive and just generally not behaving in class, so I phoned the dad to let him know, and I don't think things went very well for the boy at home'. For this reason, she now knows that 'I have to be very careful of the notes I send home. I have to be very aware that some of my students unfortunately might be subject to parenting that is not the best kind'. In this respect, she, like other teachers, sometimes faces an ethical dilemma in deciding how honest to be with some parents.

In their study of the ethical dilemmas of 26 elementary school teachers in Finland, Tirri and Husu concluded that the majority of conflicts that mostly remain unresolved are between teachers and parents, and that competing interpretations of the 'best interests of the child' provide the catalyst for such conflicts.[26] Sometimes, disagreements over the appropriateness of curricular content or pedagogical styles are the source of dilemmas for teachers. For example, Theresa acquiesced to a parent's demand that her daughter should not be involved in group work assignments because she believed it had a detrimental effect on her marks; however, for Theresa this was a bad decision because it undermined her goals to foster a sense of community and build relationships among students and because it alienated this one student who was exempted from group work at her mother's insistence.

Conflicts between parents and teachers over the substance of children's schooling may be complex and cause a good deal of moral uncertainty as to how best to resolve issues. However, for the purposes of this discussion, it is important to recognize a fundamental distinction between parents. First, there is the unreasonable or irrational parent making curricular demands on a teacher that are not supported officially (such as the neo-Nazi who wants their child exempted from exposure to the part of the history curriculum that teaches about the Holocaust). Such parents' viewpoints should not be accommodated. Second, there is the average parent, who has a right to expect schools to adhere to the spirit, intent, and content of the formally approved curriculum, but who is legitimately concerned about a teacher who deviates from it in order to promote a personal ideological or political agenda.

The ethical teacher is conscious of not becoming this latter type of teacher either directly through what is taught or indirectly through casual remarks or informal opining. By way of a fairly benign example, Shannon speaks of a dilemma she reflects on as a result of her removal from her grade three classroom of an entire set of popular reading books about circus adventures. She tells her students of her opposition to circuses because of their perceived mistreatment of animals. However, she knows that some of her students may go to circuses with their parents as a normal family activity, and she is worried about letting her strongly-felt concern for animals cross the line into a kind of activism that may be seen to indoctrinate her students against a parental choice that is both legal and generally publicly acceptable. Ethical tensions created by this kind of dilemma – the problem of determining the moral line between responsible teaching, that is always unavoidably value saturated, and the irresponsible promotion of controversial values in the classroom – are addressed in greater detail in the subsequent section of this chapter.

Controversy and politics in the classroom: when ethical knowledge disappears

The previous section describes the kinds of moral dilemmas, tensions, and challenges that teachers face as a result of school-based dynamics involving administrators, students, parents, policies, and everyday practices. Such dilemmas are seen to cause moral uncertainty that, in some cases, undermines teachers' sense of ethical knowledge and how best to use it to resolve problematic issues. Their self concept as moral agents striving to do what they believe to be in their students' best interests may suffer as a result of their actions, lack of actions, or the compromising of what they see to be right responses to specific circumstances.

This section, on the other hand, briefly outlines how some practices of some teachers may be viewed as ethically questionable in ways that potentially erode the public's perception of teachers as ethical professionals. In such cases, any evidence of the individual teacher's ethical knowledge does not merely fade, which suggests lingering self-doubt and uncertainties about behaviour; rather, it disappears entirely as the teacher pursues an activity without feeling moral qualms even though it may be controversial, inappropriate, or politically sensitive. Thus, these teachers present challenges and dilemmas to the profession as a whole in its efforts to maintain public trust. As Dickinson argues in his discussion of teachers as moral exemplars and the concept of social guardianship: 'Society *trusts* teachers to be both guardians and purveyors of knowledge, truth, and virtue', and their violation of this brings themselves and their institutions into disrepute.[27] While he focuses on legal breaches of trust, others have described other types of 'values conflicts' in which teachers are accused of 'promoting a social agenda at the expense of instructional time'.[28] In their fascinating account of 'contentious teacher behaviours' that can 'lead teachers into trouble', Piddocke et al. create a classification system that identifies not only the criminal or sex-related behaviours and others related to 'character flaws', but also 'unauthorized teaching activities' and 'contentious conduct as citizens'.[29] These behaviours include, among others, the unauthorized teaching of controversial topics, issues, or subject matter, ideological teaching, partisan politicking, the wearing of controversial symbolic material, criticism of school policy and superiors, affiliation with controversial political, social or religious associations, and the espousal of questionable beliefs. It is with reference to these latter examples of what I am arguing is unethical conduct that the subsequent discussion of the teaching of controversial issues and the expressing of political opinions is primarily concerned.

Given that teaching is inherently and unavoidably infused with aspects of social and moral inquiry, the inevitability of controversial issues emerging as routine elements of classroom discourse should not be a surprise to anyone. Many have remarked on this in their encouragement of teachers to 'welcome disagreement rather than search for ways to make contentious issues innocuous'.[30] I too endorse the sentiment that responsible teachers should not shy away from significant questions, even of a highly debatable nature, *if they are indeed relevant to the intellectual domain for which the teacher has an accepted moral authority.* However, I do so with caution and with a recommendation that we clearly distinguish between the facilitating of positive dialogue on controversial issues in a balanced and reasoned way and the either careless or deliberate expression of personal and subjective sentiment whether or not it is for the purposes of biasing students on matters that have in no way been decided publicly, historically, intellectually, philosophically, empirically, or morally.

The purpose of this brief acknowledgement to such a complex issue is not to debate the nature of what is or is not controversial.[31] Rather, it is to urge teachers to think closely about the intent and impact of the things they do and say in the classroom. The ethical teacher must confront honestly not only these implications but also significant questions about tolerance, balance, freedom of expression, and the privileged place of the teacher's voice that have been explored thoughtfully by many current authors in the field.[32] In striving to be tolerant of diverse points of view, teachers must be able to distinguish between the balancing of reasonable opinions on an issue, as Noddings so clearly explains, and the inclusion of unacceptable perspectives as more or less equal sides of the same coin.[33] There is no moral equivalency among differing opinions when one 'side' tries to argue the merits of what is otherwise known to be wrong. The thoughtful and ethical teacher should never feel the need to allow equal 'air time' in class to the neo-Nazi, for example, or the member of organized racist or terrorist groups as if their views are nothing more or less than another way of looking at things.

When ethical knowledge disappears, teachers lose their capacity to recognize such situations as much more than concerns over curriculum or pedagogy and to adjudicate either individually or collectively on what the moral limits of tolerance should be in teaching. This may lead, for some, to classroom free-for-alls in which uninformed or unsubstantiated opinions are bandied about, and accorded some level of respect and seriousness, as if students were participating in a third rate radio or television talk show. As this is neither academically nor morally defensible, teachers need to be thoughtful about their handling of controversial topics, not as a curricular issue but as a moral one.

Of course, this raises questions about how much or how little teachers should reveal about their own personal perspectives. Teachers differ over this. For example, secondary school teacher Theresa explains:

> When a subject is controversial, it's hard for me when I hear something [from the students] that I don't agree with, but I don't want to shove my opinion on them. I also don't want to hurt their feelings . . . If a student says that her parents think what I'm saying is wrong, I'll allow a discussion which presents both perspectives. I'm careful not to contradict the parents or say that they're wrong. In the end I'll try to present some basic principles that work for everybody such as 'care about each other', 'don't intentionally hurt each other'.

By comparison, Carol, who also teaches secondary school students, declares:

> On the topics of abortion or chastity or homosexuality, I love having free reign in these areas. It doesn't bother me at all. I will impart the Church's view because that's my duty as a Catholic teacher in a Catholic school, and I accept that and do it. But, then we talk as a class; there is a right and wrong according to the Church and that's fine, but I may disagree with the Church or with students. It's important for them to know what I disagree with.

I believe this latter response has the potential of crossing the line into becoming what Simon sensibly describes as 'sermonizing', those 'spontaneous

lessons on politics and society; impassioned lessons about life and controversial issues in the curriculum' that should give every teacher pause to
reflect on the appropriateness of personal declarations.[34]

The central point to be made is that, in the capacity of the professional
role, the teacher is not simply a lone individual or private citizen, free to
express opinions while being answerable only to an internal conscience.
When teachers speak, ethically they may be seen to be speaking with the
authority of the institution or the school and the profession of teaching
behind them. Their voices carry with them the power and legitimacy of their
professional position. My advice to the ethical teacher is to refrain from
saying or deliberately implying 'this is what I support or believe' on issues of
a truly controversial nature. To admit to one's opinion is a short step from
promoting it, which is another short step from alienating those students in
class who may not share the opinion or who may be unsure themselves.
Teachers are responsible to all of their students, and by extension to their
parents, not just the ones who agree with them.[35]

Additionally, some teachers may express their perspectives not directly as
personal admissions, but rather by means of presenting biased and one-sided
arguments that favour their particular points of view. I find this ethically
even more untenable, as it starts to look like indoctrination in its deceit and
intent.[36] Those who reject my arguments must be prepared to accept that, if
they assert a right to express or foster their controversial beliefs or their
political and ideological perspectives, those on the opposite side of the
spectrum with similarly controversial beliefs they find objectionable or even
offensive must be allowed the same right. Schools can become, then, political battlefields, and classrooms can become soapboxes for individuals'
causes and crusades.

I do not believe that the ethical teacher should allow this to happen,
especially in relation to the espousal of partisan political positions. I still
recall one of my own high school teachers who spoke at great length about
why Jimmy Carter should be the next President of the United States. I do not
recall anything else that she taught us, and, given that we were in both a
Canadian school and an English literature class, the immediate relevance of
this lesson escaped me. I now see it as an example of unethical, unprofessional, and inappropriate politicking in which children are held captive as an
impressionable audience. This argument is more or less consistent with the
following statement:

> Teachers cannot use the school as a platform for promoting their per-
> sonal value systems. They may have very strong personal opinions that
> are contrary to those of the students' families, but the school is not the
> place to promote personal value systems . . . Teachers are perceived as
> authorities by their students, and a teacher's personal opinion carries

weight, so there is an ethical obligation not to use the teaching position to advance personal causes or beliefs that are contrary to those of the community.[37]

However, it stands in stark contrast with those, especially of more extreme or radical ideological perspectives on all political sides, who believe the classroom is just the place to air their views often in reaction to formal policies and curricula which they regard instead as themselves a source of political indoctrination. Their perspectives usually stand in sharp opposition to those of the education authority that certifies and/or employs them as agents of the state, the elected governments who have the political mandate to set the curriculum, the majority of the members of the public who expect schools to support values consistent with those of a liberal democracy, and most parents who entrust their children to teachers with the reasonable assumption that they will not be politicized in ways that are inconsistent with their own range of more mainstream positions.[38]

In her scathing criticism of a supplementary social studies resource published and promoted by a local teacher's union in 1987, Dodds makes the point in reference to the political and controversial nature of the document that, 'It is unethical to deliberately promote biased, personal views on political matters that have not yet passed into history as accomplished fact'.[39] She refers to teachers who do this without the public mandate as being professionally unethical. By way of a more recent example, three months after the terrorist attacks on the United States of September 11, 2001, a Toronto teacher published an article addressing the attacks entitled 'Why America is hated' in the provincial secondary school teachers federation (union) newsletter that is distributed to Ontario high school teachers. The article, which was promoted as a useful classroom resource for history and geography teachers, was immediately condemned publicly as radical propaganda full of historical inaccuracies and misrepresentations originally published by 'an obscure left-wing magazine'.[40] Public outrage ensued, especially against the union that printed the piece which was seen to be slow in trying to distance itself from either the substance of the article or the alleged right of the teacher to express it. Described as a clear abuse of professional responsibility, the document alarmed many teachers. One was quoted as saying, 'I was absolutely offended. I've typically not been an activist, but I have to get in the ring with this one. These people are disseminating inaccuracies and historical revisionism, and exceeding their mandate'.[41]

The Ethical Teacher urges all such teachers, regardless of their own political suasion, to recognize the enormous dangers in allowing their schools and classrooms to be co-opted by those among them who hope to use them for political and ideological purposes beyond their public mandate, whether they represent the interests of so-called 'left wing' revolutionaries or 'right wing' white supremacists, for a polarized example, as well as those in between the extremes. The dilemma for ethical teachers is to recognize and remain vigilant against that which threatens their collective professionalism and their public image as ethical, responsible, and accountable members of an honourable, moral and trusted profession.

This chapter has addressed two broadly separate, but not altogether unrelated, areas that are a source of personal and professional ethical dilemmas, tensions, and challenges for teachers. The first section describes some of the daily, school-based realities that test teachers' limits of moral tolerance on an individual basis to situations involving administrators, students, parents, and general norms of policy and practice. Such circumstances may thrust teachers into an uneasy state of uncertainty as they try to respond to their felt sense of moral agency and responsibility for the well-being of students. The second section is, admittedly, more politically provocative. It casts as a major ethical challenge to the professionalism of teachers the demands of dealing with controversy in the classroom in honest, fair, balanced, and reasonable ways that compel them to reflect deeply on the moral lines between responsible and irresponsible behaviour. Neither catalysts of tension are easily resolvable, as they potentially have the power to undermine the ethical teacher's confidence as a moral agent. Ethical knowledge fades or disappears, and the teacher is left, usually alone, to cope with the inevitable uncertainty as best as possible. This state is greatly complicated and exacerbated by unresolved dilemmas and tensions teachers experience as a result of their associations with colleagues. The next chapter is devoted to exploring this argument.

five

Collegial fear: the dilemmas within

I can remember it being drummed into me about being ethical: Always watch what you say about another teacher.

(Fran, elementary school teacher)

Moral agency in teaching is seriously endangered by a longstanding and prevailing professional belief that 'ethical' teachers do not interfere in the business of other teachers, criticize them or their practice, or expose their negligent or harmful behaviour, even at the expense of students' well-being. Norms of loyalty, solidarity and non-interference are reinforced by both the informal dynamics of casual collegial relationships within schools and the more formalized requirements of rules and regulations established and enforced by teachers' federations or unions. Given this context, professional ethics, from the perspectives of many teachers, pertains more to how they relate to their teacher colleagues than how they uphold moral and ethical principles in their practice. Given that, as Goodlad et al. argue, 'The teacher's first responsibilities are to those being taught', such a collegial-focused interpretation of 'professionalism' is alarmingly unethical if its primary consequence is the 'covering up' of teachers' wrongdoings and the protection of those whose actions, ironically, discredit the very concept of professionalism.[1] One should be conscious of Hugh Sockett's highly significant question: 'What is the line between collegiality and toleration of inefficiency or immorality?'[2]

Unfortunately, 'inefficiency' and 'immorality' do occur in teaching. For example, in the Province of Ontario in 2001, the College of Teachers reviewed the files of 467 teachers, a 31.5% increase over the previous year, as a result of concerns raised about them. Of these, more than 190 represented formal complaints, and upon investigation, 41 were referred to hearings. The College does not investigate complaints it considers to be frivolous, vexatious or an abuse of process. Ultimately, 26 teachers were found guilty of professional misconduct, and most had their licences either revoked or suspended. These represent the most serious of offences that are also criminal in nature. Of the cases not serious enough to warrant full prosecution, there were nonetheless some exemplars of ethically questionable teacher judgement and behaviour. For example, one teacher allegedly forced three kindergarten students to walk outside in the snow without wearing shoes or coats to teach them a lesson about bringing proper footwear to school. The teacher later admitted this was 'inappropriate' (some might say cruel) and was admonished.[3]

The Ethical Teacher is not primarily focused on teachers who commit such acts, but rather on those who work with them, those who see what they do, hear what they say, are told about their practices, or harbour legitimate suspicions about their competence or treatment of others, most notably students. Those teachers, as collegial 'onlookers' to morally discomforting situations, face dilemmas about how best to respond to their knowledge or suspicions. Often, they are frustrated by their unsatisfactory responses in ways that may even undermine their own self-perception as ethical professionals.

Using empirical examples from interviews with elementary and secondary school teachers, this chapter explores teacher attitudes towards collegial loyalty and the pressures to maintain it as a source for many of significant moral and ethical dilemmas. Their voices present accounts of school life fraught with anxiety and regret for what they have done or have failed to do in response to their knowledge or suspicions of colleagues' questionable behaviour. Many are unsure and uneasy about appropriate reactions to troubling situations, and, more often than not, such situations are overlooked or ignored in the interest of maintaining friendly working relations with peers. Some allude to an overwhelming feeling of powerlessness and cowardice, fear and self-preservation, as well as a lack of clarity about limits of professional responsibility. The first section pertains to conflicts between individual teachers on a one-to-one basis, and the second section relates to the expectation that teachers maintain loyalty in a broader sense to the teacher group as a whole.

When collegial isn't ethical

There are a couple of teachers here, I'll be honest, that I can't stand. I can't stand the way they teach, I can't stand the people they are, I can't stand the way they talk to their students . . . And, I'll protect my kids.

For example, I've done it outside in the yard. I've watched teachers screaming at Tien [an ESL student], and he doesn't understand a word, so I went up to one of the teachers and said, 'he doesn't understand a thing you're saying to him so you might as well just stop now'. Like, they haul off and just yell at him because, get this, he's a grade two playing in the play area on a grade four day. As if you're going to try to explain to Tien that day one is for grade ones, and day two is for grade twos!

(Erica, grades two and three teacher)

In their study of Finnish teachers' moral conflicts, Tirri and Husu identified a third of their cases as having 'involved situations in which a colleague had behaved in a cruel way toward a child. The cruel behavior had manifested itself in hurtful use of language or purposeful actions to humiliate the child in front of others.'[4] The dilemma is for the colleague who witnesses such behaviour. Similarly, Colnerud discusses conformity in Swedish schools with the norms of the teacher group and individual collegial loyalty as the catalysts for the most 'striking' ethical dilemmas that confront teachers as they regard the violation of the, often unspoken, code of loyalty to be akin to whistle-blowing. She writes: 'Teachers sometimes witness, or are informed by others, that a colleague is treating the pupils in a harmful way. The colleague is described as e.g., cold and stern, sarcastic, unfair, offensive or humiliating. Although the teacher regards the colleague's treatment as harmful and although he or she cares about the pupils it is difficult to confront the colleague.'[5]

This is consistent with my own research in this area in which teachers are shown to be not only resistant to formally lodging a complaint against a colleague, but also highly hesitant even to confront a colleague informally and in private.[6] For example, grade seven teacher Roger recounts the following episode:

There was one absolutely critical and specific situation that I experienced. One teacher who was in a leadership position [as a chair/coordinator] happened to walk through my open class area, and I had kids working all over. I happened to look over as he walked by a couple of my kids who were being a little goofy, certainly nothing serious. And as I watched him walk by, he took his thumbnail and stuck it hard into the kid's side and then kept on walking. As the kid came back down from the ceiling and landed on the floor ready to go after this teacher, I grabbed him and tried to calm him down. I asked what happened, knowing full well what had happened but no one knew I knew. He said, 'He stuck me . . .' And the teacher turned around and said, 'I didn't touch you.' So I kind of played dumb and said I'd handle things. Anyway I went to the principal and I said that this was off the record, and that I needed some help with this. So he said to me, 'Well, this is one where you make the decision. If you're going to deal with it, then it comes from you and you have to confront him.' I was just lost. The upshot of it was that I didn't go ahead with it. When we look back at times when we chose a path that we wish we hadn't chosen, that's when I chickened out. I kind of explored it but it was in a really wishy-washy manner. And I didn't tell the youngster I knew what had really happened. And I didn't go to the teacher and say, 'I saw what you did, it was a terrible thing to do, and not only did you lie but you abused.' If we talk about the good that came out of it, it helped crystallize my own moral framework as far as what goes and what doesn't and not being afraid to say something. It was survival, but I didn't feel good.[7]

Unlike Roger, secondary school teacher Paul did confront his colleague over a significant ethical transgression involving theft, favouritism, cheating, and unfairness. However, he stopped short of taking decisive action to expose the colleague's breach of professionalism. Paul explains:

There are so many grey areas, and I've been involved in so many situations involving teachers where I know I have done the wrong thing – if I had heard that someone else had done it, I would judge and say, 'You shouldn't have done that'. For example, a friend of mine [another teacher] stole an exam of mine and gave the questions to a student who was a favourite of his but who was failing my course. When I raved about what a good exam this student had written and what a surprise it was, this teacher admitted it to me. And I was absolutely unbelievably upset. I didn't know what to do. I had passed the student on the basis of this exam, and he didn't deserve it; it was a terrible situation. And I told the person off, and it's always shaded my attitude. Things have never been the same since between us. But I didn't do the right thing. I mean the right thing would have been to march him to the principal and expose this. It's bothered me ever since.[8]

Paul tells of another incident in which he discovered that a colleague had stolen several hundred dollars from 'a fund that the students had collected for something, and [he] could skim a bit off'. As in the first example, Paul claims that he admonished the teacher for such a dishonest and illegal act and said to him, 'If I ever hear about this again, I couldn't live with it, I wouldn't be able to sleep; I would have to go to the principal, so you should put the money back.' However, while he admits that he should have reported this incident, he did not; and, furthermore, while he wishes he could say that he would act differently if it were to happen again, he knows he probably would not.

Many other teachers describe similar situations in which they fail to react to the ethically inappropriate conduct of colleagues. Despite varying levels of moral outrage that they feel, they stress the importance of being 'careful', 'tactful', and 'protective' of themselves. As Roger asks: 'Is it tattling if a child is being abused? Is it tattling if someone's professional responsibility, which could bounce back on all others, is being compromised? Yet, self-protection is a critical element here, whether we like it or not.' What exactly is it in such circumstances that teachers fear and feel the need to protect themselves from, such that it leads to what many describe as 'cowardice' and 'gutless behaviour'? It is often a combination of anxiety over the nastiness of interpersonal conflict, peer ostracism for their perceived disloyalty, and a genuine threat of retaliatory action against them in the form of a professional misconduct charge from their local union or teachers' federation. By way of example, the following is a compilation of thoughts expressed by teachers Judy, Mike, Erica and Barb who, combined, teach across all grade levels.[9] In discussing colleagues they have known to be harmful to students in a variety of ways, they state:

> That's the diciest thing of all because you're really restricted as a so-called professional teacher for what you can and can't do. When it's a peer, you feel terribly helpless. You do try to protect the kids in ways that you can but it's nearly always indirect. And there is certainly a fear of confrontation. There is a great hesitation on the part of teachers to get involved directly . . . I respect the domain of another teacher. If I suspected child molestation I would *probably* speak to the teacher personally, but I would not go outside of it. You have to be very careful, and I would give the teacher the benefit of the doubt first. Also, staff solidarity is so important. And if you drive a wedge in it, that's hard to heal. You have to be able to trust each other. And if they think there's a snitch, it's an awful life for the snitch, and it's an awful life for the staff . . . First of all, I think you get into ethics here. It's right in our rules from our Federation [union] about this. You have to be very careful . . . I just don't think I have the authority, the credibility in those situations where I'd wished I had been able to do something to intervene. Teachers just sort of fall into categories of people you wish weren't in the room beside you. It's very difficult, very dicey to go to the principal because I suppose that's like a negative report, and it really should be put in writing. Dangerous things could be going on.

This latter reference to 'a negative report' relates to a regulation in Ontario, enforced by the teachers' federation or unions, in which a teacher making an 'adverse report' against a colleague to another person, especially one in a position of authority, such as a principal, must within three days furnish the colleague with a written statement explaining the nature of the complaint.[10] While the union's formal powers to discipline members have been curtailed somewhat by the more recent creation of the College of Teachers, it is not unusual in Ontario, as elsewhere where teacher unions operate, for teachers to be reprimanded by their unions for what is often perceived as a breach of loyalty to one's co-members in the name of professional misconduct. While the original intent of such a regulation was to establish a professional and open process in which individuals are accountable to one another, and their rights to defend themselves are fully protected in the face of an accusation, the spirit of it in practice intimidates most teachers from issuing a formal complaint for fear of implicating themselves negatively, regardless of the severity of the circumstances. Teachers speak of the regulation as being protective of incompetent and even possibly abusive teachers and punitive of honest and good teachers who attempt to make a difference by becoming involved. Such a perception is further entrenched in the teacher culture by occasional information documents printed by the unions and distributed to their members which emphasize teachers' right to be protected from negative criticism and the importance of collegial support.[11] More will be said about the powerful influence of teacher unions and its implications for professional ethics in the subsequent section of this chapter.

The irony of this reality is that malicious, but informal, staffroom gossip and sniping about colleagues' practices, abilities, and character traits are rampant in many schools. While the culture seems to support such unprofessional and unethical behaviour, it suppresses the much more legitimate practice of formally and professionally exposing harmful acts committed by peers or even the less threatening step of discussing concerns face-to-face with one's colleagues in a private and productive way.

In the wake of a provincial investigation conducted in 2000, on sexual misconduct of teachers with students, the College of Teachers in Ontario has made it clear that teachers are morally and legally responsible for reporting suspicious activity by colleagues to school officials. The College's Registrar stated:

> As teachers, our duties to our colleagues are not intended to take precedence over our duty to the public interest or our duty to ensure children in our care are safe. The legislation and the ethical standards of our profession are clear. If a member of the College suspects sexual misconduct or is aware of such an allegation, that member has a duty to intervene by reporting the suspicion to the appropriate authorities.[12]

This statement is not only commendable, but also significant in its assumption that teachers may 'fail in their legal duty to report warning signs to authorities. One explanation is the ironic and mistaken belief that the *Teaching Profession Act* (which contains the Regulation on "adverse report" mentioned above) prevents teachers and administrators from doing so.'[13] While this clarity on the dilemma of reporting a colleague's behaviour is a welcome position that has been long in coming over the past decades, it may not become fully actualized in practice given the ingrained norms of collegial loyalty. And even if the norms do change according to this specific area (sexual misconduct), there is nothing to suggest that the ethical intentions embodied in the Registrar's statement will carry over into other situations of a less sensational, but nonetheless morally serious, nature. According to some of the research cited previously, such as that by Tirri and Husu, and Colnerud, this concern is certainly not restricted to the Ontario context.

Some teachers, albeit few, claim that they welcome criticism from colleagues if it means they can improve their practice or see what they are doing in a different light as possibly not the best behaviour, just as they feel free to offer the same to colleagues. Carol comments: 'You have to be careful because of the stupid union things, but I don't mind confronting a teacher. I am not going to confront the teacher in front of the students. But, students are having enough to deal with at the moment without having some idiot telling them off incorrectly. So, I have no problems telling the teacher, "I don't agree with what you did," because if I'm doing something wrong, I want somebody to tell me I'm doing something wrong.' Theresa also explains:

> I won't undermine a teacher's authority to a student or allow students to discuss the behaviour of other teachers in class. I would be hurt if another teacher allowed students to talk about me. However, if a student approaches me privately with a concern, I'm willing to discuss it. For example, if I hear about or witness another teacher being sarcastic toward a student, I would talk directly to that teacher to let him or her know the effect their manner has on the student. This way, I think I'm being loyal to the student as well as to the teacher because it's an opportunity for the teacher to live and learn.

This latter point about learning from our errors is consistent with Noddings' perspective of caring in which 'we have a primary obligation to promote our friends' moral growth'.[14] If this view were to become a new collegial norm, then pointing out a colleague's negative behaviour ethically would be interpreted as a sign of care, not as a professional attack.

However, in practice, the correcting of one's peers is not always appreciated. Grade three teacher Jasmine tells of an incident in which another teacher 'took [her] to task' for the way she treated a student who proceeded through the door before her and failed to hold the door, which consequently slammed shut on her: 'And I shouted. I used my loudest, rudest shouting voice. And he [the student] had it. He was virtually pinned up against the wall while I let him have it.' The other teacher who witnessed this (and 'didn't believe in being rude to students') complained to Jasmine who shot back that she had no context for her complaint. She further said she would never do the same to another teacher.

Elementary school teacher Bev recounts another scenario in which her 'correcting' of a colleague accelerated well beyond a casual comment to ricochet back onto her in a way that potentially could have caused her, not the teacher about whom she complained, to be charged with unprofessional conduct. She explains:

> In one situation in the learning centre, I was working with a few students from another teacher's class. I approached him about work one kid had brought down from class. I said, 'I think it would really help the student more if you looked at his work rather than having another student check it because there are things here that other students just aren't catching, and he needs more support.' So, nothing happened there. So I went to the principal, and he spoke to the teacher who started correcting a couple of students' work for a week. I did do something very uncouth then. When there was an occasional [substitute] teacher in his classroom, I said, 'When this student comes down for help, would you send me some of his books.' So – this is the worst I did actually – I got some of his books, saw where the teacher had corrected it, whipped through the corrections, and he had marked things correct that weren't correct. So I photocopied some of this to have in my records and I went to the principal again and said, 'It's great he's marking some of the work, but he's marking things right that are wrong all over the place.' Anyway I didn't go much further than that. The principal wasn't receptive at this point. I don't think he wanted me to come back a second time. He talked to the teacher and told him what I did. Now, I was going to the principal hoping to get support anonymously hoping that he would have the brains to go into the classroom and see what was happening without getting me involved. So that put some noise in the air. I guess I should have left it at the first point thinking that I had done what I can. But this poor kid was still getting kiboshed! And one day I was called into the office, and the principal said, 'You're very lucky that this teacher didn't pull you in front of the union for saying and doing the things you have done.' My feeling at this point was that I was so infuriated with the whole situation where I was thinking if it meant me going to a board of inquiry, and that this teacher would lose his job, fine, I'd go out and find another job too somewhere. It was just infuriating! And I just work with a handful of students from that class, and they're all affected by this teacher.[15]

When I present this real-life scenario to graduate students in my professional ethics course, most of whom are practising teachers, I get two very different reactions. Some feel that Bev acted ethically and responsibly, even if her methods were somewhat sneaky, because she was putting students first in her attempts to remedy a situation that was clearly detrimental to them and their academic progress. Others vehemently discredit Bev for what they see as unprofessional and unethical treatment of her colleague and maintain that she had no authority or right to question his professional ability, especially in the way that she did, even if it means that students continue to suffer from his incompetence. These opinions more or less coincide with the teachers' level of allegiance they feel for the teachers' union with the latter group being much stronger supporters and the former group being either quasi-supporters or non-supporters.

From my own perspective, the important point is that students should never be disadvantaged either emotionally or academically by a teacher's conduct, and that it is the moral responsibility of the teaching profession and its members to ensure this above all else. I cannot find it in myself to be critical of Bev, although, ideally, ethical teachers working in an ethical environment with ethical administrators should be able to sort out this type of situation more honourably. Collegial loyalty, for me, does not exist as a moral principle in such situations where students are put at risk of any kind. Union procedures or informal collegial pressures that serve to muffle this serve no good professional or ethical end.

Many teachers are unwilling to report a colleague formally or even approach the colleague personally despite their belief that they fail, in such circumstances where they suspect collegial wrongdoing, to do the right thing. They speak of 'backing off' and 'chickening out'. When they do try to confront the issue, albeit feebly in most cases, they refer to 'disloyalty', 'tattling', and 'ratting', and to themselves as 'rabble-rousers', 'a snitch', or a 'stool pigeon'. They become uneasy, apologetic, and defensive about their actions even when they are seemingly doing the ethical thing by pointing out morally objectionable behaviour for the benefit of students and the school as a whole. Most cases, however, never even reach this point. I refer to this state as 'suspended morality' in which teachers apparently conform to the collective norm, in this case collegial loyalty, even in situations in which they do not believe they should.[16]

> Suspended morality largely pertains to the compromising of individuals' subjective beliefs about right and wrong ... Compromise allows individuals to 'suspend' or abandon their sense of moral responsibility and explain their actions solely in role-based statements of false necessity; all behaviour, both good and bad, right and wrong, is justified as the outcome of simply doing one's job. This doctrine that one 'has no choice' has been seen to 'deprofessionalize' principals and teachers (Holmes, 1991). While they gain the dubious freedom to

abdicate personal responsibility for their actions, they lose the freedom associated with professional discretion.[17]

Dependence on suspended morality and false necessity as strategies for avoiding personal confrontation and keeping the collective peace among members of a teaching staff cheapens ethical knowledge and weakens the spirit of professionalism so critical to the articulation of moral agency in teaching. Teachers who succumb to the demands of unconditional collegial loyalty may find that their own ethical knowledge – the foundation of their moral intentions and aspirations – fades as a result, and their self-perception as ethical professionals becomes tarnished by their reluctance or refusal to safeguard the interests of students first.

Teachers become socialized into a culture of acceptance early in their careers, whether it is to accept unfair or inappropriate directives from an administrator (as was noted in the previous chapter) or to accept that the best way to keep out of trouble in schools is to avoid challenging colleagues on matters of ethical conduct and learn to live with the guilt over their inaction and apparent cowardice. My preservice student teachers (or teacher candidates) regularly return from their practice teaching sessions upset over experiences that made them uncomfortable on moral grounds; they are further unsettled by their own lack of response.[18] For example, one student teacher witnessed his supervising teacher hit a grade six student over the head with a textbook in order to get the attention of the student who seemed to be falling asleep at his desk. Another teacher candidate recalled how her supervising teacher walked by a grade five student who had rather large ears that protruded; the teacher flicked one of the student's ears with his finger using a snapping motion that made the ear turn pink from the assault. The student had been quietly sitting at his desk, and all the teacher said was, 'I couldn't resist', as the rest of the class chuckled in response. At the secondary level, another student teacher explained that, in the five-week session in her school, her supervising teacher came to the school on only three of the days. However, she did not report her absence and asked the student teacher to 'cover' for her with the administration. She further called the student teacher each day to get her classes' attendance records so she could 'phone them in' to the office, and, thus, pretend to be on the job. How this situation could have gone on for so long without other teachers knowing and participating in the 'covering' for a colleague, who was apparently having some personal trouble at home, I cannot fathom. As in the first two cases, the student teacher said nothing in protest either to the supervising teacher or to anyone else. Many teacher candidates further claim that they sit silently, but uncomfortably, in staffrooms listening to teachers openly criticize and disparage certain students and their families. In all such situations, the student teachers recognize these behaviours as ethically unprofessional. Yet, they also sense that any effort on their part to point this out would not in any way be welcomed or accepted. Even if they were in a more secure position as equal peers of the teachers, rather than student teachers, they doubted whether they could muster up the moral strength to 'break ranks' with their colleagues.

In his discussion of peer relations among students in schools, Power comments that, 'To report a peer is regarded as a betrayal of the in-group member to the alien out-group authority. Even to criticize a peer may be considered siding with the adults; the rule of thumb is to mind your own business.'[19] Why, as professionals, should teachers accept that such a maxim should carry over into adulthood to influence working relationships? And yet, even early educational sociologists, such as Willard Waller, confirm an entrenched belief that 'the significant people for a school teacher are other teachers . . . A landmark in one's assimilation to the profession is that moment when he decides that only teachers are important'.[20] However, there is little right about remaining loyal to a group at times when its norms and collective practices are in direct conflict with its responsibilities to others. As Piddock et al. claim, a teacher, being a member of a profession, has the duty 'to uphold the dignity of the profession by his/her actions' as well as 'the duty to duly criticize the profession and its members when they fail to abide by the profession's own proper standards'.[21]

Nonetheless, as this section has argued, a strong desire on the part of many teachers to maintain harmony among staff compels them to circumvent the moral challenge of standing alone against a colleague, and by extension the collective group norm of expected loyalty, in ethically troublesome situations. Malcolm identifies this kind of informal pressure as emanating from 'the tyranny of the group'.[22] He defines tyranny in terms of an individual's inclination to obey and conform to the perceived judgement of the majority. Informal and formal teacher groups undoubtedly would be alarmed to hear themselves described as 'tyrannical'; yet, even outwardly benign groups maintain significant pressure on their members, many of whom willingly accept it as a necessary condition of group cohesiveness and solidarity.

Solidarity

Individual teachers experience moral dilemmas and tensions not only in relation to conflicts of an ethical nature with singular colleagues but also when their convictions are at odds with the overall practices or beliefs of the collective group. Judith Boss reminds us that, 'Group mores can also weaken our motivation to do what we know is right.'[23] The previous section focused on collegial loyalty and the pressures of the informal teacher culture that inhibit teachers from taking ethical stands against one another. It also introduced the notion of individual teachers who feel threatened or intimidated by the possibility of disciplinary action against them for perceived breaches of loyalty by their federations or unions. This section builds on this introduction to address solidarity to the teacher group as a source of potential tension for individual teachers in situations that relate either directly or indirectly to the political and social realities of their mandatory membership in teachers' unions.

First, I should declare openly, if it is not already obvious, my own perspective that unionization and the normative attitudes and initiatives that flow from it endure as the single most significant hindrance to ethical professionalism in teaching. It constrains teachers' moral authority as autonomous moral agents by demanding uniformity of belief and behaviour in situations that lack ethical clarity, thus preventing individuals from pursuing courses of action that may in fact be ethically preferable. This, in turn, tarnishes the public image of teachers, further eroding the collective moral authority that should be vested in trusted professionals. This perspective, which is admittedly debatable and certainly controversial, frames the following discussion that is necessarily abbreviated. It is not the point of this section to weigh the obvious benefits to teachers of their union member status (in the form of enhanced salaries, security, and working conditions) or to describe and assess the political intricacies of their ideological battles with, usually, local or provincial or national governments. Rather, the focus of this section is on the moral dilemmas, tensions, fears, pangs of conscience, and other negative emotional reactions individual teachers experience as a result of working in environments influenced by union control and sustained by those who support this particular version of group solidarity. While the empirical examples I present reflect circumstances that are locally (Ontario) based, many of the overall issues and themes cross international lines.

As a formal extension of collegial loyalty, as addressed in the previous section, solidarity demands that union members are protective, first and foremost, of one another (except of those among them who are seen to violate this principle who may be harshly reprimanded). Union directives to teachers caution them strongly against lodging a complaint against another teacher, and at least one union in Ontario states unequivocally that it will not in any way support a member who reports on another member to the College of Teachers regardless of the professional process followed or the circumstances of the case.[24] While teachers indeed deserve protection and due process, and it is a rightful responsibility of a union to provide or ensure them, unfortunately such a strident policy and the general tone in which it is often communicated potentially feed the impression that many teachers and others express, that unions protect the incompetent, negligent, or harmful teachers and intimidate the others. This impression, if not addressed by the unions themselves in an open and candid way that acknowledges that some teachers are indeed guilty of unethical conduct, does nothing to advance a collective professional initiative on the part of teachers to be the ones accountable for maintaining the moral integrity of their profession.

From an Australian perspective, Haynes notes that, 'The union code of ethics seems at first glance to offer a different view of professional integrity, defining it in terms of loyalty to the union rather than exercising independent judgement.'[25] Loyalty to the union assumes compliance on the part of its total membership with its decisions, strategies, positions, and recommendations. Often the most dramatic and emotionally-charged of these is the decision for teachers to take strike action. While teachers, like other people, are politically and morally divided on the legitimacy of striking and picketing as a legal form of job action, the teachers who most keenly face ethical dilemmas at the time of a strike are those who fundamentally oppose the strike on principle but either comply with it in silence or break it and suffer the inevitable consequences of collegial ostracism or worse.

Hetenyi regards strike situations in teaching as ethically significant because 'the real hardship falls on the student whose education is disrupted and on the community at large . . . The real losers are the children and their parents.'[26] Unlike in private industry in which trade unions operate, in education those who suffer the most by a strike are those least able to influence the negotiating process. How, then, can teachers maintain trust as moral agents when their own actions are seen to have such a negative effect on those to whom they are most ethically responsible? As Haydon comments, from a British perspective, 'Teachers are still regarded as moral guides and exemplars, whose standards are perhaps just a little above the level of the rest of society. That is why in some minds the idea of teachers going on strike arouses a sense of betrayal.'[27] For those teachers who share this opinion, strikes create dilemmas and tensions of an ethical nature.

For example, secondary school teacher Anita comments: 'I went out on strike and I'm not very proud of it. It tore me apart. I just pray that there is never a strike again. I couldn't stand it. I went out because of my colleagues. I don't know if I'd have the guts not to go on strike and buck all my colleagues. But I sure wish I'd have.'[28] At the elementary school level, Bev describes a situation she encountered:

> Prior to the strike we all had to go down and register for it. And if we did not sign this card agreeing to follow whatever was happening, then you got taken over to this little table where there were three counsellors who would counsel you into why it was appropriate for you to follow the Federation and their strike. I saw a couple of these people, two ladies who were at these tables being 'counselled', and they were in tears because they wouldn't sign these cards. Anyway, I thought that was most interesting. I didn't agree with the strike, but I thought I'm

not going to be humiliated and go to listen to these counsellors who are going to put the pressure on me. So I guess I'm more of one to go with the flow rather than to put up the red flag.[29]

Bev further recounts an incident in which two teachers she knew of refused to strike, and 'on the first day back in the staffroom I remember hearing in one school there were two signs up, one on each side of the staff room, and one said "teachers", and the other said "scabs". It's pretty scary to think of a person who's taken the initiative and found the strike morally questionable and decided they weren't going to do it and then to have 22 other people against you.'[30] Other teachers recall how the unions publish the names of any strike-breakers and circulate them to all schools. Others tell of knowing of an occasional colleague who quits teaching altogether rather than enduring the social repercussions of being ostracized as a strike-breaker. From my perspective, ethical teachers, as a matter of personal and professional integrity and dignity, do not intimidate or bully anyone, for any reason. As perhaps an effective mechanism for compelling in others loyalty of a sort and meek compliance, it is a doomed strategy for inspiring the kind of collective ethical professionalism this book hopes to illustrate and evoke.

Labour strife, as a catalyst for moral dilemmas that confront teachers, apparently extends even beyond teachers' strikes in the interests of maintaining above all else cross-union solidarity. Elementary teacher Roy describes one situation:

> Two years ago, we had a caretakers' strike, and our [teachers'] Federation said, 'Don't you take any garbage out; you can take it out of your classroom but you're not allowed to clean the washrooms, etc. That's not your business.' A couple of teachers did clean up the bathrooms – they said the kids can't go into a dirty bathroom – which started trouble on staff. Teacher versus teacher. Some felt these others were scabbing or union breaking. It got into a big fight, and those guys' emotions never healed. I went along with the Federation. I made sure my room was clean, which I do anyway, but that was all.[31]

Work-to-rule campaigns cause similar moral tensions for teachers. Unlike during strikes, teachers continue to receive their full salaries while involved in such campaigns, in which they fulfil only the minimal conditions of their employment contracts and avoid any professional work deemed to be extra-curricular, including offering extra academic help to students and preparing lessons or marking assignments and tests during non-school time. Some teachers speak of secretly violating the requirements of such labour action by continuing to do what planning work they can in the secure privacy of their homes at night and on weekends. Others are more outspoken and garner public attention from the press. For example, one teacher refused to participate in a work-to-rule campaign by tutoring students at lunch hour and assisting with their after-school clubs. He stated that: 'Personal integrity would not allow me to desert my pupils at the request of a union. My first responsibility is to my students . . . I don't think the students should be involved in the whole union labour dispute.'[32] Since taking this stand, he has been ostracized by his peers in the school, prohibited from seeking office in the union, and could be fined by it as well.

The following three teachers have been involved in one of two work-to-rule campaigns initiated by two separate elementary teachers' unions in 2000. They all speak of the need to ensure that students do not suffer while at the same time observing more or less the conditions of the campaign; such an aim is fraught with tensions. Gina comments: 'If I had known becoming a teacher would entail this kind of politics! And I don't like to bring such business into the school because it hurts. I'm frustrated that I don't have time to prepare my lessons, but I won't bring politics into the classroom with the children.' Erica complains, 'I mean it was so ridiculous that work-to-rule. One of the things we weren't allowed to do was we weren't allowed to cut the fruit the kids get for snacks. So, the kids come to you to cut it so there'll be enough pieces for everyone. So, of course you cut it, I mean that is just like beyond ridiculous!' At the end of one school day, Shannon, who is hurrying to prepare work for the following day before having to leave the school by the deadline time imposed by the work-to-rule, comments in a panic that, 'I have to get out of here now; they'll (the union representatives in her school) be watching us.' From my perspective, again, it is alarming that professionals speak of 'not being allowed' to exercise legitimate judgement related to their practice by members of their own profession. They should not have to hide from each other, pretend to each other, and deceive each other in order to protect themselves from collegial wrath for doing what they see as their moral and professional duty. Interestingly, the teachers quoted above fundamentally supported the unions' positions on the issues of contention, but found the work-to-rule campaigns demeaning of them as professionals. Teachers, collectively, have to find more professionally honourable and respectable ways of voicing their concerns that do not compromise their role as moral agents.[33]

Kerchner and Caufman draw a distinction, relevant to this discussion, between 'old style labour unionism', which emphasizes more militant activism, the protection of teachers ('any grievant is right'), and the prevention of reform initiatives; and 'professional unionism', which emphasizes the protection of teaching, more collaborative and less adversarial relations with 'management', and a suspicion of actions politically intended to impede educational reforms.[34] In advocating the latter model, they tell of a situation in which British teachers took a 'delicate and controversial' stand, seemingly more indicative of the former model, by boycotting the government's testing programme in 1993. They summarize: 'Still, union leaders are undecided about whether teachers' venture onto the stage of public policy was simply an opportunistic tactic within a long-standing political contest with government or whether it was an assertion that teachers were taking the right and corresponding responsibility to represent the public good in the matter of testing.'[35] The relevant point for *The Ethical Teacher* is to consider the moral position individual teachers are put in by their unions compelling them, often through coercion, to support their political stands even in situations which may be illegal or subversive of the legitimate education authorities or when the teachers themselves may not share the ideological perspective they are expected to support unconditionally.

A similar scenario played out in Ontario during 2001 and 2002 in which the unions, as yet another facet of a continual and ongoing dispute with the provincial government (which in Canada has the legal jurisdiction over matters of education) instructed teachers to resist and protest against a new professional learning initiative. This initiative required teachers to enrol in and successfully complete a number of professional development courses of their choice over a period of time in order to maintain their certification as teachers licensed to teach in Ontario. The introduction of the initiative was staggered so that a fraction of the teaching force was required to commence the programme as the initial cohort. The unions objected to the initiative, among other reasons, on the grounds that it was externally mandated, threatened decertification for non-compliance, and required training in skills already deemed to have been appraised. They distributed letters of protest to teachers selected for the first cohort with the instruction that they sign and send them to the College of Teachers and thereby refuse to submit to the initiative.

One of my own graduate students was a teacher randomly chosen to be in the first cohort. She was greatly distressed by the fact that her name was disclosed to the union, informing it that she had been selected, and by the subsequent pressure she felt to challenge the mandate that she comply with the professional learning programme. For a course assignment, she presented this situation as a case study detailing a moral dilemma she faced in her professional work. She wrote: 'As a proponent of professional development, I can't understand the overwhelming resentment surrounding the Professional Learning Program. As one of the 40 000 teachers in the first cohort, I am being told by union representatives not to comply with this mandate. This action would result in the loss of my teaching certification.' She ended by asking the following question: 'Do unions, by virtue of forced association, interfere with teacher professionalism?' Other teachers reported in class that mandatory staff meetings, which union representatives made all teachers sign in and out of, were being held in most schools in which teachers were pressured to boycott the professional learning programme;

many teachers said they kept silent about being selected for the first cohort and feared that their names would be released somehow to the unions. They were afraid of being personally singled out for union attention. As this initiative evolves over several years, the issue still remains unresolved for teachers urged to resist it, even though it may put their careers in jeopardy.

As an associated action of protest against the professional learning programme, one union instructed their members to refuse to supervise student teachers from faculties of education that had agreed to be providers of the courses for the programme. By putting enormous pressure on the faculties and using our students as expendable pawns, the union hoped to force the issue with the government and the College of Teachers. Many teachers felt ethically stressed by this directive which, one week before the student teachers were scheduled to go into the schools for their practical experience, required them to renege on their professional agreement and responsibility to supervise the next generation of professional teachers.

In her discussion of professional ethics and continuous professional development, Thompson writes:

> Teachers should be committed to the systematic maintenance, improvement and broadening of their knowledge and skills and the continued development of the personal qualities necessary for the execution of their professional role . . . Teachers should be prepared to work collaboratively with colleagues as critical friends to maintain and improve professional competence . . . [they must also work to maintain and improve the competence of the professional community] by working with student teachers and other colleagues, including on their professional evaluation and assessment.[36]

Unfortunately, by comparison, union-driven protests of the kind described above not only leave a public impression that teachers have no will to be professionally accountable (despite claims to the contrary by the unions), but also cause significant moral dilemmas for individual teachers whose efforts to be personally responsible for their professional conduct seem thwarted by their collective association and the assumptions embedded in the expectation of teacher solidarity.

Ethical teachers are bound to experience moral tensions and dilemmas as a result of collegial dynamics, whether they stem from an informal culture of loyalty or more formal requirements of union membership. When the tensions are accompanied by personal fear and feelings of intimidation, anxiety and helplessness, the ethical knowledge that usually informs their practice as autonomous moral agents and defines them as ethical professionals fades. Such an erosion of ethical knowledge challenges the confidence that teachers themselves, and others, should have in teaching as a trusted profession of societal benefit and significance.

Part 3

Ethical directions

[Schools] are at once sources of moral instruction and sites of moral struggle. At the center of both source and site is the teacher, who, alone in the school's adult populace, is for long hours each day in the company of children and youths whose presence compels the making of moral choices.[1]

The aim of this third and final part of *The Ethical Teacher* is to encourage lone individual teachers who make daily moral choices to enhance the ethical knowledge that many of them already articulate. They may do this by becoming increasingly aware of the nuances of their moral agency and the moral significance of the dynamic details of teaching and by consciously applying this knowledge to the routine elements of their formal and informal practices. Its further objective is to urge teachers to work openly with one another in ways that make ethical knowledge more visible and central to all aspects of school life as a shared principle-based foundation for renewed ethical professionalism and renewed teacher cultures. In becoming more familiar with and committed to the kinds of expressions of ethical knowledge illustrated in the first part of this book, teachers may be better able to anticipate, fend off, ameliorate, or minimize the kinds of moral dilemmas and challenges, revealed in the second part, that undermine both ethical knowledge and teacher professionalism. In doing so, teachers may become more internally secure in their moral agency as well as more externally or publicly accountable for it.

The first of the following three chapters reviews briefly more formal approaches to moral accountability defined by ethical codes and standards and by the creation of regulatory associations. The second chapter, as the dominant chapter in this part, focuses on the need for teachers, individually and collectively, to become more self-determining by governing themselves as ethical professionals. This would require a significant overhaul of some prevailing norms and attitudes. It would also rely on, in part, facilitative school administrators who, as teacher professionals themselves, recognize the power of ethical knowledge to provide the guiding principles for moral decision making. The third chapter, in conclusion, summarizes the connections between ethical knowledge, moral agency, and applied professional ethics in teaching. It addresses implications for teacher education and professional development, and positions ethical knowledge as the moral measure of teacher behaviour and practice in all their forms.

six

Standards and codes

Primum non nocere [first do no harm].[1]

Moral accountability and professionalism

Increasingly, society is demanding of its professional communities more transparent and accessible evidence of their moral accountability to those they serve. As Haydon states:

> Recognizing the large and potentially very damaging influence that the members of other professions can exercise on the layperson, the general public can reasonably ask that they respect certain ethical standards. In the same way, recognizing the potential influence for good or ill that teachers can exercise towards pupils, such an expectation is equally reasonable.[2]

In many respects, the essence of professionalism is defined by the principles of ethics that govern not only the expected conduct of professionals but also the spirit of commitment and responsibility they embody as both individual practitioners and collective associates. Attempts to formalize core moral principles, that should be recognizable to us all, as well as more specialized responsibilities peculiar to certain professions have resulted in the creation of regulatory codes of ethics and professional standards and the self-governing bodies to promote and enforce them. Such official statements of ethical intent, it is hoped, both serve the public interest and provide guidance to the members of the profession. They exist to inspire confidence in the profession itself, and, even though they are not necessarily contractual in a legal sense, to symbolize a kind of moral contract between society and its trusted institutions. This chapter addresses this more official avenue to prescribing ethical conduct, as it relates to teaching, and concludes that while codes, statements, and standards, if they are crafted well, may be at least of inspirational benefit, they are insufficient vehicles for enhancing ethical knowledge as the foundational basis of the renewed professionalism of teachers.

Many of those writing in the area of moral accountability as an essential aspect of genuine professionalism remark on two specific characteristics of education that underline the need for enhanced trust between society and the profession: the exceptional vulnerability of those primarily served and the compulsory nature of schooling. Soder argues:

> Children by nature are defenseless. Children by tradition are taught to distrust strangers. But parents, in complying with compulsory school-ing laws, turn their defenseless children over to virtual strangers . . . The surrendering of children to the state's schools thus represents a con-siderable act of trust . . . Those responsible for the physical and mental health of children in schools have a moral obligation to ensure that children are kept from harm.[3]

These two conditions, the inherent susceptibility of students to teachers' actions, good or bad, and their non-voluntary presence in schools, create for students a state of inequality and dependence and for teachers a state of increased moral responsibility.[4] Such inequality and dependence on the part of students lead many to conclude that the total 'responsibility for the relationship lies with the professional, who must ensure that it benefits the other person, that power is not abused and that the relationship is not exploited'.[5] Such violations of the teacher-pupil relationship, based on a deep trust that parents individually and society collectively invest in the teaching profession, are often referred to in legal terms as a breach of fiduciary duty or a breach of trust.[6]

Hugh Sockett has written at length about the critical need to develop trust among teachers, pupils, and the public in general as a profound element of professional accountability. For Sockett, such trust is grounded in the moral principles of fidelity, veracity, friendliness, and care, and is expressed through the much needed articulation of a moral language.[7] Similarly, in her account of professional ethics as embodying an ethic of care, an ethic of competence, and an ethic of professional commitment, Thompson argues that teaching has not been adequately emphasized for being the act of trust that it is.[8]

With the endowment of trust comes the expectation of higher moral standards of behaviour. Writing broadly of professionals and others who serve the interests of society, such as teachers and police officers, Edwin

Delattre argues that those individuals who hold positions of public trust are more obligated than members of the general public to meet higher moral standards.[9] He further argues that since such individuals serve voluntarily, they 'should choose a less demanding walk of life' if they are unwilling or unable to live up to such standards.[10] It is worth considering that the notion of 'higher standards' may mean both a higher level of the same moral standards expected of anyone and different standards altogether. In the latter case, the distinction between the trusted professional (and, as in the case of the teacher, role model) and the average citizen is most sharply punctuated when the lines between accountability in one's public and private lives become blurred. As Covert states:

> Typically, teachers are not free to act in public or in private as [others] might, because they have a responsibility to uphold a moral code non-teachers need not abide by. This duty to act responsibly places teachers in the company of such other professionals as doctors, lawyers, and the clergy. Each of these professional groups are expected to behave both on and off the job in ways above moral reproach.[11]

The point that societal trust necessitates a higher standard of conduct from teachers in both professional and personal spheres than that expected of others was entrenched in Canadian law by two Supreme Court decisions in 1996:

> Both cases arose out of the teachers' conduct in their personal lives. In each case, the Supreme Court refused to draw a sharp distinction between the high standard of ethics and conduct that the community has a right to expect of teachers when they are fulfilling their public duties and the standard to be expected of teachers in their personal lives. As decisions of Canada's highest court, these two decisions are precedents that will be followed by all Canadian courts in similar cases.[12]

One case involved a teacher who wrote, published, and expressed in television interviews anti-Semitic propaganda which promoted hatred and racism. While he did not impose his views in the classroom, many in the community were fully aware of and disturbed by his actions. The other case concerned a teacher who engaged in consensual (and otherwise legal in the non-teaching community) but morally questionable, sexual activity with a 14-year-old former student during the summer holidays. Guilty verdicts in both cases led to a job dismissal ruling upheld in the first case and criminal sentencing in the second. One of the presiding judges, speaking for the unanimous Court, referred to teaching as 'uniquely important' and stated:

> Teachers are inextricably linked to the integrity of the school system.

Teachers occupy positions of trust and confidence, and exert considerable influence over their students as a result of their positions. The
conduct of a teacher bears directly upon the community's perception of
the ability of the teacher to fulfil such a position of trust and influence,
and upon the community's confidence in the public school system as a
whole.[13]

In his review of these two rulings, Mandell concludes: 'Teachers' professional bodies must send the message to their membership that there is no
room in the profession for those who cannot or will not measure up to the
high standards of personal and professional ethics that the community and
Canadian law expect'.[14] This reference to the role of teachers' professional
bodies has implications for the development of collective ethical knowledge.
While most teachers probably do not need to be reminded by their associations that immoral (by community and societal standards) or illegal
behaviour is not acceptable, cases such as those described here should serve
to highlight the importance for teachers to remain always conscious of and
alert to their role as trusted moral agents and the ethical responsibilities this
entails in more routine and less extreme contexts. From the perspective
advanced in *The Ethical Teacher*, this heightening of awareness, to the point
where both accountability and professional practice are measured in moral
terms, builds ethical knowledge. Such knowledge can be used not simply to
discipline teachers involved in such sensational cases, but to guide the
decisions of the majority of well-intentioned teachers who struggle daily
with moral choices. Professional bodies have an opportunity to address this
in ways that may benefit both individual practitioners and the collective
profession.

Professional associations in other fields are similarly engaged in the
ongoing examination of issues related to professionalism and ethics. For
example, in Ontario, a Chief Justice Advisory Committee on professionalism and what it means for lawyers states that within society, 'There is a
perception that lawyers have forsaken their professional roots and see law
more as a business than a calling. These developments create the need to
inform lawyers and the public about the nature of professionalism and to
describe the standards and values of professional service and conduct'.[15] The
Committee addresses the importance of 'personal character' and includes
among its 'building blocks of professionalism' the moral principles of integrity and honour. Similarly, the Society for Academic Emergency Medicine in
the United States issued a report on professionalism and ethics in which
medicine is defined as 'a moral enterprise grounded in a covenant of trust'.[16]
It clearly asserts that a profession is based first on ethics, and that technical
competence and knowledge of the field are not enough to ensure professional behaviour. Rather, the report refers to the need for a 'virtue-based

ethic' that includes such virtues as prudence, courage, temperance, vigilance, unconditional positive regard, charity, compassion, trustworthiness, and justice. Such virtues are equally essential in teaching, and it is notable to the promotion of ethical knowledge as the foundation of renewed professionalism that other professions are expressing a comparable conviction to the one emphasized in this discussion.

Within education internationally, regulatory bodies, self-governing organizations, colleges of teachers, teaching councils, and other such professional associations are increasingly being used or created for the purpose (among other things relating to standards of professional practice) of addressing concerns about accountability, the assertion of professionalism, and the ethical premises that should underpin both. As Strike and Ternasky state, one element that characterizes a profession as being self-governing is the fact that 'the members of a profession police their own ethics'.[17] By way of a local example, the Ontario College of Teachers was created in 1996 by an act of provincial legislation as a self-regulatory body to ensure the accountability of the teaching profession and to assume responsibility for determining and maintaining professional standards governing teachers' practice. Among its various mandates, the College approved a regulation defining professional misconduct and developed a code of ethics, that came to be called 'ethical standards', both of which the College assumes the responsibility for enforcing.[18] The ethical standards are addressed further in the subsequent section.

In her discussion of the development of a General Teaching Council in England and Wales, Meryl Thompson notes the centrality of a shared understanding and appreciation of a profession's ethical responsibilities. She wisely argues that, 'Professional ethics cannot be imposed, for by their nature they must be internalised to become part of the collective consciousness and the individual conscience'.[19] I believe it is for this reason that codes of ethics, while acceptable as a symbol of moral accountability, must not be perceived by members of the profession merely as legislated precepts or dictates detached from the realities of their daily work. Instead, they should serve as inspirational invocations to the professional ideals and moral principles imbedded in the best examples of their own practice.

Formalized standards, standardized codes

No profession can really exist without a code of ethics to guide the conduct of its members. Doctors, lawyers, and clergymen have their ethical codes, but teachers can scarcely be said to have such a code. Until they have developed a professional spirit which is characterized by loyalty to the recognized ethical standards, they cannot rank with the learned professions.

(Ontario Minister of Education, 1915)[20]

It has been nearly a century since this sentiment was expressed with such vigour and during this time, in Ontario as elsewhere, ethical codes of one sort or another have come and gone in teaching. Some support codes as a mark of status and accountability; others deride them as vacuous and useless. Yet others are ambivalent about their worth and potential contribution to a professional culture. I recall with some sense of shame how I uttered to my preservice teacher education students some jaded and cynical remark about how irksome I find politicized and bureaucratized ethical standards that do nothing to guide teachers and help them cope with the moral complexities of their work. One student quietly objected by stating that she found the standards inspiring and that they gave her a feeling of comfort just knowing they exist as a beacon of ethical intent. Perhaps she felt what the Minister in 1915 referred to as a 'professional spirit', which united her in a common moral mission with other teachers, past, present, and future, and which shook her into a sobering realization that her chosen vocation is one to be honoured and preserved for its ethical significance.

If ethical codes or standards have the power to move teachers into such a state of awareness, then I believe they can serve a vital purpose. If, by their very presence, they can enable teachers to apply a conscious ethical lens to their own view of daily practice, then they are worth promoting as an important component of professionalism. However, if they exist only as a public advertisement of presumed accountability or as a political statement seeking to be inclusive of a variety of interests and agendas, then ethical codes could cease to be seen even symbolically as professionally worthwhile. This would be certainly regrettable if, in dismissing ethical codes, we also diminish a focus on professional ethics itself. Codes of ethics and ethics should not be equated or confused. Principles of ethical behaviour, whether or not they are stated as self-evident by means of codes or standards, should reside visibly in the foreground of a teacher's consciousness. Ethical knowledge as the basis of professionalism demands this attention to moral principles *in practice*. And it is this need to make the link to actual practice that ultimately renders most codes, even those that avoid the pitfalls mentioned above, wanting as anything more than idealized goal statements.

In defining a code of ethics as 'a strategy that gives general guidelines for educational practices in particular and is open to a much wider interpretation than the law can allow', Haynes argues that codes are general by design yet more specific than the 'broad ethical principles of beneficence and non-maleficence on which they are founded', and that they should be concurrently both idealistic and practical.[21] How such principles as non-maleficence (what one should not do) and beneficence (what one should do) are expressed in an ethical code significantly influences its tone and form. Bull notes that it may be possible to 'agree upon a code of ethics for teaching that specifies what teachers should not do and that leaves open to debate precisely what teachers should do. In effect, such a code is a series of "thou shalt nots" for teachers'.[22] The distinction between presenting ethical principles from a negative/prohibitive perspective or from a positive/ imperative one highlights the complexities not only of drafting ethical codes or standards but also of trying to apply them to practice in ways that may be clearly enforceable. As I have argued elsewhere, it may be marginally easier to be more specific about what teachers should not do than about what they should do.[23] The former presumes that all behaviour is allowable unless otherwise prohibited; for enforcement purposes, one need only prove a contravention of the code. The latter necessitates the itemization of all allowable behaviour, and the potential for omission is consequently a greater risk. There is also the obvious difficulty of determining whether an individual would be in violation of the code for failing to fulfil adequately the obligations that are positively required. Different codes favour these two orientations to prescribing ethical conduct in varying ways.[24]

Ethical codes and statements of ethical standards also differ somewhat in their content and substance. It is not unusual to find in them references to honouring the worth and dignity of others, maintaining respect for such principles as justice, fairness, truthfulness, consistency of treatment, impartiality, confidentiality, and integrity, and engaging in the pursuit of excellence. Most address the need to be committed to students, parents, colleagues, other professionals, and the community at large; some refer to one's responsibilities to the profession itself and the significance of profes- sional learning. Those usually written by teachers' unions rather than professional colleges tend to emphasize both contractual obligations and the expectation that teachers remain loyal and committed to the union itself, its processes and regulations, and defend its membership. This entrenches the primacy of collective agreements, union policy, and one's fellow members.[25] Given my previously stated concerns for ethical professionalism as a result of how unions stress collegial loyalty and solidarity, I find codes skewed in such regulatory, contract-based, and process-oriented ways to be not only devoid of ethical principles, but also oppressive and deprofessionalizing for the messages they convey about their priorities.

Such ethical codes have attracted their share of criticism. Watras refers to them as being largely 'inadequate, bureaucratic, and legalistic'.[26] Strike and Ternasky see codes more generally as 'platitudinous and perfunctory'.[27] And, in their harsh criticism of the National Education Association's Code of Ethics and the American Federation of Teachers' Bill of Rights, Arends et al. recommend that the teaching profession 'revisit and revise' their standards as a minimal first step 'given the current call for a greater emphasis on teaching as moral action'.[28] They further condemn these two associations for failing to commit themselves to the advancement of a professional knowledge base and state that, 'It is more than a little troubling that the major teacher associations have produced ethical standards that are so deficient in comparison to those of other helping professions'.[29] Their observation that such codes sound more like political diatribe or job contracts could be levelled also at other codes and standards governing teaching.

Ethical codes from other 'helping professions' may be distinguished from many teaching statements in their emphasis on serving the client above all others. By way of brief example, the American School Counsellor Association's lengthy and detailed statement of ethics asserts that the primary obligation is to students, not to colleagues, parents, the profession as a whole, or the general public.[30] Similarly, the Canadian Medical Association developed and approved 'as a guide for physicians' a code of ethics based on the Hippocratic Oath in which it is stated as the first principle under 'general responsibilities' to 'consider first the well-being of the patient'.[31] The Royal College of Dental Surgeons also lists as its introductory point that ethical dentists 'will have as their first consideration the well-being of their patients'.[32] While teachers and schools frequently invoke the 'best interests of the child' as the driving motivation or indeed the justification for all decisions and actions, it is rare to find in their ethical codes such explicit and direct reference to the primacy of this moral responsibility. Ethical obligations to students are included more or less equitably along with those owed to, particularly, colleagues, and others with interests or stakes in schooling.

Whether a strong statement of primary duty in teachers' ethical codes would make much difference in practice is certainly questionable. However, it would transmit a worthy conviction of moral intent not only to the public, but also to the teachers themselves. This might provide them with a focal point around which they could individually and collectively assess their conduct and practice. Such a potential use for well designed ethical codes is reflective of Nancy Freeman's advocacy of reliance on formal ethical standards, as distinct from personal morals or instinctive reactions, as the only professional route for resolving workplace dilemmas.[33] Teachers clearly could use some professional guidance to help them navigate their way through the ethical complexities and dilemmas that impinge on them in the course of their daily practice. Perhaps a code, as suggested previously, could provide needed inspiration and contribute guiding principles.

However, regardless of how well codes or statements of ethical standards capture the essence of those principles that best define the moral dimensions of teaching, they are likely to remain insufficient, in and of themselves, as tools of professional improvement. Ethical conduct and dilemma resolution are supported ideally through an enduring respect for such dimensions based on ethical knowledge. And ethical knowledge as it is addressed here cannot be adequately represented by trying to engrave it in a code for it is not concerned solely with principles. Rather, it is built on principles as they are consciously revealed and understood in the nuances of applied practice. As Sergiovanni wisely concludes:

> Codes can provide the basis for self-regulation and can help build confidence in teachers and sustain teachers' integrity in the eyes of the public. Professional codes of ethics are helpful and necessary, but they are not enough. Conforming to a code, without making a commitment to its ideals and values, means giving only the appearance of ethical behaviour . . . Only when code-specific behaviour and underlying ideals and values are connected – only when it is accepted that what teachers do and why they do it are connected – will professional codes cease to be rules of professional etiquette and become powerful moral statements.[34]

In a similar vein, Strom, among others concerned with professional ethics, notes the potential chasm between knowing and even obeying an ethical code and living its ideals in ways that strengthen professional resolve to behave ethically. She notes that, 'The development of working knowledge goes beyond mere exposure to ethical codes, however; it requires internalization of values associated with professional performance and those related to justice, freedom, equality, truth and human dignity'.[35] The notion of 'working knowledge' is an apt descriptor for ethical knowledge.

In a not so ingenuous attempt to bridge this chasm between codified ethical standards and real dilemmas experienced by teachers, I applied, using a first-person narrative form, Ontario's Ethical Standards for the Teaching Profession to empirical data. The outcome was a series of fictitious responses to dilemma situations written from my perspective on behalf of the perplexed teachers struggling to adhere to the code.[36] Somewhat revised versions of several of these scenarios are reported below. They all relate to teachers' dilemmas described fully in Chapter 5. The exact wording of the Ethical Standards is indicated by italics. The first vignette is in response to the dilemma that secondary school teacher Paul experienced when a colleague and friend confessed to him that he had stolen an exam in order to pass it on to a failing but favoured student. If Paul were to use the standards, he might be left pondering this:

> Well, I know my friend was wrong – he violated several standards concerning *professional relationships with students, impartial respect, honesty and fairness.* But the question is, what should I do? Our standards aren't explicit about reporting a colleague's unprofessional

behaviour. The last standard says I should *advise the appropriate people*, I guess that's the principal here, *in a professional manner when policies or practices exist that should be reviewed or revised*. But, this is hardly a policy and as a practice, it can't be really reviewed or revised now. I don't think this standard could be referring to this type of problem. Also, is this *confidential information about a member that I have to respect?* It's certainly a secret, but not one I should protect, surely. The sixth standard says I should *work with other members of the College* – that's my friend and colleague – *to create a professional environment*. But, it's too late for that – the deed is done. Now it's a matter of reporting it at my own risk of losing a friend and creating a nasty collegial atmosphere that would probably undermine our ability as a faculty to work together anyway. So, maybe I'm right to keep quiet. Yet, I'm supposed to *act with honesty and integrity*. Well, I do – I would never have done what my friend did! I just wish he hadn't told me. But that wouldn't make things right for either the student who cheated or for all the other students who didn't have the same unfair advantage during the exam. I feel that honesty means you shouldn't lie. Well, by doing nothing, I'm not really lying. Who says honesty means telling something you know even when no one has asked you?

The next scenario represents a plausible reaction on the part of grade seven teacher Roger who witnessed a colleague (who was his chair/division coordinator) hurt a student by plunging his thumbnail into the child's ribs, but failed to confront the colleague or comfort the student:

Boy, did I ever display a lack of moral courage here – of course, the standards don't say I have to model that. I sure didn't show that I *recognize the privileged nature of my relationship with students* or *model respect for their dignity*. Now, at the time, neither the students nor the chair knew I saw what happened, so by not saying anything I really didn't lie and violate the principle of *honesty*. I mean I did try to *act with integrity* when I sort of reported my chair to the principal. After all, we're told to *advise the appropriate people* – it's just that the appropriate person here didn't seem to want to know about it. Maybe he thought I wasn't acting *in a professional manner*. But what does that mean? I always thought professionalism also meant maintaining loyalty to your colleagues – so perhaps I shouldn't have told on my chair in the first place. Of course, the standards don't mention that kind of loyalty the way the old union code implied. However, it doesn't say my primary moral responsibility is to the students either. I wish it did say that. And, how am I supposed to continue *working with other members of the College in a supportive professional environment* if I'm seen as a snitch?

The last brief vignette presented here could be an expression of conscience on the part of elementary teacher Roy who, unlike some of his teacher colleagues, obeyed a union directive to support a strike by school caretakers:

I can't actually find an ethical standard to support what I did, or didn't do, as the case may be. I didn't *model respect for the human dignity* of my students by accepting that they should be forced to use dirty bathrooms; and I guess I didn't *work with other members of the College and others to create a professional environment supportive of students' physical development.* The other standards just don't seem relevant to this workplace issue. So, maybe it's not a matter of ethics in this particular situation if my actions reflect a sense of responsibility to the caretakers more than to the students.

As I argue in my original presentation of these and other scenarios, this type of artificial application of an ethical code or standards to the specifics of actual dilemmas invites controversy and alternative interpretations. Theoretically, one could take the same or different standards and apply them in an entirely different way to the situations and thereby generate quite variable responses. This, however, is the key point. It highlights how minimally useful this kind of devotion to formalized ethical precepts would be in the resolution of moral conflicts. As Soltis observed in a relatively early discussion of professional ethics in teaching:

Sometimes people fail to perceive the relationship between an abstract code and a concrete situation . . . [Codes do] not offer a philosophical justification of the fundamental ethical principles embedded in the code. If rules conflict in practice or if the reasons for one's actions need to be justified, educators with only a knowledge of the code may be ill prepared to deal with the situation.[37]

It is for this reason that teachers need to heighten their ethical knowledge in ways that enable them, as individual professionals and collegial members of a collective group, to make the links between abstract principles and concrete situations.

Some imply that such a practice-oriented goal may be achieved through the designing of codes, after all, if the development process is localized rather than standardized such that those drafting the code would be those using it in their own specific context.[38] Perhaps such exercises might prove useful if only they would serve to enable teachers to discuss openly with one another matters of ethics, aspects of behaviour and practice, and how they intersect. However, at the same time, one must be attentive to Hansen's warning against codes that could serve as a disclaimer for putting too much faith in such processes. He writes:

Experienced teachers know that there is no blueprint or by-the-numbers moral code that can tell them what to do in a particular context. Students and educational settings differ a great deal, and teachers must constantly use their judgment. There is no single or best way in which to be patient, attentive, and fair-minded . . . But the fact that there exists no formula for how to be patient with or attentive to students does not mean teachers can dispense with such virtues.[39]

Rather than trying to line up one's conduct with the specificities of a formalized code, teachers should be joined in a shared mission to honour through their practice those ethical principles and virtues that capture the spirit of their professionalism and that should form the basis of the public trust invested in them as morally accountable practitioners. Schwarz argues that, 'To address teaching as ethical practice, we must conceive of teaching as *vocation* rather than profession' because professions concern specific bodies of knowledge and accountability, among other things, that obscure the moral nature of teaching.[40] However, rather than accepting this, *The Ethical Teacher* proposes that it is precisely this moral dimension that should distinguish teaching as an accountable profession. As the following chapter explains, we must harness ethical knowledge as the new body of knowledge to define professionalism in teaching. Such a renewal is not necessarily 'new' in the specific practices of many individual teachers, but in the recognition of ethical knowledge as the underlying knowledge base in teaching.

As this chapter has argued, ethical knowledge is fostered not by means of formalized codes and standards alone, but through a collective mission in which teachers become fully aware of their moral agency and of how their actions and beliefs have a profound ethical influence on students. Some teachers clearly embody this ethical orientation to their work. Sockett describes three such teachers whose practice, which he connects to a moral base grounded in virtue, he claims 'has left [him] in awe'.[41] Similarly, Richardson and Fenstermacher's Manner in Teaching Project as well as Jackson et al.'s Moral Life of Schools study, both of which were introduced in Part 1, expose us to teachers who have much to offer to our appreciation of ethical knowledge. I still vividly recall how teachers such as Marissa, Erica, and Theresa, who were introduced in Chapter 2, exude a sense of moral agency that could never fully be captured in the words of an ethical code. Such examples showcase virtues in action in all their complexities and contradictions. By making this more visible as a catalyst for ongoing professional discussion and ethical knowledge building, teachers may be able to satisfy the expectations that they be ethically competent and morally accountable. And, in summary, instead of relying on ethical standards to attempt to guide teachers' practice, we should make ethical practice the normative professional standard for teachers.

seven

Learning to create an ethical culture

Ethical knowledge as professionalism: extending the community

Throughout *The Ethical Teacher* I have argued or implied at least four central points concerning ethical knowledge. First, it seems clear that some teachers as individual practitioners possess a keen awareness of their role as moral agents, their own intentions and actions as they reflect moral principles or virtues, and the complex nuances of teaching from the seemingly mundane to the more obviously exceptional that are infused with moral and ethical significance. Second, if the consciousness of such teachers about the elements of their practice as moral expressions not only of individual character but also of practical expertise could somehow be made more visible, ethical knowledge could be shared and augmented among members of the larger teacher culture. Third, such an extension of teacher knowledge throughout the community of practitioners could well provide an applied knowledge base that could rival any other special body of teacher knowledge as the principle-based foundation of renewed professionalism in teaching. Teachers would be marked as professionals not solely for their technical competence, their mastery of subject matter, or their pedagogical success, but by the wisdom and humanity they reflect in the day-to-day realities, dilemmas, and challenges of assuming responsibility for other people's children and the hope of future societies. Fourth, it is ethical knowledge, not idealized codes, that most aptly defines applied professional ethics for the benefit of teachers themselves and for those to whom they are morally accountable.

This chapter extends these points in a focused appeal to teachers, individually and collectively, to take hold of themselves in the name of professional self-determination and embrace ethical knowledge as the measure of independent choices and the building block of renewed school cultures. This will require the examination and possible replacement of old norms and attitudes; it may initially make teachers feel more vulnerable as they share ideas, experiences, and dilemmas with each other and expose themselves to potential peer critique. This chapter also speaks briefly to school principals, not solely as administrative leaders but as professional teachers themselves, whose role in facilitating the development of ethical cultures should not be underestimated. Ultimately, while accepting the suasive power of collective norms, this chapter rests its hope on the ethical teacher as an individual professional.

There have been many conceptualizations of teacher knowledge addressed in the education literature: classroom knowledge, situational knowledge, personal knowledge, practical knowledge, personal practical knowledge, pedagogical content knowledge, process knowledge, craft knowledge, and professional craft knowledge. Relating the question of what actually constitutes a knowledge base to pressing interests to define professionalism as dependent on such a knowledge base, some remark on the tensions among these varied conceptualizations.[1]

Underlying such positions on teacher knowledge, I would argue, should be the recognition of ethical knowledge as being foundational for, as Fenstermacher claims, such things as expertise, skill, competence, validity, and assessment are not 'the concepts that capture the essential meaning of teaching. Without the specification of the moral principles and purposes of teaching, the concept amounts to little more than a technical performance to no particular point . . . The teacher's conduct, at all times and in all ways, is a moral matter. For that reason alone, teaching is a profoundly moral activity.'[2] Kerchner and Caufman claim that the knowledge base in teaching is practical in that it constitutes 'highly indeterminate and experiential' activities of the classroom, as descriptive of a craft profession, rather than the 'codified information' of expert professions.[3] Given Fenstermacher's observation that all such activities are inherently moral at their core, it is not such a dramatic conceptual leap to argue that ethical knowledge – the conscious appreciation of how moral agency is embedded in the dimensions of practice and teacher behaviour – is the foundation of teacher knowledge. This distinguishes teaching somewhat from what Kerchner and Caufman refer to as an 'expert profession' such as medicine in which, as Self and Baldwin note, there exists a 'belief and social expectation that the possession of special knowledge and skills carries with it the mandate for its moral and ethical use'.[4] In teaching, however, it is not a question of superimposing ethics onto the special knowledge and skills, but rather of contextualizing ethical practice as an integral component of the special knowledge itself. And, such special knowledge shares Hansen's description of moral knowledge which 'points neither to a specific body of facts and theories nor to a predefined content of any kind . . . the source of moral knowledge is responsiveness to human beings and their circumstances . . . moral knowledge can endure and enlighten a practitioner's work with students over a lifetime'.[5] In order for it to do so, however, it needs to be nurtured within the professional community.

In their 2002 book, Buzzelli and Johnston claim that teachers fundamentally do have a moral sense and that they 'inherently know that teaching is a moral activity'.[6] I would argue, by slight comparison, that only some teachers *know* this (in the sense of possessing ethical knowledge), and, of them, some are more aware than others of how their moral agency role influences the specific aspects of their practice and behaviour. This is not to condemn other teachers as immoral or unethical practitioners, although some may be so; rather, it suggests that ethical knowledge still resides mostly as the domain of individuals' sensibilities instead of a shared and widely acknowledged feature of the teacher's daily responsibilities. If ethical knowledge were to be more broadly expressed within the professional community at large and singular school cultures on a narrower level, perhaps those teachers who do not often make intellectual, philosophical, experiential, and practical links between core ethical principles and the idiosyncrasies of their own work may start to do so.

It is up to teachers themselves, as professionals, to assume the responsibility of cultivating ethical knowledge as the moral measure of their practice in all its aspects, planned and spontaneous, formal and informal, personal and interpersonal. They should not rely on others to define their professionalism or blame others for restricting their capacity to fulfill their moral duties. Regardless of the many constraints on teachers, it is not acceptable to use them as excuses for failing to act ethically or pursue moral inquiry in the course of their daily work. Professionals are self determining and self regulating. And, while there are many elements in a teacher's world – relating to educational bureaucracies, the establishment of curriculum standards, and other examples of overall governmental policy – for which they cannot be responsible, they surely can be so when it comes to moderating their own behaviour.[7] As Gerald Grant notes, the 'capacity for real change lies in the hands of teachers who must assume and exercise moral responsibility for their profession'.[8] In the interests of ethical professionalism, teachers need to accept this both individually and collectively.

From an individual perspective, teachers are continually exhorted to reflect on their practice, to look inward in a deep sense to examine and question the value of what they teach, how they teach, and how they can learn and improve. While much of the literature relating to teachers as reflective practitioners concerns values and beliefs, it is often silent on morals and ethics. Yet, as Buzzelli and Johnston argue in their advice to teachers to hone their moral perception: 'What makes reflection moral, then, and why reflection is important from a moral perspective is that it is an act of conscience'.[9] Opportunities for teachers to engage in such solitary reflection must be seized whenever possible in a spontaneous way since teachers, given the pressing demands of the school day, rarely have the luxury of structured time to review their actions, beliefs, and intentions.

Some seem quite proficient in maintaining an ongoing conscious evaluative focus on the moral dimensions of their classroom-based actions. For example, some of the teachers introduced in Chapters 2 and 3 commented on their decisions relating to, among other things, work assigned and students disciplined insofar as whether they were fair and respectful either as they were making these choices or shortly afterwards. Their awareness of themselves as moral agents enabled them to apply their ethical knowledge to the various challenges and situations that arose over the course of a day – or a week, a year, or a career – since their reflections have a way of enduring. These teachers make instantaneous conceptual connections between experiences they had in the past and current similar ones; they can apply non-teaching examples of ethical importance, as they relate to how human beings should treat one another, to teaching situations.

Of course, these teachers, by virtue of the fact that they were participants in a research study, also did have extra structured time to reflect on their ethical orientations to their work. One of the most rewarding aspects of the study for me was learning how much these teachers appreciated and valued the chance to speak openly during interviews about their moral beliefs and how they see them as woven into the fabric of their own teaching. They said they rarely, if ever, get to articulate things of such importance to them in a way that is practically and professionally supportive. They also commented that they felt reaffirmed as professionals to realize that what they hope to achieve in a moral sense is often readily evident to others, as proven by the research team's identified observations that lined up with the teachers' own stated intentions and perspectives on selected classroom incidents.

Not every teacher can benefit from having a research team around offering feedback and focused opportunities to be reflective. However, perhaps teachers can work collegially to achieve a similar state of moral awareness as a kind of group reflection within their school communities. After all, they collaborate on other areas of academic, social, cultural, and behavioural importance; why not expose the moral and ethical aspects of teaching to communal scrutiny? As Grant observed, 'deep-seated beliefs and attitudes' influence the 'nature of interactions between teachers and students' as well as 'the moral climate of the school' as a 'community that cannot disavow its responsibility for moral virtue'.[10] Teachers need to express and even (or in some cases, especially) debate such beliefs and attitudes as part of their collective community building.

From a collective perspective, much has been written about transforming schools from organizations into communities of various kinds. Thomas Sergiovanni has called for idealizing schools as 'covenantal communities,' guided by moral principles of justice, beneficence, and care, and grounded in the moral authority 'derived from widely shared professional and community values, ideas, and ideals'.[11] He further refers to collegiality as a form of professional virtue, and argues that professionalism must be seen to pertain not only to competence but also to the embodiment of moral virtue. The collegial sharing of ethical knowledge among teachers would make central such a professional concern with exercising virtue in the school community as a whole. In his advocacy of an 'ethical language,' Kenneth Strike argues that the fostering of such a language is integral to the development of a community in which 'we may begin to acquire the wisdom and judgment required to apply the language deftly and to deal with children in morally enlightened ways'.[12] However, he also laments what my research participants acknowledged; that is, 'Teachers are rarely asked to engage in moral dialogue with other educational professionals about the ethical issues of their practice. Their practice is often solitary'.[13] We need to find ways to bring the ethical knowledge that some teachers have to the professional culture of teaching more broadly.

However, the challenge of communicating ethical knowledge is considerable. Like Strike, Karl Hostetler concludes:

Teachers are not given the opportunity – either in their pre-service or their in-service experience – to conceive their teaching in ethical terms, to dialogue with each other and other people about ethics, to seriously engage in teaching as an ethical practice ... If conditions for ethical dialogue and action do not exist for teachers, it is likely that they do not exist for students and others either.[14]

In my own study involving some of the teachers mentioned previously, the research team discovered and identified multiple examples of how individual teachers as solitary practitioners strive to maintain an ethically professional environment in their classrooms, expressive of moral principles such as fairness, kindness, honesty, and respect, and supportive of the social, moral, and emotional development of students. However, we found no clear evidence of whether they work with other teachers, administrators, support personnel, or others to foster and extend such an environment. One of the teachers whose teaching was most illustrative of principle-based practice and who clearly articulated a firm grasp of ethical knowledge was surprised to learn that many of the ideals she put into action were also contained in her school's handbook under the title 'Vision for Staff'. She had never discussed this with any other colleague and had no sense that anyone else addressed such issues of moral responsibility. Certainly, those teachers who experienced the kinds of dilemmas, tensions, and challenges described in Chapters 4 and 5 did not have a collegial outlet for coping with the ethical complexities of their work lives. Indeed, many of these complexities were either caused or enabled by negative aspects of the prevailing collegial culture.

In his discussion of personal character and professional ethics, Delattre notes that, 'We become who we are, in many respects, in and because of the companionship of others we imitate and whose habits and dispositions we emulate – whether they are aware of it or not, and even whether we do so deliberately or unconsciously'.[15] Given this propensity for peer imitation, the teacher culture generally would benefit from a collective sharing of ethical knowledge, not just as an unintentional 'rubbing off' kind of process, but as a conscious and deliberate strategy for professional engagement. Such a strategy would apply the ethical knowledge that teachers have to varying degrees to the articulation of new ethical norms in which the primacy of teachers' moral responsibilities to students would be at their core. In making this aspect of teacher knowledge, as it is expressed in moral practices, more visible to all, perhaps those whose ethical knowledge is less formed would be influenced by a culture where such principles as fairness, kindness, honesty, and respect set the tone for in-school policies, procedures, and interpersonal relations among teachers and between teachers and students.

David Hansen describes an inner city boys' high school, challenged by enormous social problems, that seems to capture exactly this tone, in which the ethical knowledge of some quite extraordinary teachers pervades the environment. He comments that 'the everyday life of St Timothy's is charged with moral messages, from familiar admonitions such as "be respectful to others" that echo from classroom to classroom, to highly personalized counsel from individual adults. Special events and ceremonies dramatize the notion that schooling is a vehicle for the formation of character'.[16] Individual teachers seem able to foster a positive moral climate through an obviously shared vision of their ethical responsibilities and goals. However, I am curious as to whether they discuss with one another how this vision may be sustained or undermined by their own routine practices or whether the school is just fortunate to have a group of teachers with a keen individual sense of ethical knowledge that does not require further collegial cultivation.

For example, Hansen refers to one teacher, whom a troubled student particularly disliked, 'who has a reputation for being gruff with students'.[17] My question pertains to what this concept of 'reputation' implies. If this teacher is known by the other teachers to be truly harsh with students in a way that subverts their collective attempt to be adult moral models, would they intervene on the students' behalf? Or, would they even at St Timothy's, as elsewhere, respect the autonomy of a colleague and overlook such behaviour for the sake of loyalty and in the interests of keeping the peace?

The kind of ethical knowledge building proposed here would compel the teachers in a professional and collegial way to work with the other teacher to enable him to connect moral principles and ideals to his own in-class behaviour. He may not realize the effect his disposition has on some students. He may need some help coping with the difficulties he faces in class. Or, he may be sadistically inclined to bully students and exercise his authority and power over them in morally reprehensible ways that need to be confronted and stopped. I realize I am taking liberties with Hansen's data in this case. However, my purpose is to project how complex the sharing of ethical knowledge may become as teachers try to work together in non-threatening ways to address ethical professionalism, in light of their own and each other's behaviour and practices, established norms, and administrative pressures on them – all sensitive areas in their own right and made further contentious under the glare of analysis and possible criticism.

Open forum discussions in which teachers can address regularly elements of their own practice they see as ethically responsive to students, as well as moral dilemmas they experience resulting from situations with students, parents, colleagues, and administrators, may provide an outlet for their collective ethical knowledge to flourish. Concerns that one teacher has may be shared with others – I recall the ethical problem I had with the school board survey or the one Pat had with computerized report cards or the problem Daniel had with a new procedure for announcing failures. Collectively, teachers can raise such issues as being fundamentally moral in nature and, together, search for the common ground upon which to explore options for resolving them. Collectively, they can turn their existing curriculum and assessment planning meetings or committee meetings on a range of administrative policies and procedures into opportunities to evaluate the moral dimensions of their decisions and actions. By redirecting their focus on the embedded moral nature of their work, they can strive for ethically improved practice in areas that previously might not have been considered in moral or ethical terms at all. Collectively, they can muster the courage to do the most difficult of all things – face their colleagues honestly and with the professional respect that demands the exposure and correction of morally problematic behaviour, not the covering up of it.

In his recommendations for building ethical school cultures, Starratt points out the following:

> To be sure, in any organization or group there will be some antagonisms, some jealousies, some misunderstandings, some insecurity, and some unreasonable use of power and authority. Perfection eludes us all. On the other hand, despite these realities, many groups and organizations can work together in relatively effective ways when there is a sufficient level of trust that, despite the personal agendas at work,

everyone is working toward the agreed upon goal in agreed upon ways with a reasonable amount of moral integrity.[18]

In conceptualizing schools as moral communities and teaching as an ethical profession, teachers themselves may become more inspired to get beyond such realities often associated with an institutional view of the school to develop the trust and integrity needed to engage in frank discussions about their work.

As I have argued elsewhere:

> Teachers and administrators may have to declare whether they believe the students really are their first moral responsibility and what that would mean for the resolution of dilemmas involving conflicting loyalties to colleagues and competing obligations to parents and others. They may have to project the types of dilemmas mentioned and work through hypothetical case studies that would test their agreement on fundamental definitions of fairness, honesty, integrity, care and so on. They may need to ensure that procedures are in place whereby any time a new school policy is developed, it would be assessed primarily on its ethical implications. A common core of virtues may have to become the ultimate measuring stick for ethical adequacy. And, most of all, there must be an expectation among everyone that all professionals in the school community not only uphold the principles themselves, but also that they assume the responsibility of helping each other to honour the ethical norms as well, even if it leads to the exposure of others. And, in the grey areas where ethical certainty is not obvious, there must be a commitment to discussing in open forums the reasonable applicability of principles to particular cases. If such a renewed ethical culture were to become the norm of the school community, dilemmas may be avoided. Even if such incidents themselves are not completely eliminated, perhaps the apparent moral confusion among teachers surrounding what course of action is best pursued may be lifted.[19]

The force of collegial and collective reflection and discussion within individual school contexts may prove to be the best avenue for bringing the ethical knowledge of some to the wider attention of all.

However, the promotion of ethical knowledge as the basis of renewed professionalism also relies on the renewal of attitudes underpinning teacher culture more broadly. Starratt has remarked that teachers 'have been conditioned that, when it comes to school-wide decisions and policies, their opinions are not considered of much value'.[20] Similarly, Sergiovanni complains that 'the old cultural context of the school' leads to 'the reality that many teachers are reluctant to accept more responsibility for what goes on in schools, even with administrator encouragement, (which) is a vexing problem'.[21] This prevailing norm within the teacher culture, that restricts teachers from assuming the professional responsibility for promoting moral agency beyond the confines of their individual classrooms, needs to be confronted by teachers themselves.

While, admittedly, there are aspects of the administrative life of the school which teachers are not in a position to effect, they can certainly start to voice their own perspectives in the interests of their professionalism and their schools' cultures. For example, if a new school rule or policy relating to attendance, discipline or dress, that makes teachers feel uncomfortable ethically about enforcing it is introduced, they need to bring this to the attention of each other and the administration, rather than grumble churlishly about it in the staffroom. As professionals, they need to feel the collective power of their voice. This power can gain considerable credibility if their concerns are framed by reasoned ethical deliberation and thoughtful reflective arguments based on a genuine concern for the welfare of students, rather than by knee-jerk reactions to perceived encumbrances on themselves. A principle-based articulation of what professional teachers are, what they do, and what they stand for as part of the larger teacher culture should be highlighted visibly as a relevant lens through which to assess all aspects of school life.

As a necessary first step towards enhancing teachers' professional self-confidence in their assumption of greater school-based responsibilities, they need to come to terms with the crippling effect on their ethical professionalism that the prevailing norms of collegial loyalty and non-interference have. This is one area where teachers, alone, have the opportunity to make a difference to their culture, independent of administrators, governments, local authorities, students, parents, budget issues, curriculum standards, testing initiatives, and so on. Only teachers themselves can try to break free from the anxiety, fear and demoralizing helplessness of wanting to protect students from harm caused by the incompetent, negligent, or hurtful behaviour of some colleagues but not knowing how to do so. Haunted by such terms as 'tattling', 'snitch', 'whistle-blowing', 'stool pigeon', 'scab', and other unappealing labels associated with the pressures of peer culture and union solidarity, good teachers find themselves adopting a 'none of my business' or 'it's not my job' attitude that blinds them to ethical problems around them.

To be clear, this is not to advocate a culture in which teachers spy and report on each other regularly in threatening and oppressive ways reminiscent of the worst examples of societal dictatorships. Rather, it is to encourage the cultivation of a professional climate in which individual teachers feel free to tell each other about their concerns, to offer to work with one another to improve practice, to point out ethically problematic styles and the effects they have on students, and to do so in ways that are enabling and not rejected by defensive colleagues. Collectively, they need to work towards enhancing the ethical knowledge of all. Peer reviews must be seen as professionally enriching, not personally insulting, for who is better placed to assess and help teachers establish morally sound practices than other teachers? In those extreme cases where a colleague does not need to be helped, but instead should be disciplined or dismissed from the profession altogether for unethical conduct, teachers must feel supported by formal professional processes that do not punish them for exposing or testifying against one another. Other professions acknowledge the responsibility of peers to involve, rather than remove, themselves in such delicate situations as a means of safeguarding the profession itself. If teachers abdicate their moral responsibility for students' well-being to the initiative of administrators, parents, or others, and 'if teachers generally do not consider the "policing" of their profession to be a legitimate obligation either as individuals or as a collective group, it may be argued that they are neither self-regulating nor fully accountable as professionals'.[22] Increasingly, professional associations, such as colleges of teachers, are promoting this moral responsibility and enforcing ethical standards of conduct by means of formal disciplinary procedures.

However, this does not necessarily lead to a renewal of teachers' attitudes and norms that guide their informal collegial relations within the contexts of individual schools. Only teachers themselves within the comfort of those schools can devise ways to overcome the social stigmas and fears of engaging in professional dialogues that are widely interpreted as unwelcome criticism.

In this regard, teachers could use some help from their unions or federations since it is largely due to enduring traditional stances of the unions themselves that teachers feel intimidated from taking any action that might be viewed as 'breaking rank'. If unions are to continue to exist in teaching, they must not be seen to be working *against* professionalism in ways such as those described in Chapter 5. Others have written of the need for teachers' unions to redefine themselves 'in ways that depart from industrial work norms and authority patterns' and embrace a 'professional teacher unionism' which, among other things, would approve forms of teacher participation in the evaluation and peer coaching of other teachers.[23] Similarly, Covert proposes the idea of establishing peer tribunals and peer review to address specifically the moral conduct of teachers; he argues, 'Teachers as professionals should have a greater say in defining the moral standards of the profession and should have greater control over the discipline of professional misconduct'.[24] And in a broader discussion of the role of a 'new teacher unionism,' Hargreaves and Fullan argue that, 'It should also be an act of individual moral courage that leads you [teachers] to question colleagues or parents whenever you see them do harm to students . . . it is important to express moral outrage towards colleagues when warranted'.[25]

In a spirit of professionalism, teachers need to share their ethical knowledge, not only in descriptive ways that offer advice on how to fulfil the demands of moral agency more competently, but also in critical ways that do not shrink from exposing for collective scrutiny bad practices that should be eliminated.

Others have offered recommendations for achieving such objectives. For example, Betty Sichel writes at length about the advantages of creating 'school ethics committees'.[26] Comparing this initiative to current models established in many health care institutions, she states that, since 'many moral problems in schools cannot be understood or resolved with the knowledge and skills of any one person, but require multidimensional input and the expertise of various specialists and school personnel', school ethics committees would draw on multiple beliefs and knowledge.[27] She dismisses as 'the remains of old attitudes and outdated ways of governing schools' the potential objections of administrators who may feel a loss of personal authority, unions who stand opposed to any change not negotiated by contractual agreement, and teachers who may resist the extra responsibility these committees would entail.[28] Sichel describes three significant purposes of school ethics committees: an educational purpose, a policy purpose, and a consultative purpose, and she concludes that teachers would 'become part of communicative networks that would allow for increased discussion about professional ethical matters and greater understanding of professional moral dilemmas'.[29] Such a proposal offers concrete ideas for addressing both locally significant moral issues of the school community and broader ethical concerns of the professional teacher culture. It is crucial to combine both of these avenues of discussion, and Sichel's plan parallels well my hopes for open forum discussions, ethical reflection on an individual and community-wide basis, and the replacement of prevailing norms and attitudes as central to the sharing of teachers' ethical knowledge.

By way of comparison, Gerald Grant also offers three suggestions on how to engage teachers within their schools in moral reflection and action. One way is called 'seminaring'; he writes, 'a collegial seminar experience would strengthen consensus about the moral responsibilities of teachers and model a form of teaching that is sadly neglected in most schools'.[30] The other two involve 'shadowing', in which teachers spend a day shadowing a pupil to see what is wrong in the school as stimulus for reflection and discussion, and 'researching', in which aspects of school life are discovered, also as substance for moral reflection. Also, similar to Sichel's suggestions, Paul et al. have assembled a collection of edited chapters on ethics and decision making that stress the importance of ethical deliberation in school-based decision-making committees as 'a positive force in developing schools as ethical learning communities'.[31]

If such suggestions are to be realized in practice, the onus falls on teachers primarily to be receptive to the exploration of how ethical knowledge should influence their routine and not-so-routine work lives. However, the role of the school administration is critical to the success of teachers' site-based efforts to reconceptualize their professional responsibilities in moral terms. Principals and other administrators, through their own quality of leadership, can either support and facilitate such efforts or thwart and subvert them. As this book is about the ethical teacher, not the ethical principal, I will resist delving into the increasingly expansive body of literature on the ethics of leadership and educational administration.[32] However, the following abbreviated discussion focuses on the significance of two clear roles for principals: to facilitate efforts by teachers to enhance and share ethical knowledge; and to ensure that their own behaviour, attitudes, decisions, and leadership practices contribute positively to an overall ethical environment rather than to a dysfunctional community that places little premium on professionalism and moral agency.

Principals need to be responsible for both these objectives not as some long-range, strategic planning proposal for organizational effectiveness, but as an immediate and human assertion of virtue-based wisdom that compels them to remember first who they are as professional teachers themselves. It is a shame that traditionally much of the research and literature related to administration and leadership and that concerned with teaching and teacher education rarely emanate from the same source or even cross-reference one another. Perhaps their interdependence may become more obvious when viewed through the perspective of ethical professionalism and moral agency and accountability.

In his discussion of the roots of school leadership, Thomas Sergiovanni states that 'school leadership is about connecting people morally to each other and to their work. The work of leadership involves developing shared purposes, beliefs, values, and conceptions themed to teaching and learning, community building, collegiality, character development, and other school issues and concerns'.[33] Principals can 'connect' teachers and be facilitative of their moral growth by providing opportunities for them to engage in activities, such as those mentioned previously (e.g., ethics committees, peer review, seminaring), in which ethical reflection would dominate the agenda. Notwithstanding the notable impediments caused by structural, temporal, and other institutional constraints, principals could help teachers engage creatively in the collegial sharing of ethical knowledge by finding their own creative ways to restrict the number of administrative demands they make daily on teachers. It is likely that this would require them to rearrange organizational priorities.

School administrators would also enable a growth in teachers' moral awareness of their work by establishing and maintaining an ethical tone in schools, implied above by Sergiovanni, as a first principle of organizational leadership.[34] By way of example, Fenstermacher recalls that the principals of two schools involved in the Manner in Teaching Project were so particularly forceful in promoting virtue-based school goals that the teachers were all similarly driven to articulate and foster moral climates in their classrooms.[35] It is critical to the enhancement of ethical tone within schools that the administrators have a sense of ethical knowledge themselves and that they are both willing and committed to apply it to their own practice. If principals do not consider their actions, decisions, policies, procedures, habits, inclinations, personal styles, and attitudes from a perspective of moral agency before subjecting them on teachers and students, they injure the chance to foster truly moral communities.

Ethical knowledge for principals can be expressed in seemingly simple and routine ways, such as being respectful of teachers' and students' classroom work by minimizing intrusive interruptions. It may frame a principal's willingness to review and change personal decisions related to school policies at the request of teachers who point out morally troublesome implications of them. Ethical knowledge influences how principals speak to students and staff, as well as more serious problems related to how they cope with teachers seen as incompetent and how they handle complaints from parents. If teachers perceive their school's leadership not to be ethical, then efforts to create the kind of moral community in which teachers' ethical knowledge can flourish will be stalled.

Unfortunately, much of the administrative and organizational theory upon which principal leadership programmes have been established focuses on instrumental, technical, managerial, political and strategic models of decision making rather than on moral and ethical principles. Increasingly, critics of the field have lamented this void for, as McKerrow states, excluding 'by default, serious consideration of ethics in a profession whose mission is fundamentally moral but whose practice is not'.[36] One principal remarked on his problem-solving style by acknowledging, 'Ethically, you don't have a really good basis for making decisions and you have to hunt around and build a value set . . . Until you have the experience, you tend to back off so sometimes you find yourself allowing things you think are wrong, but you don't think you have a basis to act on'.[37] If school leaders tend to make intuitive and experience-based administrative decisions without a firm appreciation of the moral and ethical dimensions of their responsibilities, they are left to rely, not on a professional sense of ethical knowledge, but on what Marshall refers to as 'seat-of-the-pants ethics'; she writes that this approach to ethics 'does not work, [but] gives us stressed administrators unable to make decisions with any sense of professional guidance or support'.[38]

Empirical studies have indicated that school leaders would welcome more training in ethical decision making as an important element of their professional preparation, and the literature in the area is increasingly responding.[39]

This is important since, as Reitz argues, 'we cannot realistically hope to reinvigorate the moral climate of the schools . . . if schools are not managed ethically'.[40] From the perspective of teachers' ethical knowledge, principals would be well advised to recall their own practice as teachers and consider how it was or was not expressive of core moral principles; as a point of reflection, such recollection may enable them to augment their ethical knowledge as it applies to the daily administrative choices that they make in ways that are sensitive to the moral dimensions, not solely of school leadership, but of teaching more broadly.

Just as the individual school administrator can make a difference to the ethical tone of the school, so too does the individual teacher, through the expression of ethical knowledge, make a difference to the moral tone of the classroom and possibly the school, and potentially to the teacher culture's conception of professional ethics. While, ideally, the collective sharing of ethical knowledge among the professional members of school communities may be hoped for, ultimately personal responsibility for moral behaviour rests squarely on the ethical teacher as a solitary practitioner.

A return to the individual professional

> Professional teacher ethics primarily concentrates on improving an individual teacher's ethical reasoning and judgments. Accordingly, a teacher should be an autonomous moral agent who individually makes and carries out ethical judgments. The existence of a just, humane, and caring school is dependent on each teacher becoming just, humane, and caring. With this additive approach, the sum of all just and humane teachers equals a just and humane school. The onus of moral responsibility is on each teacher.[41]

The author of this statement acknowledges that her perspective tends to obscure the inevitable institutional factors relating to school culture and governance that are bound to influence the individual teacher's perspective and orientation to the moral nature of school life. I, too, accept that individuals are inescapably affected by the external forces that press on them.[42] However, systemic realities, while obviously important, should not provide an easy rationale for individual professionals to neglect the ethical obligations embedded in their accountable moral agency.[43] The focus of *The Ethical Teacher* as a discussion of professional ethics is not on systems and organizations, but on individual teachers working alone and together to cultivate a deeper sense of their moral agency as it is expressed in practice – in other words, their ethical knowledge, as the basis of both renewed teacher professionalism and renewed teacher cultures.

This conceptual emphasis is consistent with Sommers' description of 'earlier moralists' who 'were working in a tradition in which it was assumed that the practical end of all moral theory was the virtuous individual'.[44] It is further consistent with her comparative criticism of more recent perspectives that assert that moral action and social justice forms of activism should be 'politically directed' to mould not the personally responsible individual, but society's civic institutions instead.[45]

Of course, this position begs the questions posed in Chapter 1 regarding whether ethical teachers could exist in unethical schools and, conversely, whether teachers could conduct themselves in unethical ways within school contexts that promote ethical accountability. Admittedly, it is easier for individuals to conduct themselves in ways that are compatible with the contexts in which they live and work. However, I believe there is ample experiential evidence to support both the above possibilities – the extraordinary teacher striving to achieve morally exceptional goals in bleak and unsupportive educational environments; and the corrupt teacher secretly using for personal advantage the authority position of the role despite having the security of a morally sound school life.

Ultimately, the individual acquisition of ethical knowledge may reduce down to a matter of personal character. However, this is not the whole answer. Many individual teachers, despite being people of integrity having virtuous intentions, may fail to grasp how the moral principles embedded in their orientations to their lives translate into professional practices that guide their daily conduct as teachers. Failing to grasp the moral significance of the dimensions of schooling may not signal a lack of moral fibre in such individuals; it may be, instead, that they need their consciousness jogged – they need to develop their ethical knowledge. As will be addressed in the next and final chapter, this is an area in which a renewal of teacher education and professional learning opportunities, that prioritizes moral and ethical issues in teaching, may contribute greatly to the collective strengthening of professional ethical knowledge.

As a brief addendum to this chapter, I offer the following anecdote which I found quite touching and illuminating. During the time I was writing this book, the world-renowned philosopher, John Rawls, died at the age of 82. Rawls's professional work in the area of justice, it was noted in one obituary, could be seen as an extension of his character: 'Dr Rawls's concern for justice and individual happiness is seen in a story from Harvard. When a candidate was defending his dissertation, Dr Rawls noticed the sun shining in his eyes. He positioned himself between the candidate and the sunlight for the rest of the session'.[46] This quiet application of kindness, consideration and respect to what may be regarded as a professional teaching situation is nothing less than what is described here as ethical knowledge.

eight

Using ethical knowledge to inform practice

Fostering ethical professionalism through teacher education

Ethical knowledge as the applied basis of professional ethics in teaching should be used by teachers in their self-examinations of the moral nature of their actions, decisions, and overall attitudes to students and to the professional obligations of teaching more generally. They need to question why they do what they do, what the moral impact is of their behaviour towards others, whether aspects of their routine practices could be indicative of careless, negligent, insensitive, or essentially inadequate conduct, and so on. Collectively, they need to consider such questions from the perspective of shared ethical knowledge as they may apply to the normative practices in their own schools. In this respect, the previous chapter addressed both the imperative for individual self-reflection and the hope for a collective use of ethical knowledge as a lens through which to assess all aspects of teaching and schooling. Consequently, it argued that ethical knowledge can provide the basis of renewed professionalism in teaching and renewed school cultures.

This concluding chapter proposes that the concept of ethical knowledge should also provide the theoretical and practical framework for renewed teacher education and professional learning. For if ethical knowledge is to be the moral gauge of teachers' practices, then simultaneously, practices should be designed to cultivate teachers' ethical knowledge. And the practice of teacher education, in all its various forms, is the obvious sphere from which to launch such a cultivation of the core of ethical professionalism.

As I have argued elsewhere, teacher education programmes must develop 'ways to enable student teachers to understand their future role and anticipate the moral and ethical significance of their practice. Moral agency is not simply an inevitable state resulting from being a teacher but instead a professional quality exemplifying ethically good practice. This should not be left to chance but developed in a deliberate way through the teaching of ethics to preservice teachers.'[1] Some of those writing of ethics and teacher education raise the issue of whether or not moral dispositions can really be fostered and developed in individuals through programmatic means.[2] For example, in invoking Plato's *Meno* and the classical question about whether virtue can be taught, Kenneth Strike concludes that 'academic instruction in professional ethics has little redemptive potential', in that it is unlikely to influence positively those inclined to do bad things.[3] However, he acknowledges that such instruction is not pointless if it focuses on the engagement in ethical dialogue as a process of community formation. In a previous discussion, he also asserts that ethical instruction must move beyond abstract courses in philosophy to examine the daily realities of school life.[4] It is in part because of such arguments that *The Ethical Teacher* has not been concerned with trying to correct those who would conduct their professional lives in deliberately unethical or immoral ways. Rather, its focus is on the majority of teachers of essentially good will and intention, many of whom may not fully appreciate the moral and ethical nature of the nuances of their work – as Strike notes, the daily realities. In drawing attention to these nuances and realities within a principle-based framework, teacher educators can introduce to preservice and inservice teachers the concept of ethical knowledge, thus increasing the awareness of one's practice so essential to the building and strengthening of the knowledge base itself.

Scholars in the field agree that teacher education programmes have tended to ignore the moral and ethical dimensions of teaching and that, unlike in other professions, it is rare to find any formal attempt to acquaint students with the professional ethics of their chosen vocation. In education, there is the additional pressure on teachers to conduct themselves morally not only for the sake of professionalism but also for the purpose of being moral exemplars to their own students. This dual expectation parallels the double nature of moral agency addressed in the first part of this book. It further distinguishes teachers from lawyers, doctors, architects, accountants, engineers and other professionals who do not need to be concerned with modelling behaviour for the educative enrichment of their clients. Yet, still, teacher education programmes have also been 'silent about the teacher as a moral exemplar'.[5] In this respect, applied professional ethics and moral education are essentially connected in a conceptual and practical sense. As I have claimed elsewhere in an exploration of the function of teacher education to prepare teachers to recognize the moral and ethical demands of their role:

To be guides for the young in morality and ethics, teachers must understand the complex moral role that they occupy as ethical professionals and appreciate the significance of their own actions and decisions on the students in their care. *Moral education* is a term applicable to the preparation of future teachers, as much as to children and adolescent students.[6]

In recent years, given the increased attention in the literature to the need to include ethics instruction in preservice teacher education programmes, some attempts to introduce ethics components have been made beyond merely pointing to the relevant local ethical code. However, many still complain that ethical considerations are rarely addressed as anything other than an add-on to programme areas seen as more critical. Instead, the instructional focus on technical competence and skills dominant in most teacher education faculties neglects any serious discussion of ethical issues in teaching and fails to integrate even an awareness of such issues into broader perspectives on curriculum and instruction, assessment, or classroom management.

In a recent study, Cummings et al. criticize this concentration on technique at the expense of moral instruction and make the disturbing confirmation of other studies' troublesome findings that 'preservice education students demonstrate lower principled moral reasoning than college students with other majors'.[7] They further blame their participants' 'significantly lower' level of moral reasoning that affects their ethical behaviour more generally on the fact that their professional programmes do not provide them with opportunities 'to reason about and respond to the many moral and ethical issues that arise daily in the context of the dynamic public school classroom'.[8]

Those who propose that teacher education programmes (and to a lesser degree ongoing teacher development processes) should be formally structured to nurture the 'moral sensibilities' such as 'moral perception', 'moral imagination', and 'moral courage' invariably promote the significant role of *moral reflection* as a means of heightening one's powers of moral and ethical reasoning and judgement.[9] For example, in their articulation of teacher 'manner' as expressive of moral virtue in the classroom, Richardson and Fallona note:

> One thing that can be done is to provide preservice teachers with new ways of looking at teaching and their roles as educators. This includes moving preservice teachers beyond considerations of method to considerations of manner. Teacher educators should help future teachers understand that teaching is a moral endeavour ... the relationship between student and teacher is at the heart of teaching and, thus, at the heart of organizing and managing the classroom environment.

Therefore, through their teacher education programs, students should be asked to reflect upon their beliefs about teaching and the attributes of their style that may be indicative of their manner.[10]

Similarly, Hamberger and Moore claim that, 'Teacher educators must enable students to become professionals who reflect, as a matter of practice, on three key questions: What are my values and how do these values guide my actions? Who am I? How do I resolve the value conflicts within myself and with others as I perform the role of teacher?'[11]

I, too, share these authors' enthusiasm for reflection and dialogue as valuable ways of enhancing our awareness of moral and ethical considerations in teaching. However, we should recognize that embedded in this enthusiasm are at least two fairly sizeable assumptions. First, one must assume that teacher educators themselves possess the level of ethical knowledge needed to enable them to address teachers' moral agency and how it influences the practical dynamics of teaching. In stimulating reflection and discussion, they must appreciate both the philosophically complex questions about moral and ethical principles as they translate into professional activities and the routine elements of teaching and schooling that may, at first blush, seem remote from deliberate efforts to fulfil one's obligations as a moral agent. Second, one must also assume that most teacher candidates are morally reasonable people who, while differing perhaps in their values and beliefs about elements of morality, fundamentally possess an innate or intuitive ability to know what is harmful to others, dishonest, and unfair, and, by contrast, what is kind, truthful, and just; all they need is the professional prompt to make conceptual and practical links between their appreciation of the virtues and the details of teaching.

However, interpretations of ethical principles vary, and in teaching, as in life, there are 'grey areas' that defy moral certainty more than other situations where right and wrong are obvious to most rational people. Recognition of this need not plunge us into a relativist mire that defeats our efforts to address moral issues. It merely confirms what many of those writing in this area accept – moral reflection and discussion are inevitably fraught with debates, uncertainties, and conflicts that, within the context of the teacher education environment, should provide the substance for intellectual, professional, and experiential growth. It is far better to debate the moral and ethical dimensions of teaching than to pretend they do not exist.

Teacher educators, drawing on the expertise of philosophers and practitioners, can help strengthen the ethical knowledge base and apply it to their programmatic objectives.[12] For example, traditional 'foundations' courses in educational philosophy and law should bring to the forefront moral questions as they pertain directly to the practical realities of schooling rather than leaving complex theories to speak for themselves. Additionally, curriculum and methods courses should challenge prospective teachers to view as moral choices their designing of lesson plans, their selection of materials and texts, their preferred pedagogical approaches, their assessment strategies, and their discipline styles. They should ask themselves what their purposes are in making these choices and how they can support the fair treatment of students, the honest belief that they are serving the overall best interests of the students, a respectful attitude towards students as fellow humans, and the kind sensitivity students deserve in their position of dependency and even vulnerability.[13] From a negative perspective, prospective teachers need to scrutinize, among other concrete aspects of their practice, any inclination that they might have to assign work they know to be inappropriate in order to frighten or punish students; to impose surprise tests with the sole intention of asserting their authority; to discipline innocent students in an effort to get badly-behaved ones to improve through the peer pressure that results from group punishment; to use marks and grades as favours and bribes unrelated to academic goals; to speak to students as lesser beings in the misguided belief that this will win their respect; to allocate privileges in class without considering principles of impartiality, consistency, constancy, and fairness; and ultimately to assume that, in doing what admittedly may be at times a frustrating and threatening job, they are exempted from applying the high standard of integrity expected of all professionals. And, perhaps most important yet most elusive of all, prospective teachers need considerable exposure to examples of the fleeting, unplanned, and spontaneous moments both in and out of the classroom that require teachers to muster up all the ethical knowledge they can to deal morally with such incidents, some of which may seem fairly benign and normative and others of which may become catalysts for perplexing moral dilemmas. Such experiential moments and incidents should be 'frozen' for ethical analysis, reflection, and debate within teacher education classes and seminars.

Some advocate the use of more formal frameworks and methods to structure ethical reflection and discussion. For example, in his work in applied ethics relating broadly to the ethics of professions and organizations, philosopher Michael McDonald proposes a five-stage process for engaging in ethical decision making.[14] It includes the identification of a moral problem; the specification of feasible alternatives to resolve the problem in which good and bad consequences are examined; the use of ethical resources (such as ethical principles, maxims of autonomy, beneficence, non-maleficence, and justice, contextual features, and moral models) to identify morally significant factors of each alternative; the testing of these possible resolutions; and ultimately the making of the decision in which one is instructed to 'live with it' and 'learn from it'. Within teacher education, Nancy Freeman proposes a similar five-step process for ethical decision making that she calls the Systematic Reflective Case Debriefing Method.[15]

Such frameworks provide the teacher educator with a methodical way of exploring the moral and ethical dimensions and dilemmas in teaching with teacher candidates. These methods should combine rigorous attention to profound philosophical questions from the field of ethical theory with the practical consideration of the detailed realities of teaching. Abstract conceptual discussions without obvious application to 'real-life' practice are unhelpful and ineffectual.similarly, speculating on practical situations without grounding one's opinions in the detached foundation of scholarship leads to potential pontification more reminiscent of soapbox sermonizing than of the professional teacher education classroom.

As another structured format for acquainting preservice teachers with the ethical realities and dilemmas in schools, the case study method of instruction is now widely recommended.[16] Based in part on 'the business school model', the case study method was seen in the 1990s as 'a relatively new phenomenon in teacher education'.[17] As Strike argues, 'Teachers must be taught how to apply ethical principles to concrete situations by learning to perceive a situation as involving an ethical issue and by reflecting on how principles are appropriately applied to the case', and case study approaches may be quite effective in meeting this need.[18] I too support and use case studies in my own teacher education classes, both preservice and graduate, despite being wary of their potential to foster relativistic slides into values clarification-type discussions.[19]

Karl Hostetler, whose book on ethical judgement in teaching is entirely structured around a series of case studies dealing with issues of discipline, evaluation and testing, religion in the school, cultural diversity, and the teaching of controversial curricula, warns of another danger in focusing only on moral crises or dilemmas; because 'it is in the protracted, everyday, seemingly mundane features of classrooms and teaching that ethical judgment is most often called for', case studies requiring dilemma resolution may only limit student teachers' introduction to the many moral and ethical aspects of teaching.[20] It is for this reason, I would propose, that teacher educators would gain much by working with practising teachers to capture in case study form those snapshots of their daily work in which their ethical knowledge is most obvious. Imagine taking the words and beliefs of teachers such as Marissa, Theresa, Shannon and Erica and creating non-dilemma based classroom scenarios to share with preservice teachers. We can do this by means of highlighting our empirical research in our classrooms; we can also try to engage more directly our 'participants' with our students, thus bringing the field closer to our programmes in ways not exclusively the domain of the practicum component.

The focus of this discussion is clearly on the preservice induction forms of teacher education. However, most of the recommendations for programme development to make central ethical reflection and decision making may be applied also to the ongoing professional learning of experienced teacher practitioners.[21] As was addressed in the previous chapter, teachers need to engage within their own school communities in the sharing of ethical knowledge. As well as being a process of ethical renewal within school cultures, such collective sharing could provide substance for in-service workshops, professional development days, and other forums where teachers come together to discuss their work. In particular, case study approaches are an appealing method of stimulating thoughtful exploration and debate. My own graduate students, for the most part all experienced teachers themselves, continually remark on how the case study work they do, combined with the academic literature, makes them aware of their own practices in ethical terms that had never before occurred to them. Thus, such concentrated study of familiar elements of their work through an unfamiliar lens serves to enhance and exalt their own sense of ethical knowledge.

If teachers can become more competent in expressing, as some already do, their moral and ethical orientations to their practice, and if they can identify with greater clarity situations in which virtues and principles are either embedded or violated, then they would be contributing, to an ethical knowledge base, those descriptors of moral agency that may be teachable and learnable within the context of teacher education. Renewed teacher education, structured around the centrality of moral agency and ethical professionalism, both relies on existing ethical knowledge and augments it in ways that may influence future practice.

By way of conclusion, I offer the following rather informal and by no means complete list of suggestions and reflections that I created and distributed to my preservice students last year as a small part of our discussion about professional ethics:

- Always identify core principles (honesty, fairness, kindness . . .) relevant to each situation and/or dilemma and ask yourself, 'Are they being upheld or compromised?'
- Listen to your conscience. What is your first reaction and why? Don't do anything you believe is wrong just because someone or some group is pressuring you or assuring you that it's really acceptable because 'everybody here does it'.
- Reflect and anticipate: before teaching curricular material, assigning a test or piece of work, making a class rule, disciplining a student, etc., think ahead to its potential consequences that may create ethical dilemmas for you or others. Ask, 'If I do this, could this happen . . .?'
- Put students first (individually and collectively) even though this seems to be easier said than done, especially in the context of situations involving colleagues.
- Ultimately, you are not simply a private individual doing a job; you are a

public professional, personally accountable and embodying the entire authority of the profession of teaching and the institution of school. You don't speak and act as independent person X; your role accords you greater authority than that – and culpability. 'The teacher says so, so it must be right.' Consequently: think about the difference between address-ing controversial issues in the classroom and indoctrinating; don't feel compelled to give your own personal opinion on truly contestable issues (in fact, avoid doing so); ask yourself if your 'cause' is political, and, if so, is the classroom really the place to air it?

- Don't compromise moral principles in the way you act around students (re: use of language, personal or intimate stories told, attitudes expressed, humour used, etc.) because you think they'll otherwise see you as 'un-cool' or because you think you'll 'reach them' better if you pretend to be part of their peer culture – you're not part of it and you shouldn't try to be.
- Be familiar with school rules, acceptable norms, policies, and know when to access legal information, if needed.
- You are not alone. You are part of a profession and a member of a school staff. Seek advice and help in difficult situations formally and informally from your colleagues and administrators.
- Don't do, say, or condone anything that you wouldn't want 'the world' to know about, but remember, integrity means 'doing right where there is no one to make you do it but yourself' (John Fletcher Moulton 1924).[22]
- Don't use *Boston Public* as your role model for ethical decision making![23]

The ethical teacher: a concluding statement

> Many people believe that the beginning and end of doing ethics is to act in good personal conscience. They are right that this is the beginning, but wrong that it is the end. We all need to do ethics and, therefore, to learn how to do it. But doing ethics is not always a simple task: It is a process, not an event, and, in many ways, a life-long learning experience.[24]

By all accounts, 'doing ethics', to borrow Somerville's phrase, in teaching is a complex pursuit embedded, for the most part, in the layered and often unintentional dynamics of classroom and school life. This book has sought to make some of the moral and ethical dimensions of teaching and school-ing more visible by calling on the obvious recognition that some teachers express regarding their moral agency to advance the deliberate and con-scious renewal of ethical professionalism in education. What has emerged is an argument for bringing to the forefront of our thinking about teaching that which some teachers, more than others, *know* about their formal and informal practices as moral agents – in other words, their ethical knowledge.

Moral agency, as it is addressed here, concerns the dual, but interrelated, commitment of the teacher to be both a moral person and a moral educator and, by means of combining the two, an inevitable exemplar and model of virtuous conduct and attitude. How teachers behave generally towards others in classroom and school contexts should reflect those principles that they aspire to impart to students in their care. Some teachers seem to have a keen awareness of this, and they articulate their insight into the details of their own practice and intentions with reflective precision. They identify ways that their daily work intersects with their own moral orientations to their professional responsibilities, and many apply this consciousness to their own critical self-assessments.

This ethical knowledge of such teachers, albeit incomplete and ever evolving, is principle based. It illustrates their devotion to living through their actions, core moral and ethical principles descriptive of our common human legacy in all its complexities and even apparent contradictions. Ethical knowledge is not a relative concept; instead, it is situated firmly in an appreciation of the moral significance of such principles as justice and fairness, honesty and integrity, kindness and care, empathy and respect for others. Simply stated, applied professional ethics, as a collective expression of ethical knowledge, merely confirms moral and ethical principles as they are woven into the professional conduct of practitioners engaged in the specific elements of their own distinct work. In conceptualizing professional ethics in this applied and practice-rooted way, *The Ethical Teacher* proposes that ethical knowledge, as *the* specialized knowledge base of teaching expertise, be the foundation of a renewed sense of professionalism.

By building on what some teachers know individually, groups of teachers can collectively share and strengthen the ethical knowledge base that may lead to renewed school cultures as well. As I have explained elsewhere:

> It is important for educators to feel the power of their collective will to do good things in schools. The force of shared expectations should be their guide in this respect. An individual teacher without support or assurance that his or her beliefs are consistent with the group's norms, even though the moral imperative seems clear, may hesitate to take decisive ethical action.[25]

Concerted efforts within individual school communities and professional organizations more broadly to augment ethical knowledge may provoke the kind of discussion and debate needed to highlight teaching as a moral pursuit. This, in turn, may lend support to the lone teacher struggling to cope without much guidance with the dilemmas and tensions that unavoidably surface when one is engaged in the moral domain.

Efforts to clarify professionalism, rooted in teachers' ethical knowledge, and to foster school communities centred on the ongoing attention to it will require teachers to look inward – not only individually, but also as a collective body of professionals. This will force them to tackle tough social, political and ideological questions about collegiality and to confront those aspects of the teacher culture that may be seen to stifle or compromise professionalism rather than nurture it. As Coles asks in his discussion of moral intelligence, 'What is the point of knowing good if you don't keep trying to become a good person? . . . Moral reasoning is not to be equated with moral conduct.'[26] Ethical knowledge is necessarily action-oriented. It needs to underpin new norms of collective professional practice. A renewal of teacher education, both preservice and inservice professional learning, could be the most promising step towards the cultivation of such norms.

As a tripartite introduction to ethical knowledge, *The Ethical Teacher* first examines the concept as it is revealed in the morally supportive empirical descriptions of teachers at work. We see their beliefs and actions, attitudes and intentions articulated and exhibited in their daily concern with being principled practitioners. Second, ethical knowledge is shown to be challenged and subverted by moral dilemmas, uncertainties, tensions, and complexities that unfold in schools as a result of organizational practices, interpersonal relations, and individuals' proclivities. Third, ethical knowledge is shown to be usable, sharable, and learnable in ways that would enable more teachers, who despite being essentially good people do not naturally or intuitively connect their moral dispositions to details of their professional work, to appreciate the essence of moral agency. Teachers are urged to embrace an element of morally accountable self-determination in the one area where they have the most control – in the regulation of their own professional conduct. And this conduct is not only classroom based, but also extends to the good that teachers can achieve on behalf of students through their relationships with other teachers, administrators, parents, teacher educators, and others within their sphere of influence.

This book has emphasized the role of the individual teacher working with students in a solitary capacity and with other teachers as a member of a collective professional community. The focus on the moral accountability of practitioners as individuals and as groups of individuals, rather than on the culpability of systems and organizations, is deliberate. We often hear of how one teacher 'made a difference' in someone's life. Perhaps the difference relates to a student's academic achievement, future direction, personal feelings of self-worth, general outlook on life, the promise of possibilities, or a sense of security provided that simply 'got' him or her through each day. Invariably, the teacher responsible for such a 'difference' is described in ethical terms as one who is kind, understanding, fair, honest, wise, giving, empathetic, demanding in the best sense of the word, responsible, reliable, courageous, indefatigable in the pursuit of intellectual and moral excellence, and possessing of other qualities of fine character.

The impact of the individual should never be underestimated. In a negative sense, many can recall also, as Marissa and Carol did, those individual teachers who stood out in their lives for their cruelty and lack of sensitivity, favouritism, negligence, or careless disregard for either students or their work. They too teach moral lessons, but these messages do nothing to inspire and everything to demoralize others around them, both students and colleagues. Fortunately, more teachers, I believe, occupy the former category of difference-makers than the latter one. However, as Jackson and his team found in their well known and respected study of the moral life of schools, 'The truth is that no teacher is morally perfect, no matter what perspective on his or her work we might choose to adopt. Nor is anyone else, quite obviously, including [themselves].'[27] Nonetheless, ethical teachers need not be perfect. They do need, however, to be receptive to the development and enrichment of their own ethical knowledge. And united in the professional goal of enhancing collective ethical knowledge, teachers may work to *perfect* both the sense of moral accountability and the overall practice of the profession itself.

There is no one uniform or generic model of the ethical teacher who comes in many forms, reflective of the uniqueness of individuals. However, ethical teachers do share a similar sense of moral agency and purpose framed by a deep regard for core moral and ethical principles such as those primarily addressed here – justice, kindness, honesty, and respect for others.

The ethical teacher, like Marissa, Erica, Sarah, or Theresa, speaks to students with care and consideration, firmly insisting that right be done, yet calmly and with equanimity accepting of all students as people even when they do wrong. Ever empathetic, the ethical teacher is similarly conscious not only of what is said and the tone in which it is said, but also of the power of body language and eye contact to encourage and engage students and to afford them the respect and interest they should be able to expect. Like Jean, Lori, and Robert, the ethical teacher is aware of the surrounding classroom environment as a source of comfort and reassurance so needed to foster safe learning.

Just as Tracy and Daniel strive to protect their students from public embarrassment in front of peers, the ethical teacher respects the privacy and dignity of students and their families. Perhaps, like Gina, the ethical teacher remembers to wear glasses to class on occasion to help self-conscious adolescents feel less conspicuous about their own need to wear glasses. Or, like Shannon whose concern for a teased child with a speech impediment leads her to tell her class about her own struggle with language and speech when she was a child, the ethical teacher remains sensitive to the vulnerability of others and acts to protect them from emotional harm. Intolerant of meanness, the ethical teacher impresses on students the imperatives of care and respect for others, including, as Farideh and Theresa explain, the custodians and other members of the school staff.

For the ethical teacher, like Bob, a sign of respect is the careful reading or marking of students' work as well as its prompt return. Or, like Theresa, the ethical teacher may keep unclaimed student projects for several years in case former students come back searching for their work. As Theresa notes, respecting students' 'stuff' is a sign of one's respect for them personally and for the importance of the work they do.

Like Marissa, Erica, Shannon, Sean, and so many others, the ethical teacher consciously and continually weighs, balances, and adjudicates between the specific needs of individual students and the general common good of the whole class; constantly concerned with being above all else fair-minded and just in one's actions, such a teacher applies the lenses of equality, impartiality, and consistency to even the most routine behaviour from allocating classroom duties and privileges to the equitable enforcement of school rules and policies. As does Theresa, the ethical teacher regards the assigning of group work not only as an academically focused aspect of pedagogy, but also a matter of fairness to ensure that all students are equally well served in their working groups or partnerships.

Like Carol, Marissa, and Erica, the ethical teacher feels the compelling moral need to be honest and avoid any form of deception not only in the area of relational and interpersonal exchanges, but also in matters of student evaluation and the accurate representation of subject matter. Curriculum resources and materials are chosen with care and thought regarding their moral significance as well as their educative potential. By extension, the ethical teacher follows Shannon's example by not letting the strength of personal convictions (in Shannon's case concerning animal rights) lapse into controversial forms of political or ideological activism intended to influence the perspectives of students. Similarly, the ethical teacher, as Gina explains, refuses to bring partisan political issues, including those related to educational policy and contractual agreements, into the classroom or school to impose them on unsuspecting students who should never be put either directly or indirectly in the position of pawn in disputes obviously beyond their control.

Within the larger school context, the ethical teacher attends to the same principles of honesty, respect, fairness, and kindness, in dealing with colleagues and administrators on behalf of the best interests of students. Strengthened by an ethical school community that does not use such principles and others such as loyalty as a rationale for covering up moral errors, the ethical teacher has the courage, for example, to inform the principal about unfair grading policies or practices, as Karl did; or, like Roger and Bev, the ethical teacher refuses to ignore the harmful or negligent conduct of a colleague because of the effect it is seen to have on students. However, unlike Karl, Roger, and Bev, the ethical teacher would find ways to address dilemmas that would garner the professional support of a community of ethical teachers determined to work together for the benefit of all, including those who cause the dilemmas by their faulty conduct.

Even though this kind of ethical community needs to be further developed and nurtured, there are, within other regular school communities, many ethical teachers similar to the example of the ethical teacher profiled here. Daily, they make decisions and engage in practices that deliberately advance and reinforce core ethical principles through the intricacies of their curricular and pedagogical work with students and their interpersonal relationships in schools. And they do this within the context of a highly complex and morally layered environment. It is time to make these teachers more visible – to exemplify their collective disposition, attitudes, and practice as the standard of applied professional ethics for all teachers and to showcase their ethical knowledge as the attainable foundation of professionalism in teaching.

Notes

Preface

1 For a more detailed description of this incident, see E. Campbell (1997a) Administrators' decisions and teachers' ethical dilemmas: implications for moral agency, *Leading & Managing*, 3(4): 245–57.
2 E. Campbell (1992) Personal morals and organizational ethics: how teachers and principals cope with conflicting values in the context of school cultures. Unpublished PhD thesis, University of Toronto.

Part 1: Moral agency and ethical knowledge

1 P.W. Jackson, R.E. Boostrom and D.T. Hansen (1993) *The Moral Life of Schools*. San Francisco, CA: Jossey-Bass.
2 Ibid., p. 2.
3 H. Sockett (1993) *The Moral Base for Teacher Professionalism*, p. 108. New York: Teachers College Press.
4 This will be addressed in the latter part of the book with specific reference to Munby, Russell and Martin's chapter on teacher knowledge in the *Handbook of Research on Teaching*, 4th edn (2001). They write that 'Interestingly, there seems to have been little empirical research into the moral appropriateness of the content of teachers' knowledge and beliefs', p. 899.
5 G. Fenstermacher (1990) Some moral considerations on teaching as a profession, in J. Goodlad et al. (eds) *The Moral Dimensions of Teaching*, p. 132. San Francisco, CA: Jossey-Bass.
6 See D.T. Hansen (2001a) Teaching as a moral activity, in V. Richardson (ed.) *Handbook of Research on Teaching*, 4th Edn, pp. 826–57. Washington, DC: American Educational Research Association.

7 K.A. Strike and P.L. Ternasky (eds) (1993) *Ethics for Professionals in Education: Perspectives for Preparation and Practice*, p. 220. New York: Teachers College Press.
8 I first coined the phrase 'suspended morality' in Campbell 1992, op. cit.
9 K.D. Hostetler (1997) *Ethical Judgment in Teaching*, pp. 195–6. Boston: Allyn and Bacon.

Chapter 1 – Introduction to ethics in teaching

1 A. Weston (1997) *A Practical Companion to Ethics*, p. 2. New York: Oxford University Press, original emphasis.
2 Ibid., p. 4.
3 P. Benn (1998) *Ethics*, p. 59. Montreal and Kingston: McGill-Queen's University Press.
4 M.W. Baron, P. Pettit and M. Slote (1997) *Three Methods of Ethics: A Debate*, p. 229. Oxford: Blackwell.
5 C.A. Buzzelli and B. Johnston (2002) *The Moral Dimensions of Teaching: Language, Power and Culture in Classroom Interaction*, p. 9. New York and London: Routledge Falmer.
6 For an extensive review of relevant literature up to 1992, see H. Sockett (1992) The moral aspects of the curriculum, in P.W. Jackson (ed.) *Handbook of Research on Curriculum*. New York: MacMillan. Also see Hansen (2001a) op. cit. for a similarly extensive literature review updated to 2001.
7 E. Campbell (1997b) Connecting the ethics of teaching and moral education, *Journal of Teacher Education*, 48(4), p. 256.
8 Hansen (2001a) op. cit., p. 826.
9 S. Todd (2001) 'Bringing more than I contain': ethics, curriculum and the pedagogical demand for altered egos, *Journal of Curriculum Studies*, 33(4), p. 437.
10 J.R. Coombs (1998) Educational ethics: are we on the right track? *Educational Theory*, 48(4): 555–69. Also, for a diverse range of essays on professional ethics and moral development in a variety of occupations (college teaching, nursing, counselling, accounting, dentistry, medicine, veterinary medicine, sports, journalism) see J.R. Rest and D. Narváez (eds) (1994) *Moral Development in the Professions: Psychology and Applied Ethics*. Hillsdale, NJ: Lawrence Erlbaum Associates.
11 I originally addressed this issue in E. Campbell (2001) Let right be done: trying to put ethical standards into practice, *Journal of Educational Policy*, 16(5): 395–411.
12 C.J.B. MacMillan (1993) Ethics and teacher professionalization, pp. 189–90 in K.A. Strike and P.L. Ternasky (eds) op. cit.
13 M.D. Bayles (1981) *Professional Ethics*. Belmont, CA: Wadsworth.
14 Coombs (1998) op. cit., p. 569.
15 E.J. Delattre (1998) *Leadership: A Position? An Activity? And . . .?: Ethics in Policing*, p. 2. Ottawa: The Police Leadership Forum, Occasional Papers Collection.

16 As Jonas Soltis observed in his 1986 article on teaching professional ethics in the *Journal of Teacher Education* (37(3): 2–4) 'One is not a free individual when one accepts membership in a profession. The very act of becoming a professional commits one to the ethical principles and standards of membership in the community of that profession and to the service of its general purposes' (p. 3). More recently, in a 1997 monograph written for the General Teaching Council (England and Wales), Meryl Thompson argues that any member of a profession 'voluntarily accepts to be bound by another set of ethical dimensions relating to the clients, the public, the employing institution and fellow professionals' (p. 8).

17 See particularly Sockett's description of four dimensions of moral professionalism and five virtues central to an understanding of the practice of teaching: honesty, courage, care, fairness, practical wisdom, (1993) op. cit. For an adaptation of the four main principles of medical ethics to the teaching profession, see T.J. Lovat (1998) Ethics and ethics education, *Curriculum Perspectives*, 18(1): 1–7.

18 See the Medical Student Online Service, The University of Kansas School of Medicine. www.kumc.edu/som/medsos/pd.htm

19 See L. Colero (undated) *A Framework For Universal Principles of Ethics*. www.ethics.ubc.ca/papers/invited/colero.html (accessed 3 April 2000).

20 Strike and Ternasky (1993) op. cit., p. 2.

21 Soltis (1986) op. cit., pp. 2–3.

22 L.P. Nucci (2001) *Education in the Moral Domain*. Cambridge: Cambridge University Press.

23 Ibid., p. 19.

24 For a particularly good discussion of the philosophical distinctions among universalist theories of ethics, relativist theories, moral and ethical subjectivism, cultural relativism, and other branches of ethics see J.A. Boss (1998) *Ethics for Life: An Interdisciplinary and Multicultural Introduction*. Mountain View, CA: Mayfield.

25 G.D. Fenstermacher (2001) On the concept of manner and its visibility in teaching practice, *The Journal of Curriculum Studies*, 33(6), pp. 640–1.

26 C.M. Clark (1990) The teacher and the taught: moral transactions in the classroom, in J. Goodland et al. op. cit., p. 252, original emphasis.

27 R.J. Starratt (1994) *Building an Ethical School: A Practical Response to the Moral Crisis in Schools*. London: Falmer. Also, F. Haynes (1998) *The Ethical School*. London: Routledge.

28 M. Somerville (2000) *The Ethical Canary: Science, Society and the Human Spirit*. Toronto: Viking.

29 D.J. Reitz (1998) *Moral Crisis in the Schools: What Parents and Teachers Need to Know*, p. 21. Baltimore, MD: Cathedral Foundation Press.

30 D.J. Fasching (1997) Beyond values: story, character, and public policy in American schools, in J.L. Paul et al. (eds) *Ethics and Decision Making in Local Schools: Inclusion, Policy, and Reform*, p. 99. Baltimore, MD: Paul H. Brookes.

31 J.D. Hunter (2000) *The Death of Character: Moral Education in an Age Without Good or Evil*, p. xiii. New York: Basic Books.

32 Hostetler (1997) op. cit., p. 10.

33 K.A. Sirotnik (1990) Society, schooling, teaching, and preparing to teach, in J. Goodlad et al. (eds) op. cit., p. 320.

34 The objective of this book is to focus on professional ethics as contextualized in the real life practice of teachers, rather than framing the discussion in theoretical arguments that parallel those found in the literature of moral and ethical philosophy. However, for reference, the bibliography lists some excellent sources from the more philosophical tradition that distinguish between varying theories of ethics.

35 Sockett (1993) op. cit., p. 90. See also Benn (1998) op. cit., pp. 7–8, who refers to the 'moral expert' and to 'moral knowledge' as 'a kind of instrumental knowledge, an ability to judge how to achieve what we desire'.

36 D. Carr (1993) Questions of competence, *British Journal of Educational Studies*, XXXXI(3), p. 265, original emphasis.

37 T.R. Sizer and N.F. Sizer (1999) *The Students are Watching: Schools and the Moral Contract*. Boston: Beacon Press.

38 C.H. Sommers (1984) Ethics without virtue: moral education in America, *The American Scholar*, 53(3), p. 387.

39 J.M. Halstead and M.J. Taylor (2000) Learning and teaching about values: a review of recent research, *Cambridge Journal of Education*, 30(2), p. 177.

40 D.T. Hansen (1993) From role to person: the moral layeredness of classroom teaching, *American Educational Research Journal*, 30(4), p. 669, original emphasis.

Chapter 2 – The teacher as a moral person

1 E.A. Wynne and K. Ryan (1997) *Reclaiming Our Schools: Teaching Character, Academics, and Discipline*, 2nd Edn, p. 139. Upper Saddle River, NJ: Prentice Hall.

2 L.S. Wiley (1998) *Comprehensive Character-building Classroom: A Handbook for Teachers*, p. 38. De Bary, FL: Longwood Communications.

3 D.T. Hansen (2001b) *Exploring the Moral Heart of Teaching: Towards a Teacher's Creed*. New York: Teachers College Press. See page 21 where moral sensibility is defined as 'a disposition of mind and feeling centered around attentiveness to students and their learning'.

4 V. Richardson and G. Fenstermacher (2001) Manner in teaching: the study in four parts, *Journal of Curriculum Studies*, 33(6): 631–7. See this entire issue for related articles on the Manner in Teaching Project by members of the research team.

5 V. Richardson and G. Fenstermacher (2000) *The Manner in Teaching Project*. www-personal.umich.edu/~gfenster (accessed 10 May 2000).

6 Ibid.

7 I gratefully acknowledge the Social Sciences and Humanities Research Council of Canada for its funding of the research project, entitled, The moral and ethical bases of teachers' interactions with students (1998–2002). E. Campbell, principal investigator and D. Thiessen, co-investigator.

8 J. M. Halstead and M.J. Taylor (2000) Learning and teaching about values: a review of recent research, *Cambridge Journal of Education*, 30(2), p. 178.

9 M. Borba (2001) *Building Moral Intelligence: The Seven Essential Virtues that Teach Kids to Do the Right Thing*, p. 4. San Francisco, CA: Jossey-Bass.

10 Much has been written about the ethical imperative for teachers to be intellectually rigorous themselves as well as competent and effective pedagogues. The moral aspect of the curriculum as worthwhile content and of the teaching act as a kind of moral initiation of students on the part of teachers similarly stand out in the education literature. *The Ethical Teacher* acknowledges the significance of these perspectives, but does not focus on them since its primary concern is with the actions and beliefs of teachers as individuals and as part of a collective profession rather than on the actual teaching process itself.

11 See D.T. Hansen (1993) From role to person: the moral layeredness of classroom teaching, *American Educational Research Journal*, 30(4), p. 658, where he discusses the moral complexity of hand-raising. He claims that 'how a teacher routinely handles turn-taking can influence students' feelings and beliefs about schooling and learning'.

12 P.W. Jackson, R.E. Boostrom and D.T. Hansen (1993) *The Moral Life of Schools*, p. 216. San Francisco, CA: Jossey-Bass.

13 D.C. Bricker (1989) *Classroom Life as Civic Education: Individual Achievement and Student Cooperation in Schools*, p. 28. New York: Teachers College Press.

14 G. Colnerud (1997) Ethical conflicts in teaching, *Teaching and Teacher Education*, 13(6), pp. 631–2.

15 C. Fallona (2000) Manner in Teaching: a study in observing and interpreting teachers' moral virtues, *Teaching and Teacher Education*, 16(2000), p. 692.

16 L.P. Nucci (2001) *Education in the Moral Domain*, p. 88. Cambridge: Cambridge University Press.

17 See also T.A. Thorkildsen (1989) Justice in the classroom: the student's view, *Child Development*, 60(2): 323–34. On page 324, she writes that 'young students would view justice in school in terms of simple equality of rewards or learning. Only older students would endorse equity and reject practices that treat everyone the same or produce equal learning.'

18 For a particularly good collection of essays on the ethic of justice/ethic of care debate, see M.S. Katz, N. Noddings, and K.A. Strike (eds) (1999) *Justice and Caring: The Search for Common Ground in Education*. New York: Teachers College Press.

19 M.S. Katz (1999) Teaching about caring and fairness: May Sarton's *The Small Room*, in Katz et al. ibid., p. 61.

20 K.A. Strike (1999) Justice, caring, and universality: in defence of moral pluralism, in Katz et al. ibid., pp. 21–36.

21 D.J. Reitz (1998) *Moral Crisis in the Schools: What Parents and Teachers Need to Know*, p. 127. Baltimore, MD: Cathedral Foundation Press.

22 R. Groves, J. Wallace, and W. Louden conducted a study about sincerity as a moral principle, a moral disposition that is seldom addressed in teaching. See their paper entitled, Measuring the unmeasurable: moral dispositions and the teaching standards conundrum, presented to the 2002 Annual Meeting of the American Educational Research Association, New Orleans.

23 For an expanded discussion of this point as it unfolds morally and intellectually in the instructional practices of the mathematics classroom, see E. Wall, J.M. Lewis, and D.L. Ball (2000) Moral work in teaching: the treatment of right and wrong answers in mathematics class. Paper presented to the Annual Meeting of the American Educational Research Association, New Orleans.

24 R. DeVries and B. Zan (1994) *Moral Classrooms, Moral Children: Creating a Constructivist Atmosphere in Early Education*, p. 58. New York: Teachers College Press.

25 C.M. Dunn (1999) The ordinary schoolteacher, in D.E.W. Fenner (ed.) *Ethics in Education*, pp. 69–80. New York: Garland Publishing.

26 J.A. Boss (1998) *Ethics for Life: An Interdisciplinary and Multicultural Introduction*, p. 186. Mountain View, CA: Mayfield, original emphasis.

27 P.W. Jackson, R.E. Boostrom, and D.T. Hansen (1993) *The Moral Life of Schools*, p. 44. San Francisco, CA: Jossey-Bass.

28 D.T. Hansen (1993) From role to person: the moral layeredness of classroom teaching, *American Educational Research Journal*, 30(4): 651–74.

29 M. Thompson (1997) *Professional Ethics and the Teacher: Towards a General Teaching Council*, p. 11. Stoke on Trent: Trentham Books Limited.

30 M.G. Sanger (2001) Talking to teachers and looking at practice in understanding the moral dimensions of teaching, *The Journal of Curriculum Studies*, 33(6): 683–704.

31 Marissa exemplifies what Purkey and Novak describe as the 'intentionally inviting' level of ethical functioning which is the highest of four levels teachers can attain. See their article on how teachers may be ethically inviting or disinviting, either intentionally or unintentionally, in the classroom. W.W. Purkey and J.M. Novak (1998) An invitational approach to ethical practice in teaching, *The Educational Forum*, 63(1): 37–43.

32 C.A.Buzzelli and B. Johnston (2002) *The Moral Dimensions of Teaching: Language, Power, and Culture in Classroom Interaction*, p. 125. New York and London: Routledge Falmer.

33 K.A. Strike (1995) Professional ethics and the education of professionals, *educational HORIZONS*, 74(1), p. 31.

34 K.A. Strike and P.L. Ternasky (1993) *Ethics for Professionals in Education: Perspectives for Preparation and Practice*, p. 225. New York: Teachers College Press.

Chapter 3 – The teacher as a moral educator

1 R.J. Starratt (1994) *Building an Ethical School: A Practical Response to the Moral Crisis in Schools*, p. 12. London: The Falmer Press. See also G. Fenstermacher's discussion of teachers as moral agents and moral educators who model for their students virtuous traits that are observed, discussed, and imitated by the students in J. Goodlad et al. (1990) *The Moral Dimensions of Teaching*, pp. 130–51. San Francisco, CA: Jossey-Bass.

2 E. Campbell (1997b) Connecting the ethics of teaching and moral education, *Journal of Teacher Education*, 48(4), p. 261.

3 K. Ryan (1993a) Mining the values in the curriculum, *Educational Leadership*, 51(3), p. 17.

4 P.W. Jackson, R.E. Boostrom and D.T. Hansen (1993) *The Moral Life of Schools*. San Francisco, CA: Jossey-Bass.

5 M.W. Berkowitz (2000) Civics and moral education, in B. Moon, S. Brown, and M. Ben-Peretz (eds) *Routledge International Companion to Education*, pp. 897–909. New York: Routledge.

6 V. Richardson and C. Fallona (2001) Classroom management as method and manner, *Journal of Curriculum Studies*, 33(6): 705–28.

7 G.D. Fenstermacher (2001) On the concept of manner and its visibility in teaching practice, *The Journal of Curriculum Studies*, 33(6): 639–53.

8 See Brian McCadden's 1998 account of one kindergarten classroom as a complex moral construction in which the 'moral milieu' is social rather than individual. *It's Hard to Be Good: Moral Complexity, Construction, and Connection in a Kindergarten Classroom*. New York: Peter Lang.

9 In *Voices: The Educational Formation of Conscience*, Thomas Green refers to moral education as the formation of conscience, a word that is not widely used anymore. (1999, Notre Dame, IN: University of Notre Dame Press).

10 R. Coles (1997) *The Moral Intelligence of Children: How to Raise a Moral Child*, p. 105. New York: Plume.

11 For a more detailed description of 'Sarah' and her classroom, see D. Thiessen (2002) Developing a conscience: the moral base of one kindergarten teacher. Paper presented to the Annual Meeting of the American Educational Research Association, New Orleans.

12 Larry Nucci describes the five most prevalent modes of teacher response to classroom transgressions by students that include both admonitions and censures. For a fuller description, see L.P. Nucci (2001) *Education in the Moral Domain*. Cambridge: Cambridge University Press.

13 Fenstermacher (2001) op. cit., p. 646. As an apparent opposite of 'call outs', 'showcasing' as a method of fostering moral conduct is also described in which the teacher praises a student for good behaviour as an example to one's peers. Fenstermacher cautions about the use of showcasing specific students if it leads to favouritism.

14 N. Noddings (2002) *Educating Moral People: A Caring Alternative to Character Education*, p. 144. New York: Teachers College Press.

15 Ibid., p. 142

16 Fenstermacher (2001) op. cit., p. 643.

17 See Nathan M. Greenfield's book review of Vigen Guroian's *Tending the Heart of Virtue* in *The Globe and Mail*, August 29, 1998.

18 See Nucci (2001) op. cit. Also, for a particularly good comparison, see N. Noddings (2002) op. cit., p. 2 where she writes, 'Character educators tend to favor heroes and inspirational accounts; care theorists lean toward stories that problematize ethical decisions and arouse sympathies.'

19 E. McClellan (1999) *Moral Education in America: Schools and the Shaping of Character from Colonial Times to the Present*, p. 90. New York: Teachers College Press.

This book provides a thoughtful history on moral instruction in schools and traces the character education movement back to earlier times.

20 L.S. Wiley (1998) *Comprehensive Character-building Classroom: A Handbook for Teachers*, p. 19. DeBary, FL: Longwood Communications.

21 Ibid., p. 18.

22 See Noddings (2002) op. cit. See also R.J. Nash (1997) *Answering the 'Virtuecrats': A Moral Conversation on Character Education*. New York: Teachers College Press.

23 See the empirical results of studies conducted by Nucci (2001) op. cit.; McCadden (1998) op. cit.; and K. Quinn-Leering (2000) Fostering prosocial behavior as an aspect of teaching. Paper presented to the Annual Meeting of the American Educational Research Association, New Orleans.

24 McCadden (1998) op. cit., p. 77.

25 Berkowitz (2000) op. cit., p. 906.

Part 2: Challenges to ethical professionalism

1 J.I. Goodlad, R. Soder, and K.A. Sirotnik (1990) *The Moral Dimensions of Teaching*, p. xii. San Francisco, CA: Jossey-Bass.

2 R.J. Nash (1996) *'Real World' Ethics: Frameworks for Educators and Human Service Professionals*, p. 63. New York: Teachers College Press.

3 D. Young (1995) Understanding ethical dilemmas in education, *educational HORIZONS*, 74(1), p. 39.

4 J.A. Boss (1998) *Ethics for Life: An Interdisciplinary and Multicultural Introduction*, p. 71. Mountain View, CA: Mayfield.

5 J.Knutson (1995) D is for dilemma, *educational HORIZONS*, 74(1), p. 2.

6 C.E. Campbell (1994) Personal morals and organizational ethics: a synopsis, *The Canadian Administrator*, 34(2), p. 1.

7 K.A. Strike and J.F. Soltis (1992) *The Ethics of Teaching*, 2nd edn. New York: Teachers College Press.

8 W. Hare (1997) Review of *Ethical Judgment in Teaching* by K.D. Hostetler, *Journal of Educational Administration and Foundations*, 12(2), p. 62.

9 For an expanded argument of how the serving of the best interests of students is both a moral imperative and an ideal that should 'lie at the heart of any professional paradigm for educational leaders' (p. 23) see J.P. Shapiro and J.A. Stefkovich (2001) *Ethical Leadership and Decision Making in Education: Applying Theoretical Perspectives to Complex Dilemmas*. Mahwah, NJ: Lawrence Erlbaum Associates.

10 K.D. Walker (1995) A principled look at 'the best interests of children', *The Canadian School Executive*, 15(5): 3–8.

11 Ibid., p. 3

12 B.M. McCadden (1998) *It's Hard to Be Good: Moral Complexity, Construction, and Connection in a Kindergarten Classroom*, p. 15. New York: Peter Lang.

Chapter 4 – Dilemmas in teaching

1 K.A. Strike (1990) The legal and moral responsibility of teachers, in J. Goodlad et al. (eds) *The Moral Dimensions of Teaching*, pp. 207–8. San Francisco, CA: Jossey-Bass.
2 See particularly some of the research conducted in Sweden by Gunnel Colnerud. For example, G. Colnerud (2001) Aristotle and teacher ethics, *Nordic Educational Research*, 21(3): 149–56. Also, G. Colnerud (1997) Ethical conflicts in teaching, *Teaching and Teacher Education*, 13(6): 627–35.
3 For an expanded discussion of this point, see my section on moral and ethical indecision originally published in: E. Campbell (1996a) Suspended morality and the denial of ethics: how value relativism muddles the distinction between right and wrong in administrative decisions, in S.L. Jacobson et al. (eds) *School Administration: Persistent Dilemmas in Preparation and Practice*, pp. 63–74. Westport, CA: Praeger.
4 D.J. Reitz (1998) *Moral Crisis in the Schools: What Parents and Teachers Need to Know*, p. 48. Baltimore, MD: Cathedral Foundation Press.
5 E. Campbell (1994) Personal morals and organizational ethics: a synopsis, *The Canadian Administrator*, 34(2), p. 8.
6 For discussions of ethics in teaching that focus on the more criminal aspects of unprofessional behaviour, see the survey results reported in J.W. Boothe et al. (1992) Questions of ethics, *The Executive Educator*, 14(2): 17–24. See also references to bribery and nepotism in education in J. Kalish and D. Perry (1992) Setting ethical standards, *The Executive Educator*, 14(2): 24–6. Additionally, in his description of moral crisis in schools, Donald Reitz itemizes a range of unethical actions of teachers that include such serious behaviour: Reitz (1998) op. cit. In the Province of Ontario, the regular newsletter of the College of Teachers, which is the professional association for teachers in the province, reports the ongoing findings of its Discipline Committee regarding complaints laid against individual teachers. In a recent issue, ten teachers were identified for a variety of offences, mostly of a criminal nature. See Ontario College of Teachers (2002) *Professionally Speaking*, June issue, pp. 33–6.
7 As Kenneth Strike notes in his discussion of ethical expectations for teachers that include standards that cannot be legally enforced, 'It is hoped that we should expect more of our teachers than that they not be felons or abuse their students.' He further refers to abuse laws, as being, while obviously crucial, hardly a sufficient guide to the ethics of teaching. Strike (1990) op. cit., p. 189 and p. 206.
8 This collegial issue of ethics is central to the description of teachers' dilemmas and is discussed at length in Chapter 5.
9 N. Lyons (1990) Dilemmas of knowing: ethical and epistemological dimensions of teachers' work and development, *Harvard Education Review*, 60(2), p. 170.
10 S. Todd (2001) 'Bringing more than I contain': ethics, curriculum and the pedagogical demand for altered egos, *Journal of Curriculum Studies*, 33(4), p. 434.
11 F. Haynes (1998) *The Ethical School*, p. 40. London: Routledge.
12 Many of the subsequent empirical illustrations are reported in my specific examination of principals' decision making on teachers' ethical sensibilities. See

E. Campbell (1997a) Administrators' decisions and teachers' ethical dilemmas: Implications for moral agency, *Leading & Managing*, 3(4): 245–57.

13 Reitz (1998) op. cit., p. 42.

14 Campbell (1997a) op. cit., p. 252.

15 Ibid., p. 251.

16 Ibid., p. 253.

17 Colnerud (1997) op. cit.

18 For example, see Margaret Wente's column in *The Globe and Mail*, March 6, 2000, in which she reports on a range of unfair student suspensions imposed thoughtlessly by schools 'gripped by panic over safety and hysteria over violence'. She concludes that, 'Zero-tolerance policies are being enforced with zealous mindlessness all across North America'.

19 Campbell (1997a) op. cit., p. 252.

20 A version of this case was published originally in E. Campbell (1997b) Connecting the ethics of teaching and moral education, *Journal of Teacher Education*, 48(4), p. 261.

21 Campbell (1997a) op. cit., p. 250.

22 Ibid., p. 250.

23 This anecdote was originally published as a case study in Campbell (1997b) op. cit., p. 260. It was revised in first person narrative form and appears also in E. Campbell (2001) Let right be done: trying to put ethical standards into practice, *Journal of Educational Policy*, 16(5), p. 405.

24 In the Province of Ontario, Canada, where Erica teaches, teachers (among others) are required by the *Child and Family Services Act* to report promptly to a children's aid society any suspicion 'on reasonable grounds' that a child has suffered physical or emotional harm or neglect.

25 Colnerud (1997) op. cit., p. 631.

26 K. Tirri and J. Husu (2002) Care and responsibility in 'the best interest of the child': relational voices of ethical dilemmas in teaching, *Teachers and Teaching: theory and practice*, 8(1): 65–80.

27 G.M. Dickinson (2001) Teachers, trust, and the law: the matter of sexual misconduct, *Orbit*, 32(2), p. 15, original emphasis.

28 See a description of a self-esteem programme that parents were particularly concerned by in J. Vondra (1996) Resolving conflicts over values, *Educational Leadership*, 53(7), p. 76.

29 S. Piddocke, R. Magsino, and M. Manley-Casimir (1997) *Teachers in Trouble: An Exploration of the Normative Character of Teaching*. Toronto: University of Toronto Press.

30 P.L. Ternasky (1995) Why should we talk to them?: the ethics of disagreement, *educational HORIZONS*, 74(1), p. 19.

31 For the most part, my conceptualization of what is controversial is consistent with such publicly debated issues of contention as abortion, capital punishment, animal rights, the environment, and so on. See G. Haydon (1997) *Teaching About Values: A New Approach*. London: Cassell, for a valuable discussion on this. Almost any social issue can be a source of disagreement and controversy as well. By contrast, I do not share the view of those who regard the teaching of the accepted or official curriculum or values reflective of mainstream Western society

to be more controversial than the promotion of ideological or political positions reflective of radical social advocacy, protest, and activism. For a particularly good description of the ideological distinctions among such competing moralities based on controversy and doctrine see C.H. Sommers (1984) Ethics without virtue, *The American Scholar*, 53(3): 381–9.

32 See especially the chapters on controversy in the classroom, edited by Hare and Portelli, that highlight significant questions about what the teacher's role should be, whether all viewpoints should be tolerated, whether some issues should be excluded from the classroom, and whether the teacher should remain neutral. W. Hare and J.P. Portelli, (eds) (1996) *Philosophy of Education: Introductory Readings*, 2nd end Calgary, Alberta: Detselig Enterprises Ltd.

33 N. Noddings (2002) *Educating Moral People: A Caring Alternative to Character Education*, p. 43. New York: Teachers College Press.

34 K. Simon (2002) If schools teach values, whose values shall they teach? Paper presented to the Annual Meeting of the American Educational Research Association, New Orleans.

35 In a recent court challenge that reached the Supreme Court of British Columbia, Canada, a teacher and his sympathizers fought a previous decision that had three storybooks about same-sex families banned from his kindergarten and grade one classroom. He argued against parents who initiated the complaint, by stating, 'People have a right to their own belief system – but not to impose it on other people's children in the classroom.' The irony of this statement is that it should apply both ways. Do teachers have any more right to impose their beliefs on other people's children? See the article by Kirk Makin in *The Globe and Mail*, June 11, 2002, p. A10.

36 Haydon (1997) op. cit., p. 121 defines indoctrination as 'any process which leaves people accepting certain ideas which they are incapable of subjecting to any rational assessment'.

37 L.S. Wiley (1998) *Comprehensive Character-building Classroom: A Handbook for Teachers*, p. 22. DeBary, FL: Longwood Communications.

38 As an example of the kind of politicization to which I am referring, see Robert Nash's compelling description and critique of 'the liberationist initiative' in R.J. Nash (1997) *Answering the 'Virtuecrats': A Moral Conversation on Character Education*. New York: Teachers College Press. For a further example of such an 'initiative' in practice see L.E. Beyer (1991) Schooling, moral commitment, and the preparation of teachers, *Journal of Teacher Education*, 42(3): 205–15 and L.E. Beyer (1997) The moral contours of teacher education, *Journal of Teacher Education*, 48(4): 245–54.

39 E. Dodds (1988) The ethics of peace education, *Ethics in Education*, 8(1), p. 11.

40 M. Wente (2001) Why America's hated: all that and more from your teachers union. *The Globe and Mail*, 6 December.

41 Ibid.

Chapter 5 – Collegial fear: the dilemmas within

1 J.I. Goodlad, R. Soder, and K.A. Sirotnik (1990) *The Moral Dimensions of Teaching*, p.xii. San Francisco, CA: Jossey-Bass.

2 H. Sockett (1990) Accountability, trust, and ethical codes of practice, in J.I. Goodlad et al. (eds) ibid., p. 241.

3 Ontario College of Teachers (2002) *The Blue Pages, Professionally Speaking* (June issue), pp. 33–40. Toronto: Ontario College of Teachers.

4 K. Tirri and J. Husu (2002) Care and responsibility in 'the best interest of the child': relational voices of ethical dilemmas in teaching, *Teachers and Teaching: theory and practice*, 8(1), p. 72.

5 G. Colnerud (1997) Ethical conflicts in teaching, *Teaching and Teacher Education*, 13(6), p. 631.

6 E. Campbell (1996b) Ethical implications of collegial loyalty as one view of teacher professionalism, *Teachers and Teaching: theory and practice*, 2(2): 191–208.

7 Ibid., pp. 201–2. Also E. Campbell (2001) Let right be done: trying to put ethical standards into practice, *Journal of Educational Policy*, 16(5), p. 403.

8 Campbell (1996b) op. cit., p. 201; Campbell (2001) op. cit., p. 402.

9 Campbell (1996b) op. cit., pp. 202–3, added emphasis.

10 See the description of 'Adverse Report' in *Professional Conduct and the Professional Teacher* (1986), a publication issued by the Relations and Discipline Committee of the Ontario Teachers' Federation.

11 See, for example, the 1996 Federation of Women Teachers Association of Ontario piece on 'Addiction: What to do if a colleague shows an addiction problem', in which it is clearly stated that, 'Although you are not obliged to be involved, if you handle things sensitively you certainly may offer confidential support.'

12 J. Atkinson, as quoted in Ontario College of Teachers (2001) Sexual misconduct and the teaching profession, *Professionally Speaking* (March issue), p. 26.

13 Ibid., p. 26.

14 N. Noddings (2002) *Educating Moral People: A Caring Alternative to Character Education*, p. 98. New York: Teachers College Press.

15 Campbell (1996b) op. cit., pp. 197–8.

16 For an expanded discussion of the state of 'suspended morality' or the action of 'suspending morality', see the following: E. Campbell (1994) Personal morals and organizational ethics: a synopsis, *The Canadian Administrator*, 34(2): 1–10; E. Campbell (1996a) Suspended morality and the denial of ethics, in S.L. Jacobson et al. (eds) *School Administration: Persistent Dilemmas in Preparation and Practice*, pp. 63–74. Westport, CT: Praeger; E. Campbell (1996b) op. cit.

17 Campbell (1994) op. cit., p. 3. See also my discussion of the 'false necessity trap' as a 'method of justifying unethical or immoral conduct on the grounds that it is "vital," "crucial," or "essential," and that to do otherwise would yield disastrous results' Campbell (1996a) op. cit., p. 71.

18 Some might charge that my encouragement of student teachers to discuss their practice teaching experiences publicly in class is, itself, unethical in that it fosters unprofessional conduct against teacher colleagues. I refute such a charge and

have no will to contribute to the culture of silence and cover-ups in matters of ethical significance. Students discuss issues and ideas, not persons, and we observe professional standards and take care to ensure that individuals are neither identified nor slandered. If we are to work towards creating more ethical teaching cultures, such concerns need to be addressed openly so that new teachers can anticipate the moral complexities of their professional role. Applied professional ethics is best explored through the application of moral inquiry to real contexts.

19 F.C. Power (1993) Just schools and moral atmosphere, p. 153 in K.A. Strike and P.L. Ternasky (eds) *Ethics for Professionals in Education: Perspectives for Preparation and Practice*. New York: Teachers College Press.

20 W. Waller (1932) *The Sociology of Teaching*, p. 389. New York: John Wiley and Sons.

21 S. Piddocke, R. Magsino, and M. Manley-Casimir (1997) *Teachers in Trouble: An Exploration of the Normative Character of Teaching*, p. 224. Toronto: University of Toronto Press.

22 A. Malcolm (1973) *The Tyranny of the Group*. Toronto: Clarke, Irwin and Co. See also my discussion of his work in E. Campbell (1995) Raising the moral dimension of school leadership, *Curriculum Inquiry*, 25(1): 87–99, and Campbell (1996b) op. cit.

23 J. A. Boss (1998) *Ethics for Life: An Interdisciplinary and Multicultural Introduction*, p. 224. Mountain View, CA: Mayfield.

24 See two documents (undated) produced by the Ontario English Catholic Teachers' Association (OECTA) on investigations under the Ontario College of Teachers. See also the pamphlet entitled *Guidelines for Members* (undated) issued by the Ontario Secondary School Teachers' Federation (OSSTF) which states, 'If you are considering laying a complaint against another member, OSSTF advises you to explore all possible avenues before taking this serious step. If you do lay a complaint, you must provide that member with a copy. **OSSTF does not provide assistance to members laying complaints at the College of Teachers**' (original emphasis).

25 F. Haynes (1998) *The Ethical School*, p. 112, London: Routlege.

26 L. Hetenyi (1978) Unionism in education: the ethics of it, *Educational Theory*, 28(2), pp. 91–2.

27 G. Haydon (1997) *Teaching About Values: A New Approach*, pp. 4–5. London: Cassell.

28 Campbell (1996b) op. cit., p. 200.

29 Ibid.

30 Ibid., pp. 199–200.

31 Ibid., p. 204 and Campbell (2001) op. cit., p. 405.

32 A.M. Owens (1999) Union could fine teacher for tutoring students, *National Post*, June 23, p. A4.

33 Judyth Sachs refers to one possibly relevant approach as 'activist professionalism'. She writes that 'An activist teacher professionalism will also require new forms of affiliation and association between systems and union officials, as well as opportunities for all parties to come together on "neutral" ground that has not been tainted by previous experiences, prejudices and left-over ideological

baggage . . . For union officials and people working in educational bureaucracies, activist professionalism demands that they develop new strategies for communicating with their constituencies, which are collegial, respectful and strategic.' See J. Sachs (2000) The activist professional, *Journal of Educational Change*, 1(1), p. 92.

34 C.T. Kerchner and K.D. Caufman (1995) Lurching toward professionalism: the saga of teacher unionism, *The Elementary School Journal*, 96(1): 107–22.

35 Ibid., p. 110.

36 M. Thompson (1997) *Professional Ethics and the Teacher: Towards a General Teaching Council*, pp. 50–4. Stoke on Trent: Trentham Books.

Part 3: Ethical directions

1 B.R. Thomas (1990) The school as a moral learning community, in J. Goodlad et al. (eds) *The Moral Dimensions of Teaching*, p. 267. San Francisco, CA: Jossey-Bass.

Chapter 6 – Standards and codes

1 This oft-quoted first principle of professional ethics is associated with the field of medicine, but is also frequently applied to other professions. While by no means all-inclusive of one's ethical responsibilities, this precept is of as primary significance to the teacher as it is to the physician. Translation cited in M. Somerville (2000) *The Ethical Canary: Science, Society and the Human Spirit*, p. xiv. Toronto: Viking.

2 G. Haydon (1997) *Teaching About Values: A New Approach*, p. 157. London: Cassell.

3 R. Soder (1990) The rhetoric of teacher professionalization, in J. Goodlad et al. (eds) op. cit., p. 73.

4 Barry Bull writes that 'students are particularly vulnerable to their teachers' actions and motivations and, therefore, that teachers have special moral responsibilities toward their students'. See B. Bull (1993) Ethics in the preservice curriculum, in K.A. Strike and P.L. Ternasky (eds) *Ethics for Professionals in Education: Perspectives for Preparation and Practice*, p. 72. New York: Teachers College Press.

5 G. Colnerud (2001) Aristotle and teacher ethics, *Nordic Educational Research*, 21(3), p. 155.

6 In his discussion of fiduciary duty, Greg Dickinson refers to students under the age of 16 who are compelled by law to attend school as 'captives of the state'. See G.M. Dickinson (2001) Teachers, trust, and the law: The matter of sexual misconduct, *Orbit*, 32(2): 15–19.

7 H. Sockett (1993) *The Moral Base for Teacher Professionalism*. New York: Teachers College Press. See also my review essay based on this book in: E.

Campbell (1996c) The moral core of professionalism as a teachable ideal and a matter of character, *Curriculum Inquiry*, 26(1): 71–80.

8 M. Thompson (1997) *Professional Ethics and the Teacher: Towards a General Teaching Council*. Stoke on Trent: Trentham Books.

9 E.J. Delattre (1998) *Leadership: A Position? An Activity? And...?: Ethics in Policing*. Ottawa: The Police Leadership Forum, Occasional Papers Collection.

10 Ibid., p. 25.

11 J.R. Covert (1993) Creating a professional standard of moral conduct for Canadian teachers: a work in progress, *Canadian Journal of Education*, 18(4), p. 442.

12 Mandell (1997) Personal and professional ethics and conduct: the cases of Malcolm Ross and Yves Audet, *Viewpoint* (published by the Ontario Public School Teachers' Federation), 18 November, p. 2.

13 Ibid., p. 6.

14 Ibid., p. 11.

15 Chief Justice of Ontario Advisory Committee on Professionalism (2001) *Defining Professionalism* (draft October 2001, revised December 2001), p. 1.

16 T.A. Schmidt and J.G. Adams (1998) *Professionalism and Ethics*, p. 1. Lansing, MI: Society for Academic Emergency Medicine. www.Saem.org/publicat/chap13.htm

17 K.A. Strike and P.L. Ternasky (1993) *Ethics for Professionals in Education: Perspectives for Preparation and Practice*, p. 3. New York: Teachers College Press.

18 For a more detailed discussion of the Ontario College of Teachers and its role in developing ethical standards for the teaching profession, see the following discussion paper I wrote for the College: E. Campbell (1999) Thinking about ethical standards: issues and complexities. Toronto: Ontario College of Teachers, pp. 1–8. See also the following two articles: E. Campbell (2000) Professional ethics in teaching: towards the development of a code of practice, *Cambridge Journal of Education*, 30(2): 203–221; E. Campbell (2001) Let right be done: trying to put ethical standards into practice, *Journal of Educational Policy*, 16(5): 395–411.

19 Thompson (1997) op. cit., p. 1.

20 Ontario Minister of Education (1915) Teachers' code of ethics, *School Management: Ontario Normal School Manuals*. Toronto: The Ryerson Press.

21 F. Haynes (1998) *The Ethical School*, pp. 41–2. London: Routledge.

22 Bull (1993) op. cit., p. 76.

23 Campbell (2000) op. cit., pp. 209–12.

24 For a more detailed discussion of the ethical codes of the National Education Association (US), the American Federation of Teachers (US), the Ontario College of Teachers (Canada), and the Australian College of Education, see Campbell (2000) op. cit. and Campbell (2001) op. cit.

25 For a strongly union-focused code, see the Code of Ethics written by the British Columbia Teachers' Federation (2000) in which five of the ten items relate directly to the collective and individual obligations and duties incurred as a result of union membership and local collective agreements. (www.bctf.bc.ca)

26 J. Watras (1986) Will teaching applied ethics improve schools of education? *Journal of Teacher Education*, 37(3), p. 13.

27 Strike and Ternasky (1993) op. cit., p. 2.
28 R. I. Arends, N.E. Winitzky, and M.D. Tannenbaum (1998) *Exploring Teaching*, 1st edn, pp. 426–8. Boston: McGraw-Hill.
29 Ibid., p. 426.
30 American School Counselor Association (1998) *Ethical Standards For School Counselors*. www.schoolcounselor.org/ethics/standards.htm
31 Canadian Medical Association (1996) *Code of Ethics of the Canadian Medical Association*. Ottawa.
32 Royal College of Dental Surgeons of Ontario (1999) *Code of Ethics*. www.rcdso.org
33 N.K. Freeman (1998) Morals and character: the foundations of ethics and professionalism, *The Educational Forum*, 63(1): 30–6.
34 T.J. Sergiovanni (1992) *Moral Leadership: Getting to the Heart of School Improvement*, pp. 54–5. San Francisco, CA: Jossey-Bass.
35 S.M. Strom (1989) The ethical dimension of teaching, in M.C. Reynolds (ed.) *Knowledge Base for the Beginning Teacher*, p. 270. Oxford: Pergamon Press.
36 For the complete series of scenarios, see my article entitled, Let right be done, Campbell (2001) op. cit.
37 J.F. Soltis (1986) Teaching professional ethics, *Journal of Teacher Education*, 37(3), p. 2.
38 Of particular interest are Kalish and Perry's recommendations for drafting a code of ethical conduct, in which they state: 'The attempt to reach consensus on basic professional responsibilities has a way of reinforcing commitment to ethical conduct in general, and the increased awareness of where you might stumble decreases the likelihood of unethical conduct, thereby helping to restore public trust in your school system' (p.25). J. Kalish and D. Perry (1992) Setting ethical standards, *The Executive Educator*, 14(2): 24–6. See also the eight-statement code of the individual teacher proposed in R.L. Calabrese and G. Nunn (1993) A teacher code of ethics: defining what students can expect, *NASSP Bulletin*, 77(551): 50–6.
39 D.T. Hansen (1998) The moral is in the practice, *Teaching and Teacher Education*, 14(6), p. 649.
40 G.E. Schwarz (1998) Teaching as vocation: enabling ethical practice, *The Educational Forum*, 63(1), p. 23, original emphasis.
41 Sockett (1993) op. cit., p. 1.

Chapter 7 – Learning to create an ethical culture

1 See the comprehensive discussion of teacher knowledge in H. Munby, T. Russell, and A.K. Martin (2001) Teachers' knowledge and how it develops, in V. Richardson (ed.) *Handbook of Research on Teaching*, 4th edn, pp. 877–904. Washington, DC: American Educational Research Association.
2 G. Fenstermacher (1990) Some moral considerations on teaching as a profession, in J. Goodland et al. (eds) *The Moral Dimensions of Teaching*, p. 133. San Francisco, CA: Jossey-Bass.

3 C.T. Kerchner and K.D. Caufman (1995) Lurching toward professionalism: the saga of teacher unionism, *The Elementary School Journal*, 96(1), p. 109.
4 D.J. Self and D.C. Baldwin, Jr. (1994) Moral reasoning in medicine, in J.R. Rest and D. Narváez (eds) *Moral Development in the Professions: Psychology and Applied Ethics*, p. 147. Hillsdale, NJ: Lawrence Erlbaum Associates.
5 D.T. Hansen (2001a) Teaching as a moral activity, in V. Richardson (ed.) op. cit., pp. 849–50.
6 C.A. Buzzelli and B. Johnston (2002) *The Moral Dimensions of Teaching: Language, Power, and Culture in Classroom Interaction*, p. 156. New York and London: Routledge Falmer.
7 'Because the questions to be raised about values are far from simple, there is no substitute for serious, careful, hard thinking. The teaching profession needs to recognize this for itself, if it is not to be always responding to a moral agenda set from outside.' G. Haydon (1997) *Teaching About Values: A New Approach*, p. xiii. London: Cassell.
8 G. Grant (1993) Discovering how you really teach, in K.A. Strike and P.L. Ternasky (eds) *Ethics for Professionals in Education: Perspectives for Preparation and Practice*, p. 135. New York: Teachers College Press.
9 Buzzelli and Johnston (2002) op. cit., p. 127.
10 Grant (1993) op. cit., pp. 135–9.
11 T.J. Sergiovanni (1992) *Moral Leadership: Getting to the Heart of School Improvement*, p. 42. San Francisco, CA: Jossey-Bass. See also my review of this book in E. Campbell (1995) Raising the moral dimension of school leadership, *Curriculum Inquiry*, 25(1): 87–99.
12 K.A. Strike (1995) Professional ethics and the education of professionals, *educational HORIZONS*, 74(1), p. 33.
13 Ibid., p. 34.
14 K.D. Hostetler (1997) *Ethical Judgment in Teaching*, p. 205. Boston: Allyn and Bacon.
15 E.J. Delattre (1998) *Leadership: A Position? An Activity? And . . .?: Ethics in Policing*, p. 12. Ottawa: The Police Leadership Forum, Occasional Papers Collection.
16 D.T. Hansen (2002) The moral environment in an inner-city boys' high school, *Teaching and Teacher Education*, 18(2), p. 201.
17 Ibid., p. 196.
18 R.J. Starratt (1994) *Building an Ethical School: A Practical Response to the Moral Crisis in Schools*, p. 82. London: The Falmer Press.
19 E. Campbell (2001) Let right be done: trying to put ethical standards into practice, *Journal of Educational Policy*, 16(5), p. 408.
20 Starratt (1994) op. cit., p. 132.
21 T. J. Sergiovanni (1996) *Leadership for the Schoolhouse: How Is It Different? Why is it Important?* p. 155. San Francisco, CA: Jossey-Bass.
22 E. Campbell (1996b) Ethical implications of collegial loyalty as one view of teacher professionalism, *Teachers and Teaching: theory and practice*, 2(2), p. 206.
23 Kerchner and Caufman (1995) op. cit., p. 107. On pages 115–16, they further note that, 'Unions have been traditionally built on internal cohesion: Solidarity!

Placing a union member in a position of judgment over another violates the existing norms of solidarity, and many unionists hold to the belief that it will wreck the organization.'

24 J.R. Covert (1993) Creating a professional standard of moral conduct for Canadian teachers: a work in progress, *Canadian Journal of Education*, 18(4), pp. 443–4.

25 A. Hargreaves and M. Fullan (1998) *What's Worth Fighting For Out There?* p. 100. Mississauga, Canada: Ontario Public School Teachers' Federation.

26 B.A. Sichel (1993) Ethics committees and teacher ethics, in Strike and Ternasky (eds) op. cit., pp. 162–75.

27 Ibid., p. 165.

28 Ibid.

29 Ibid., p. 172.

30 Grant (1993) op. cit., p. 141.

31 J.L. Paul, N.H. Berger, P.G. Osnes, Y.G. Martinez, and W.C. Morse (eds) (1997) *Ethics and Decision Making in Local Schools: Inclusion, Policy, and Reform*, p. xi. Baltimore, MD: Paul H. Brookes Publishing Co.

32 In previous articles on ethics and educational leadership, I have reviewed some of the then current literature on administration. See: E. Campbell (1997a) Administrators' decisions and teachers' ethical dilemmas: implications for moral agency, *Leading & Managing*, 3(4): 245–7; E. Campbell (1997c) Ethical school leadership: problems of an elusive role, *Journal of School Leadership*, 7(3): 287–300.

33 T.J. Sergiovanni (1994) The roots of school leadership, *Principal*, November, p. 7.

34 See the description of a school involved in an initiative in Ontario called 'Together We Light the Way', spearheaded by the principal, in which respect as a moral principle became the dominant focus of all in-school conduct and expectations: 'If the students were to show respect for themselves and others, they would also have to be respected. Teachers were forbidden to yell at children or use the S word: shut up . . . When the program started a year ago, she (the principal) wondered how staff would respond to the challenge of treating students more respectfully. "It's a total shift in philosophy", she said.' See: S. Fine (2000) The three Rs plus respect equals results, *The Globe and Mail*, 10 October, p. A9.

35 G.D. Fenstermacher (2001) On the concept of manner and its visibility in teaching practice, *The Journal of Curriculum Studies*, 33(6): 639–53.

36 K. McKerrow (1997) Ethical administration: an oxymoron?, *Journal of School Leadership*, 7(2), p. 210.

37 Campbell (1997a) op. cit., p. 254.

38 C. Marshall (1992) School administrators' values: a focus on atypicals, *Educational Administration Quarterly*, 28(3), p. 383.

39 See a study reported by J.W. Boothe et al. (1992) Questions of ethics, *The Executive Educator*, 14(2): 17–24. Two books that address ways to improve the ethical practice of school administrators are as follows: R. Rebore (2001) *The Ethics of Educational Leadership*. Upper Saddle River, NJ: Prentice-Hall; J.P. Shapiro and J.A. Stefkovich (2001) *Ethical Leadership and Decision Making in*

Education: Applying Theoretical Perspectives to Complex Dilemmas. Mahwah, NJ: Lawrence Erlbaum Associates.
40 D.J. Reitz (1998) *Moral Crisis in the Schools: What Parents and Teachers Need to Know*, p. 49. Baltimore, MD: Cathedral Foundation Press.
41 Sichel (1993) op. cit., p. 162.
42 For example, one of the researchers in the Manner of Teaching Project concluded that notions of virtuous teaching could be understood only in the context of wider school level influences. See: T.K. Chow-Hoy (2001) An inquiry into school context and the teaching of the virtues, *The Journal of Curriculum Studies*, 33(6): 655–82.
43 The legacy of the Nuremberg war trials provides profound evidence that individuals cannot avoid being held culpable for their own actions by arguing their innocence on the basis of apparent organizational imperatives.
44 C.H. Sommers (1984) Ethics without virtue: moral education in America, *The American Scholar*, 53(3), p. 388.
45 For a good example of this latter emphasis, see J. Oakes et al. (2000) *Becoming Good American Schools: The Struggle for Civic Virtue in Education Reform.* San Francisco, CA: Jossey-Bass.
46 D. Martin (2002) John Rawls: a concern for justice and fairness, *The Globe and Mail*, 27 November, p. R7.

Chapter 8 – Using ethical knowledge to inform practice

1 E. Campbell (1997b) Connecting the ethics of teaching and moral education, *Journal of Teacher Education*, 48(4), p. 257.
2 See, for example, Deborah Yost's discussion that concludes that teacher education programmes with a 'clearly defined mission based on the moral dimensions of teaching' can indeed exert a considerable influence on the moral dispositions of preservice teachers: D.S. Yost (1997) The moral dispositions of teaching and preservice teachers: can moral dispositions be influenced? *Journal of Teacher Education*, 48(4): 281–92.
3 K.A. Strike (1995) Professional ethics and the education of professionals, *educational HORIZONS*, 74(1), p. 35.
4 K.A. Strike and P.L. Ternasky (1993) *Ethics for Professionals in Education: Perspectives for Preparation and Practice.* New York: Teachers College Press.
5 K. Ryan (1993b) Why a center for the advancement of ethics and character, *Journal of Education*, 175(2), p. 6. For an expanded discussion of Ryan's argument, see also: K. Ryan and K.E. Bohlin (1999) *Building Character in Schools: Practical Ways to Bring Moral Instruction to Life.* San Francisco, CA: Jossey-Bass.
6 Campbell (1997b) op. cit., p. 255.
7 R. Cummings, L. Dyas, C.D. Maddux, and A. Kochman (2001) Principled moral reasoning and behavior of preservice teacher education students, *American Educational Research Journal*, 38(1), p. 143.
8 Ibid., p. 153.

9 C.A. Buzzelli and B. Johnston (2002) *The Moral Dimensions of Teaching: Language, Power, and Culture in Classroom Interaction*, p. 18. New York and London: Routledge Falmer.

10 V. Richardson and C. Fallona (2001) Classroom management as method and manner, *Journal of Curriculum Studies*, 33(6), p. 725.

11 N.M. Hamberger and R.L. Moore, Jr (1997) From personal to professional values: conversations about conflicts, *Journal of Teacher Education*, 48(4), p. 303.

12 See, for example, Stengel and Tom's description of the valued end of teacher education as being the integration of technical proficiencies of teaching with care and moral courage. They advocate an interdisciplinary programme which breaks down traditional subject-based boundaries and encourages reflective practice as a form of moral self-education. They even suggest making admission and retention decisions on the basis of the moral fitness of teacher candidates in relation to 'professional virtues' such as honesty, caring, courage, fairness, and practical wisdom. B. Stengel and A. Tom (1995) Taking the moral nature of teaching seriously, *The Educational Forum*, 59(2): 154–63.

13 For a description of how one teacher educator has her students in a graduate certification programme identify assumptions about the moral teacher (which reflect the principles addressed here) see: P.B. Joseph (2000) Teaching about 'the moral classroom': a moral lens for reflecting on practice. Paper presented to the Annual Meeting of the American Educational Research Association, New Orleans, April.

14 Michael McDonald's work with the Centre for Applied Ethics at the University of British Columbia, Canada, which includes a number of ethical frameworks and worksheets, may be reviewed at the following website addresses: www.ethics.ubc.ca/mcdonald/decisions.html
www.ethics.ubc.ca/education

15 N.K. Freeman (1998) Morals and character: the foundations of ethics and professionalism, *The Educational Forum*, 63(1): 30–6.

16 See especially the case study books, dealing with ethical issues, authored by Kenneth Strike and Jonas Soltis for use in professional education classrooms.

17 R. Silverman, W.M. Welty, and S. Lyon (1996) *Case Studies for Teacher Problem Solving*. 2nd edn, p. xvii. New York: McGraw-Hill.

18 K.A. Strike (1990) The legal and moral responsibility of teachers, in J. Goodlad et al. (eds) *The Moral Dimensions of Teaching*, p. 208. San Francisco, CA: Jossey-Bass.

19 For detailed descriptions of how I use case study instruction to teach professional ethics as well as an explanation of my reservations about case studies, see: Campbell (1997b) op. cit., and E. Campbell (1997c) Ethical school leadership: problems of an elusive role, *Journal of School Leadership*, 7(3): 287–300.

20 K.D. Hostetler (1997) *Ethical Judgment in Teaching*, p. 11. Boston: Allyn and Bacon.

21 In their empirical study of teachers' interpersonal conflict solving, Oser and Althof raised the question of 'whether the fundamental ethical orientations of teachers can be influenced and changed' (p.253). Through this 'interventional' study, they concluded that it is possible by means of professional development to

do so and thus 'help teachers develop their conceptual frames of professional responsibility' (p.273) See: F. Oser and W. Althof (1993) Trust in advance: on the professional morality of teachers, *Journal of Moral Education*, 22(3): 253–75.

22 John Fletcher Moulton, as cited in E.J. Delattre (1998) *Leadership: A Position? An Activity? And . . .?: Ethics in Policing*, p. 2. Ottawa: The Police Leadership Forum, Occasional Papers Collection.

23 Apologies to those who find this US television drama series (that deals questionably with morally sensitive and sensationalized issues within the context of one high school) a source of enjoyable entertainment. My point is simply that it should be seen only as that, and not as a reflection of the realities of teaching or as a source of ethical professional development. I am struck by how much and how often some of my preservice students make reference to this show as well as to other popular movies and fictitious shows about teaching and life in schools.

24 M. Somerville (2000) *The Ethical Canary: Science, Society and the Human Spirit*, p. 284. Toronto: Viking.

25 E. Campbell (2001) Let right be done: trying to put ethical standards into practice, *Journal of Educational Policy*, 16(5), p. 409.

26 R. Coles (1997) *The Moral Intelligence of Children: How to Raise a Moral Child*, p. 181. New York: Plume.

27 P.W. Jackson, R.E. Boostrom and D.T. Hansen (1993) *The Moral Life of Schools*, p. 143. San Francisco, CA: Jossey-Bass.

Bibliography

American School Counselor Association (1998) *Ethical standards for school counselors.* www.schoolcounselor.org/ethics/standards.htm (accessed 29 March 2000).

Arends, R.I., Winitzky, N.E. and Tannenbaum, M.D. (1998) *Exploring Teaching*, 1st edn. Boston: McGraw-Hill.

Aurin, K. and Maurer, M. (1993) Forms and dimensions of teachers' professional ethics – case studies in secondary schools, *Journal of Moral Education*, 22(3): 277–96.

Ball, D.L. and Wilson, S.M. (1996) Integrity in teaching: recognizing the fusion of the moral and intellectual, *American Educational Research Journal*, 33(1): 155–92.

Baron, M.W., Pettit, P. and Slote, M. (1997) *Three Methods of Ethics: A Debate.* Oxford: Blackwell.

Bayles, M.D. (1981) *Professional Ethics.* Belmont, CA: Wadsworth.

Beck, L.G. and Murphy, J. (1994) *Ethics in Educational Leadership Programs.* Thousand Oaks, CA: Corwin Press.

Benn, P. (1998) *Ethics.* Montreal and Kingston: McGill-Queen's University Press.

Bergem, T. (1993) Examining aspects of professional morality, *Journal of Moral Education*, 22(3): 297–312.

Berkowitz, M.W. (2000) Civics and moral education, in B. Moon, S. Brown, and M. Ben-Peretz (eds) *Routledge International Companion to Education*, pp. 897–909. New York: Routledge.

Beyer, L.E. (1991) Schooling, moral commitment, and the preparation of teachers, *Journal of Teacher Education*, 42(3): 205–15.

Beyer, L.E. (1997) The moral contours of teacher education, *Journal of Teacher Education*, 48(4): 245–54.

Boothe, J.W., Bradley, L.H., Flick, T.M., Keough, K.E. and Kirk, S.P. (1992) Questions of ethics, *The Executive Educator*, 14(2): 17–24.

Borba, M. (2001) *Building Moral Intelligence: The Seven Essential Virtues that Teach Kids to Do the Right Thing.* San Francisco, CA: Jossey-Bass.

Boss, J.A. (1998) *Ethics for Life: An Interdisciplinary and Multicultural Introduction.* Mountain View, CA: Mayfield.

Bricker, D.C. (1989) *Classroom Life as Civic Education: Individual Achievement and Student Cooperation in Schools.* New York: Teachers College Press.

British Columbia Teachers' Federation (2000) BCTF code of ethics. www.bctf.bc.ca (accessed 14 May 2001).

Bull, B. (1993) Ethics in the preservice curriculum, in K.A. Strike and P.L. Ternasky (eds) *Ethics for Professionals in Education: Perspectives for Preparation and Practice*, pp. 69–83. New York: Teachers College Press.

Bull, B.L. and McCarthy, M.M. (1995) Reflections on the knowledge base in law and ethics for educational leaders, *Educational Administration Quarterly*, 31(4): 613–31.

Buzzelli, C.A. and Johnston, B. (2002) *The Moral Dimensions of Teaching: Language, Power, and Culture in Classroom Interaction.* New York and London: Routledge Falmer.

Calabrese, R.L. and Nunn, G. (1993) A teacher code of ethics: defining what students can expect, *NASSP Bulletin*, 77(551): 50–6.

Campbell, E. (1992) Personal morals and organizational ethics: how teachers and principals cope with conflicting values in the context of school cultures. Unpublished PhD thesis, University of Toronto.

Campbell, E. (1994) Personal morals and organizational ethics: a synopsis, *The Canadian Administrator*, 34(2): 1–10.

Campbell, E. (1995) Raising the moral dimension of school leadership, *Curriculum Inquiry*, 25(1): 87–99.

Campbell, E. (1996a) Suspended morality and the denial of ethics: how value relativism muddles the distinction between right and wrong in administrative decisions, in S.L. Jacobson, E.S. Hickcox and R.B. Stevenson (eds) *School Administration: Persistent Dilemmas in Preparation and Practice*, pp. 63–74. Westport, CA and London: Praeger.

Campbell, E. (1996b) Ethical implications of collegial loyalty as one view of teacher professionalism, *Teachers and Teaching: theory and practice*, 2(2): 191–208.

Campbell, E. (1996c) The moral core of professionalism as a teachable ideal and a matter of character, *Curriculum Inquiry*, 26(1): 71–80.

Campbell, E. (1997a) Administrators' decisions and teachers' ethical dilemmas: implications for moral agency, *Leading & Managing*, 3(4): 245–57.

Campbell, E. (1997b) Connecting the ethics of teaching and moral education, *Journal of Teacher Education*, 48(4): 255–63.

Campbell, E. (1997c) Ethical school leadership: problems of an elusive role, *Journal of School Leadership*, 7(3): 287–300.

Campbell, E. (1999) Thinking about ethical standards: issues and complexities. Toronto: Ontario College of Teachers.

Campbell, E. (2000) Professional ethics in teaching: towards the development of a code of practice, *Cambridge Journal of Education*, 30(2): 203–21.

Campbell, E. (2001) Let right be done: trying to put ethical standards into practice, *Journal of Educational Policy*, 16(5): 395–411.

Canadian Medical Association (1996) *Code of Ethics of the Canadian Medical Association.* Ottawa.

Carr, D. (1993) Questions of competence, *British Journal of Educational Studies*, xxxxi (3): 253–71.

Carr, D. (2000) *Professionalism and Ethics in Teaching*. London: Routledge.

Carr, D. and Steutel, J. (eds) (1999) *Virtue Ethics and Moral Education*. London: Routledge.

Chief Justice of Ontario Advisory Committee on Professionalism (2001) *Defining Professionalism* (draft October 2001, revised December 2001), Toronto.

Chow-Hoy, T.K. (2001) An inquiry into school context and the teaching of the virtues, *The Journal of Curriculum Studies*, 33(6): 655–82.

Clark, C.M. (1990) The teacher and the taught: moral transactions in the classroom, in J.I. Goodlad, R. Soder and K.A. Sirotnik (eds) *The Moral Dimensions of Teaching*, pp. 251–65. San Francisco, CA: Jossey-Bass.

Colero, L. (undated) *A Framework for Universal Principles of Ethics*. www.ethics.ubc.ca/papers/invited/colero.html (accessed 3 April 2000).

Coles, R. (1997) *The Moral Intelligence of Children: How to Raise a Moral Child*. New York: Plume.

Colnerud, G. (1997) Ethical conflicts in teaching, *Teaching and Teacher Education*, 13(6): 627–35.

Colnerud, G. (2001) Aristotle and teacher ethics, *Nordic Educational Research*, 21(3): 149–56.

Coombs, J.R. (1998) Educational ethics: are we on the right track?, *Educational Theory*, 48(4): 555–69.

Covert, J.R. (1993) Creating a professional standard of moral conduct for Canadian teachers: a work in progress, *Canadian Journal of Education*, 18(4): 429–45.

Cummings, R., Dyas, L., Maddux, C.D. and Kochman, A. (2001) Principled moral reasoning and behavior of preservice teacher education students, *American Educational Research Journal*, 38(1): 143–58.

Delattre, E.J. (1998) *Leadership: A Position? An Activity? And . . .?: Ethics in Policing*. Ottawa: The Police Leadership Forum, Occasional Papers Collection.

Delattre, E.J. and Russell, W.E. (1993) Schooling, moral principles, and the formation of character, *Journal of Education*, 175(2): 23–43.

DeVries, R. and Zan, B. (1994) *Moral Classrooms, Moral Children: Creating a Constructivist Atmosphere in Early Education*. New York: Teachers College Press.

Dickinson, G.M. (2001) Teachers, trust, and the law: the matter of sexual misconduct, *Orbit*, 32(2): 15–19.

Dodds, E. (1988) The ethics of peace education, *Ethics in Education*, 8(1): 11–13.

Dunn, C.M. (1999) The ordinary schoolteacher, in D.E.W. Fenner (ed.) *Ethics in Education*, pp. 69–80. New York: Garland.

Fallona, C. (2000) Manner in teaching: a study in observing and interpreting teachers' moral virtues, *Teaching and Teacher Education*, 16(2000): 681–95.

Fasching, D.J. (1997) Beyond values: Story, character, and public policy in American schools, in J.L. Paul, N.H. Berger, P.G. Osnes, Y.G. Martinez and W.C. Morse (eds) *Ethics and Decision Making in Local Schools: Inclusion, Policy, and Reform*, pp. 99–122. Baltimore, MD: Paul H. Brookes.

Federation of Women Teachers Association of Ontario (1996) Addiction: what to do if a colleague shows an addiction problem. Toronto: FWTAO.

Fenstermacher, G.D. (1990) Some moral considerations on teaching as a profession, in J.I. Goodlad, R. Soder and K.A. Sirotnik (eds) *The Moral Dimensions of Teaching*, pp. 130–51. San Francisco, CA: Jossey-Bass.

Fenstermacher, G.D. (2001) On the concept of manner and its visibility in teaching practice, *The Journal of Curriculum Studies*, 33(6): 639–53.

Fine, S. (2000) The three Rs plus respect equals results, *The Globe and Mail*, 10 October, p. A9.

Freeman, N.K. (1998) Morals and character: the foundations of ethics and professionalism, *The Educational Forum*, 63(1): 30–6.

Freitas, D.J. (1991) Successfully resolving ethical dilemmas in the school, *NASSP Bulletin*, 75(531): 86–90.

Gecan, C. and Mulholland-Glaze, B. (1993) The teacher's place in the formation of students' character, *Journal of Education*, 175(2): 45–57.

Goldman, A.H. (1980) *The Moral Foundations of Professional Ethics*. Totowa, NJ: Rowman and Littlefield.

Goodlad, J.I., Soder, R. and Sirotnik, K.A. (eds) (1990) *The Moral Dimensions of Teaching*. San Francisco, CA: Jossey-Bass.

Goodman, J.F. and Lesnick, H. (2001) *The Moral Stake in Education: Contested Premises and Practices*. New York: Longman.

Grace, G. (1995) *School Leadership: Beyond Education Management*. London: The Falmer Press.

Grant, G. (1993) Discovering how you really teach, in K.A. Strike and P.L. Ternasky (eds) *Ethics for Professionals in Education: Perspectives for Preparation and Practice*, pp. 135–47. New York: Teachers College Press.

Green, T. (1999) *Voices: The Educational Formation of Conscience*. Notre Dame, IN: University of Notre Dame Press.

Greenfield, N.M. (1998) Review of Vigen Guroian's *Tending the Heart of Virtue* in *The Globe and Mail*, 29 August.

Groves R., Wallace, J. and Louden, W. (2002) Measuring the unmeasurable: moral dispositions and the teaching standards conundrum. Paper presented to the Annual Meeting of the American Educational Research Association, New Orleans, April.

Halstead, J. M. and Taylor, M.J. (2000) Learning and teaching about values: a review of recent research, *Cambridge Journal of Education*, 30(2): 169–202.

Hamberger, N.M. and Moore, Jr., R.L. (1997) From personal to professional values: conversations about conflicts, *Journal of Teacher Education*, 48(4): 301–10.

Hansen, D.T. (1993) From role to person: the moral layeredness of classroom teaching, *American Educational Research Journal*, 30(4): 651–74.

Hansen, D.T. (1998) The moral is in the practice, *Teaching and Teacher Education*, 14 (6): 643–55.

Hansen, D.T. (2001a) Teaching as a moral activity, in V. Richardson (ed.) *Handbook of Research on Teaching*, 4th edn, pp. 826–57. Washington, DC: American Educational Research Association.

Hansen, D.T. (2001b) *Exploring the Moral Heart of Teaching: Towards a Teacher's Creed*. New York: Teachers College Press.

Hansen, D.T. (2001c) Reflections on the manner in teaching project, *The Journal of Curriculum Studies*, 33(6): 729–35.

Hansen, D.T. (2002) The moral environment in an inner-city boys' high school, *Teaching and Teacher Education*, 18(2): 183–204.

Hare, W. (1993) *What Makes a Good Teacher?* London, Ontario: Althouse Press.

Hare, W. (1997) Review of *Ethical Judgment in Teaching* by K.D. Hostetler, *Journal of Educational Administration and Foundations*, 12(2): 61–6.

Hare, W. and Portelli, J.P. (eds) (1996) *Philosophy of Education: Introductory Readings*, 2nd edn. Calgary, Alberta: Detselig Enterprises Ltd.

Hargreaves, A. and Fullan, M. (1998) *What's Worth Fighting For Out There?* Mississauga, Canada: Ontario Public School Teachers' Federation.

Haydon, G. (1997) *Teaching About Values: A New Approach*. London: Cassell.

Haynes, F. (1998) *The Ethical School*. London: Routledge.

Hetenyi, L. (1978) Unionism in education: the ethics of it, *Educational Theory*, 28(2): 90–95.

Hodgkinson, C. (1991) *Educational Leadership: The Moral Art*. Albany: State University of New York Press.

Holmes, M. (1991) Alasdair MacIntyre and school administration: after the collapse of the common school. Paper presented to the Canadian Society for the Study of Education, Kingston, Ontario, June.

Hostetler, K.D. (1997) *Ethical Judgment in Teaching*. Boston: Allyn and Bacon.

Hunter, J.D. (2000) *The Death of Character: Moral Education in an Age Without Good or Evil*. New York: Basic Books.

Jackson, P.W., Boostrom, R.E. and Hansen, D.T. (1993) *The Moral Life of Schools*. San Francisco, CA: Jossey-Bass.

Joseph, P. and Efron, S. (1993) Moral choices/moral conflicts: teachers' self-perceptions, *Journal of Moral Education*, 22(3): 201–20.

Joseph, P.B. (2000) Teaching about 'the moral classroom': a moral lens for reflecting on practice. Paper presented to the Annual Meeting of the American Educational Research Association, New Orleans, April.

Kalish, J. and Perry, D. (1992) Setting ethical standards, *The Executive Educator*, 14(2): 24–6.

Katz, M.S. (1999) Teaching about caring and fairness: May Sarton's *The Small Room*, in M.S. Katz, N. Noddings and K.A. Strike (eds) *Justice and Caring: The Search for Common Ground in Education*, pp. 59–73. New York: Teachers College Press.

Katz, M.S., Noddings, N. and Strike, K.A. (eds) (1999) *Justice and Caring: The Search for Common Ground in Education*. New York: Teachers College Press.

Kelly, T.E. (2001) Discussing controversial issues: four perspectives on the teacher's role, in W. Hare and J.P. Portelli (eds) *Philosophy of Education: Introductory Readings*, 3rd edn, pp. 221–42. Calgary, Alberta: Detselig Enterprises Ltd.

Kerchner, C.T. and Caufman, K.D. (1995) Lurching toward professionalism: the saga of teacher unionism, *The Elementary School Journal*, 96(1): 107–22.

Kirby, P.C., Paradise, L.V. and Protti, R. (1992) Ethical reasoning of educational administrators: structuring inquiry around the problems of practice, *Journal of Educational Administration*, 30(4): 25–32.

Knutson, J. (1995) 'D' is for dilemma, *educational HORIZONS*, 74(1): 2.

Kohn, A. (1996) What's wrong with character education? *ASCD Education Update*, 38(3): 5.

Kohn, A. (1997) How not to teach values, *The Education Digest*, May, pp. 12–17.

Leicester, M., Modgil, C. and Modgil, S. (eds) (2000) *Education, Culture and Values. Volume IV: Moral Education and Pluralism*. London: Falmer Press.

Lickona, T. (1991) *Educating for Character: How our Schools can Teach Respect and Responsibility*. New York: Bantam.

Lovat, T.J. (1998) Ethics and ethics education: professional and curricular best practice, *Curriculum Perspectives*, 18(1): 1–7.

Lyons, N. (1990) Dilemmas of knowing: ethical and epistemological dimensions of teachers' work and development, *Harvard Education Review*, 60(2): 159–79.

Macmillan, C.J.B. (1993) Ethics and teacher professionalization, in K.A. Strike and P.L. Ternasky (eds) *Ethics for Professionals in Education: Perspectives for Preparation and Practice*, pp. 189–201. New York: Teachers College Press.

Makin, K. (2002) B.C. banned-books case reaches Supreme Court, *The Globe and Mail*, 11 June.

Malcolm, A. (1973) *The Tyranny of the Group*. Toronto: Clarke, Irwin, and Co.

Mandell, A. (1997) Personal and professional ethics and conduct: the cases of Malcolm Ross and Yves Audet, *Viewpoint* (published by the Ontario Public School Teachers' Federation), 18 November, pp. 2–11.

Marshall, C. (1992) School administrators' values: a focus on atypicals, *Educational Administration Quarterly*, 28(3): 368–86.

Martin, D. (2002) John Rawls: a concern for justice and fairness, *The Globe and Mail*, 27 November, p. R7.

McCadden, B.M. (1998) *It's Hard to Be Good: Moral Complexity, Construction, and Connection in a Kindergarten Classroom*. New York: Peter Lang.

McClellan, E. (1999) *Moral Education in America: Schools and the Shaping of Character from Colonial Times to the Present*. New York: Teachers College Press.

McDonald, M. (undated) www.ethics.ubc.ca/mcdonald/decisions.html (accessed 3 April 2000).

McDonald M. (undated) www.ethics.ubc.ca/education (accessed 3 April 2000).

McKerrow, K. (1997) Ethical administration: an oxymoron? *Journal of School Leadership*, 7(2): 210–25.

Ministry of Community and Social Services (2000) *Reporting Child Abuse and Neglect*. Toronto: Queen's Printer for Ontario.

Munby, H., Russell, T. and Martin, A.K. (2001) Teachers' knowledge and how it develops, in V. Richardson (ed.) *Handbook of Research on Teaching*, 4th edn, pp. 877–904. Washington, DC: American Educational Research Association.

Murphy, M.M. (1998) *Character Education in America's Blue Ribbon Schools: Best Practices for Meeting the Challenge*. Lancaster, PA: Technomic Publishing Company.

Nash, R.J. (1996) *'Real World' Ethics: Frameworks for Educators and Human Service Professionals*. New York: Teachers College Press.

Nash, R.J. (1997) *Answering the 'Virtuecrats': A Moral Conversation on Character Education*. New York: Teachers College Press.

Noblit, G.W. and Dempsey, V.O. (1996) *The Social Construction of Virtue: The Moral Life of Schools*. Albany: State University of New York Press.

Noddings, N. (1984) *Caring: A Feminine Approach to Ethics and Moral Education*. Berkeley, CA: University of California Press.

Noddings, N. (2002) *Educating Moral People: A Caring Alternative to Character Education*. New York: Teachers College Press.

Nucci, L.P. (2001) *Education in the Moral Domain*. Cambridge: Cambridge University Press.

Oakes, J., Quartz, K.H., Ryan, S. and Lipton, M. (2000) *Becoming Good American Schools: The Struggle for Civic Virtue in Education Reform*. San Francisco, CA: Jossey-Bass.

Ontario College of Teachers (2001) Sexual misconduct and the teaching profession, *Professionally Speaking*, March, pp. 21–30. Toronto: Ontario College of Teachers.

Ontario College of Teachers (2002) *Professionally Speaking*, June. Toronto: Ontario College of Teachers.

Ontario English Catholic Teachers' Association (undated) *Allegations, Investigations and Legal Process*. Toronto: OECTA.

Ontario English Catholic Teachers' Association (undated) *What You Should Know about Investigations and Discipline under the Ontario College of Teachers*. Toronto: OECTA.

Ontario Minister of Education (1915) Teachers' code of ethics, *School Management: Ontario Normal School Manuals*. Toronto: The Ryerson Press.

Ontario Secondary School Teachers' Federation (undated) *Guidelines for Members: The College of Teachers, Assault or Sexual Harassment, Suspected Child Abuse, Search and Seizure*. www.osstf.on.ca (accessed 3 April 2000).

Ontario Teachers' Federation (1986) *Professional Conduct and the Professional Teacher*, Toronto: OTF.

Oser, F. and Althof, W. (1993) Trust in advance: on the professional morality of teachers, *Journal of Moral Education*, 22(3): 253–75.

Owens, A.M. (1999) Union could fine teacher for tutoring students, *National Post*, 23 June.

Paul, J.L., Berger, N.H., Osnes, P.G., Martinez, Y.G. and Morse, W.C. (eds) (1997) *Ethics and Decision Making in Local Schools: Inclusion, Policy, and Reform*. Baltimore, MD: Paul H. Brookes.

Peters, R.S. (1966) *Ethics and Education*. London: George Allen and Unwin.

Piddocke, S., Magsino, R. and Manley-Casimir, M. (1997) *Teachers in Trouble: An Exploration of the Normative Character of Teaching*. Toronto: University of Toronto Press.

Power, F.C. (1993) Just schools and moral atmosphere, in K.A. Strike and P.L. Ternasky (eds) *Ethics for Professionals in Education: Perspectives for Preparation and Practice*, pp. 148–61. New York: Teachers College Press.

Pring, R. (2001) Education as a moral practice, *Journal of Moral Education*, 30(2): 101–112.

Purkey, W.W. and Novak, J.M. (1998) An invitational approach to ethical practice in teaching, *The Educational Forum*, 63(1): 37–43.

Quinn-Leering, K. (2000) Fostering prosocial behavior as an aspect of teaching. Paper presented to the Annual Meeting of the American Educational Research Association, New Orleans, April.

Rebore, R. (2001) *The Ethics of Educational Leadership*. Upper Saddle River, NJ: Prentice-Hall.

Reitz, D.J. (1998) *Moral Crisis in the Schools: What Parents and Teachers Need to Know.* Baltimore, MD: Cathedral Foundation Press.

Rest, J.R. and Narváez, D. (eds) (1994) *Moral Development in the Professions: Psychology and Applied Ethics.* Hillsdale, NJ: Lawrence Erlbaum Associates.

Richardson, V. and Fallona, C. (2001) Classroom management as method and manner, *Journal of Curriculum Studies,* 33(6): 705–28.

Richardson, V. and Fenstermacher, G.D. (2000) The Manner in Teaching Project. www-personal.umich.edu/~gfenster (accessed 10 May 2000).

Richardson, V. and Fenstermacher, G.D. (2001) Manner in teaching: the study in four parts, *Journal of Curriculum Studies,* 33(6): 631–7.

Royal College of Dental Surgeons of Ontario (1999) *Code of Ethics.* www.rcdso.org (accessed 4 August 2002).

Ryan, K. (1993a) Mining the values in the curriculum, *Educational Leadership,* 51(3): 16–18.

Ryan, K. (1993b) Why a center for the advancement of ethics and character? *Journal of Education,* 175(2): 1–11.

Ryan, K. and Bohlin, K.E. (1999) *Building Character in Schools: Practical Ways to Bring Moral Instruction to Life.* San Francisco, CA: Jossey-Bass.

Sachs, J. (2000) The activist professional, *Journal of Educational Change,* 1(1): 77–95.

Sanger, M.G. (2001) Talking to teachers and looking at practice in understanding the moral dimensions of teaching, *The Journal of Curriculum Studies,* 33(6): 683–704.

Schmidt, T.A. and Adams, J.G. (1998) *Professionalism and Ethics.* Lansing, MI: Society for Academic Emergency Medicine. www.saem.org/publicat/chap13.htm (accessed 2 November 2002)

Schwarz, G.E. (1998) Teaching as vocation: enabling ethical practice, *The Educational Forum,* 63(1): 23–9.

Self, D.J. and Baldwin, Jr, D.C. (1994) Moral reasoning in medicine, in J.R. Rest and D. Narváez (eds) *Moral Development in the Professions: Psychology and Applied Ethics,* pp. 147–62. Hillsdale, NJ: Lawrence Erlbaum Associates.

Sergiovanni, T.J. (1992) *Moral Leadership: Getting to the Heart of School Improvement.* San Francisco: Jossey-Bass.

Sergiovanni, T.J. (1994) The roots of school leadership, *Principal,* November, pp. 6–9.

Sergiovanni, T.J. (1996) *Leadership for the Schoolhouse: How is it Different? Why is it Important?* San Francisco, CA: Jossey-Bass.

Shapiro, J.P. and Stefkovich, J.A. (2001) *Ethical Leadership and Decision Making in Education: Applying Theoretical Perspectives to Complex Dilemmas.* Mahwah, NJ: Lawrence Erlbaum Associates.

Sichel, B.A. (1993) Ethics committees and teacher ethics, in Strike and Ternasky (eds) *Ethics for Professionals in Education: Perspectives for Preparation and Practice,* pp. 162–75. New York: Teachers College Press.

Silverman, R., Welty, W.M. and Lyon, S. (1996) *Case Studies for Teacher Problem Solving,* 2nd edn. New York: McGraw-Hill.

Simon, K. (2002) If schools teach values, whose values shall they teach? Paper presented to the Annual Meeting of the American Educational Research Association, New Orleans, April.

Sirotnik, K.A. (1990) Society, schooling, teaching, and preparing to teach, in J.I. Goodlad, R. Soder and K.A. Sirotnik (eds) *The Moral Dimensions of Teaching*, pp. 296–327. San Francisco, CA: Jossey-Bass.

Sizer, T.R. and Sizer, N.F. (1999) *The Students are Watching: Schools and the Moral Contract*. Boston: Beacon Press.

Smith, R. and Standish, P. (eds) (1997) *Teaching Right and Wrong: Moral Education in the Balance*. Stoke on Trent: Trentham Books.

Sockett, H. (1990) Accountability, trust, and ethical codes of practice, in J.I Goodlad, R. Soder and K.A. Sirotnik (eds) *The Moral Dimensions of Teaching*, pp. 224–50. San Francisco, CA: Jossey-Bass.

Sockett, H. (1992) The moral aspects of the curriculum, in P.W. Jackson (ed.) *Handbook of Research on Curriculum*, pp. 543–69. New York: MacMillan.

Sockett, H. (1993) *The Moral Base for Teacher Professionalism*. New York: Teachers College Press.

Soder, R. (1990) The rhetoric of teacher professionalization, in J.I. Goodlad, R. Soder and K.A. Sirotnik (eds) *The Moral Dimensions of Teaching*, pp. 35–86. San Francisco, CA: Jossey-Bass.

Soltis, J.F. (1986) Teaching professional ethics, *Journal of Teacher Education*, 37(3): 2–4.

Somerville, M. (2000) *The Ethical Canary: Science, Society and the Human Spirit*. Toronto: Viking.

Sommers, C.H. (1984) Ethics without virtue: moral education in America, *The American Scholar*, 53(3): 381–9.

Starratt, R.J. (1994) *Building an Ethical School: A Practical Response to the Moral Crisis in Schools*. London: Falmer.

Stengel, B. and Tom, A. (1995) Taking the moral nature of teaching seriously, *The Educational Forum*, 59(2): 154–63.

Strike, K.A. (1990) The legal and moral responsibility of teachers, in J.I. Goodlad, R. Soder and K.A.Sirotnik (eds) *The Moral Dimensions of Teaching*, pp. 188–223. San Francisco, CA: Jossey-Bass.

Strike, K.A. (1995) Professional ethics and the education of professionals, *educational HORIZONS*, 74(1): 29–36.

Strike, K.A. (1999) Justice, caring, and universality: in defence of moral pluralism, in M.S. Katz, N. Noddings and K.A. Strike (eds) *Justice and Caring: The Search for Common Ground in Education*, pp. 21–36. New York: Teachers College Press.

Strike, K.A. and Soltis, J.F. (1992) *The Ethics of Teaching*, 2nd edn. New York: Teachers College Press.

Strike, K.A. and Ternasky, P.L. (eds) (1993) *Ethics for Professionals in Education: Perspectives for Preparation and Practice*. New York: Teachers College Press.

Strike, K.A., Haller, E. and Soltis, J. (1988) *The Ethics of School Administration*. New York: Teachers College Press.

Strom, S.M. (1989) The ethical dimension of teaching, in M.C. Reynolds (ed.) *Knowledge Base for the Beginning Teacher*, pp. 267–76. Oxford: Pergamon Press.

Ternasky, P.L. (1995) Why should we talk to them?: the ethics of disagreement, *educational HORIZONS*, 74(1): 13–20.

Thiessen, D. (2002) Developing a conscience: the moral base of one kindergarten teacher. Paper presented to the Annual Meeting of the American Educational Research Association, New Orleans, April.

Thomas, B.R. (1990) The school as a moral learning community, in J.I. Goodlad, R.Soder and K.A. Sirotnik (eds) *The Moral Dimensions of Teaching*, pp. 266–95. San Francisco, CA: Jossey-Bass.

Thompson, M. (1997) *Professional Ethics and the Teacher: Towards a General Teaching Council*. Stoke on Trent: Trentham Books.

Thorkildsen, T.A. (1989) Justice in the classroom: the student's view, *Child Development*, 60(2): 323–34.

Tippins, D., Tobin, K. and Hook, K. (1993) Ethical decisions at the heart of teaching: making sense from a constructivist perspective, *Journal of Moral Education*, 22(3): 221–40.

Tirri, K. and Husu J. (2002) Care and responsibility in 'the best interest of the child': relational voices of ethical dilemmas in teaching, *Teachers and Teaching: theory and practice*, 8(1): 65–80.

Todd, S. (2001) 'Bringing more than I contain': ethics, curriculum and the pedagogical demand for altered egos, *Journal of Curriculum Studies*, 33(4): 431–50.

Tom, A.R. (1984) *Teaching as a Moral Craft*. New York: Longman.

Vondra, J. (1996) Resolving conflicts over values, *Educational Leadership*, 53(7): 76–9.

Walker, K.D. (1995) A principled look at 'the best interests of children', *The Canadian School Executive*, 15(5): 3–8.

Wall, E., Lewis, J.M. and Ball, D.L. (2000) Moral work in teaching: the treatment of right and wrong answers in mathematics class. Paper presented to the Annual Meeting of the American Educational Research Association, New Orleans, April.

Waller, W. (1932) *The Sociology of Teaching*. New York: John Wiley and Sons.

Watras, J. (1986) Will teaching applied ethics improve schools of education? *Journal of Teacher Education*, 37(3): 13–16.

Wente, M. (2000) Zero tolerance and zero sense: the Fall River Rebellion and other dastardly school-yard crimes, *The Globe and Mail*, 6 March.

Wente, M. (2001) Why America's hated: all that and more from your teachers union. *The Globe and Mail*, 6 December.

West, S. (1993) *Educational Values for School Leadership*. London: Kogan Page.

Weston, A. (1997) *A Practical Companion to Ethics*. New York: Oxford University Press.

White, P. (1996) *Civic Virtues and Public Schooling: Educating Citizens for a Democratic Society*. New York: Teachers College Press.

Wiley, L.S. (1998) *Comprehensive Character-building Classroom: A Handbook for Teachers*. DeBary, FL: Longwood Communications.

Wynne, E.A. and Ryan, K. (1997) *Reclaiming Our Schools: Teaching Character, Academics, and Discipline*, 2nd edn. Upper Saddle River, NJ: Prentice Hall.

Yost, D.S. (1997) The moral dispositions of teaching and preservice teachers: can moral dispositions be influenced? *Journal of Teacher Education*, 48(4): 281–92.

Young, D. (1995) Understanding ethical dilemmas in education, *educational HORIZONS*, 74(1): 37–42.

Index

THE ACTIVIST TEACHING PROFESSION
Judyth Sachs

This is a thoughtful, provocative and important book. Clear, concise, articulate and pulling no punches, Judyth Sachs maps out an agenda for a new 'transformative professionalism' which celebrates the complexities of teacher identities and work, and acknowledges the tensions between standards of accountability and autonomy. She argues persuasively for a reorientation of policy from managerial to a democratic and radical reconceptualisation of teacher education programmes and notions of teacher professionalism. Her text, richly supported by case studies of practice, will appeal to teachers and teacher educators worldwide who are committed to principles of active participation, trust and community.

Professor Chris W. Day, University of Nottingham

- What forms of professionalism are shaping the teaching profession?
- How can the concept of teacher professionalism be revitalized so that it is relevant to the needs and aspirations of teachers working in increasingly difficult and constantly changing work environments?

The Activist Teaching Profession examines the issue of teacher professionalism as a social and political strategy to enhance the status and activities of the teaching profession. The book is contextualized within current debates, both government policy and scholarly, about teacher professionalism. Evidence to support the development of alternative forms of teacher professionalism utilizing new structural arrangements with various stakeholders through collaboration and cooperation, is represented using examples from Australia and elsewhere. Teacher inquiry is presented as an initiative whereby teacher professionalism can be developed. A strategy for re-establishing the moral and intellectual leadership of the teaching profession along activist lines is developed in the last section of the book. Issues surrounding teacher professional identity are examined in the light of the discourses that are shaping teacher professionalism. Rethinking professional identity provides a basis for developing new forms of teacher professionalism. *The Activist Teaching Profession* is both a wake up call and a call to action for teachers and the community alike.

Contents

192pp   0 335 20818 5 (Paperback)   0 335 20819 3 (Hardback)

ENGAGING TEACHERS
TOWARDS A RADICAL DEMOCRATIC AGENDA
FOR SCHOOLING
Trevor Gale and Kathleen Densmore

Engaging Teachers reclaims the education discourse captured by new right politics and connects it with a radical democratic agenda for schooling. The authors concentrate on five areas central to schooling:

- Markets in education
- Education policy
- Leadership
- Professionalism
- Communities

By engaging with these topics, teachers are invited to become involved in reconstructing schooling in democratic ways for socially just purposes. This is not simply a matter of acquiescence or of resistance but a demonstration of the benefits that can result when teachers, students and parents work collectively to make things happen rather than having things done to them. This book is key reading for advanced undergraduate and masters students of education, teacher educators and policymakers.

Contents
Foreword by Simon Marginson – Introduction: to a politics of engagement – Markets: an increasingly visible hand – Policy: the authoritative allocation of values – Leadership: taking a radical democratic stance – Professionalism: a framework for just social relations – Community: reconnecting school and society – References – Index

144pp   0 335 21026 0 (Paperback)   0 335 21027 9 (Hardback)

TEACHING LEARNING FOR EDUCATIONAL CHANGE
A SYSTEMS THINKING APPROACH
Garry F. Hoban

Hoban pays careful attention to the dynamic interplay between personal, social and contextual conditions for learning in his Professional Learning System by valuing extended time frames and learning communities in his quest for real teacher change. But beyond his theory, persuasive arguments and compelling examples is the learning through reflection that he embodies himself in this book. A wonderful read.

J. John Loughran, Faculty of Education, Monash University, Australia

How many teachers (including academics) understand the dynamic relationship between learning and teaching? In this highly readable account of teacher learning for educational change, Hoban provides both the theory and the detailed examples for a rich and engaging new perspective on teachers' professional learning. This is essential reading for all who would improve their own teaching or provide meaningful support and leadership for such teachers.

Tom Russell, Professor of Education, Queen's University, Canada

This book presents a new mindset for teacher learning and educational change. When viewed from a conventional mechanistic paradigm, educational change is a linear step-by-step process that is supported by a simplistic approach to teacher learning. Although this approach often produces disappointing results, rarely is an alternative one proposed. What is new in this book is that educational change and teacher learning are viewed from a paradigm based on complexity theory, assuming that change is a nonlinear process that needs to be supported by a framework for long-term teacher learning. The central question of this book, therefore, is 'What conditions will help to establish a framework for long-term teacher learning to support educational change?' To address this question, a systems thinking approach is used to draw together ideas from existing learning perspectives into a new theoretical framework called a Professional Learning System. This framework is not a formula, but a new mindset to help us understand the nonlinear dynamics of educational change and teacher learning.

Contents

208pp   0 335 20953 X (Paperback)   0 335 20954 8 (Hardback)